...and Summer

WHO'S AFRAID OF VIRGINIA WOOLF?

TREETCAR DESIRE

death of a

TRAGEDY
AND FEAR

WHY MODERN TRAGIC DRAMA FAILS

TRAGEDY
AND FEAR

WHY MODERN TRAGIC DRAMA FAILS

by John von Szeliski

The University of North Carolina Press • Chapel Hill

Manufactured in the United States of America
Printed by Heritage Printers, Inc.
ISBN 0-8078-1177-7
Library of Congress Catalog Card Number 70-156136

FOR KARLENE

CONTENTS

PREFACE

People are constantly writing about tragedy, it seems, and there is plenty of danger of duplication in new work on the subject. While inevitably I will comment on some of the old issues ceaselessly discussed, rest assured that I am not trying to answer writers already in print so much as to do a fresh and reasonably thorough study on the essential issue which has been curiously neglected—that is, whether tragedy must presuppose some distinct attitude toward life and whether this should be positive or negative. It is this deceptively simple problem that needs attention, not another reinterpretation of the *Poetics* or our five-hundred-and-first look at *Oedipus the King* or *Hamlet* as ideal tragedies. I think there are some very large implications in the problem beyond literary-aesthetic matters (given the kind of world we must deal with today and the art that is offered to express it), and I hope all readers will interpret and follow these according to their own insights and experience.

The academic reader will be interested in the background of the pessimism-optimism debate and the substantiation of my method for going at such a seemingly subjective project. Hence the introduction (and related material in the appendixes, plus the quick "overviews" of my theorems which open chapters 3 through 9). The general reader might skip the introduction, at least once he has the gist of my purpose. As for the overall shape of the book, part one is necessary background to the history of the problem and a general description of the unique weaknesses I have noted in seeing and reading modern attempts at tragedy. Part two consists of chapters which are intended as a fairly comprehensive survey of just what "fear" (or pessimism) does to tragic expression. In part three I want to bring the practical problems and the common-man philosophical problems together to reach some conclusions about how tragedy (and much serious art) should now move man—literally and aesthetically. The two chapters here, amounting to frankly subjective essays, can be looked on as my cure for the illness. In the appendixes, I have included material that might be of interest to students and others wishing a clearer idea of the backgrounds or raw materials for my study.

I began work on *Tragedy and Fear* in 1960, and the bulk of the book was completed in the late 1960s. Critical works referred to include major publications on the subject through 1970, but the plays under discussion still date to the early and mid-sixties. Tragedy is even more clearly "off-duty" now than it appeared to be a few years ago.

I am grateful to Williams College for assistance which made possible some final stages of research and provided time for the editing and re-writing which put original drafts of *Tragedy and Fear* into book form. Specifically, I acknowledge the special assistant professor leave I had in 1968, the summer Humanities Grant program, and aid from the Class of 1900 Fund.

TRAGEDY AND FEAR

WHY MODERN TRAGIC DRAMA FAILS

INTRODUCTION

Tragedy and Fear stems mostly from speculating on two questions. First, isn't the most crucial failure of modern tragic art its unprecedented insistence on a terrified, wailing, pessimistic view of existence (and thereby don't we have a strong clue as to the heart of authentic tragic spirit)? Second, just what is it that the special view of life in tragic art does for man in his real world? That is, isn't the tragic vision inextricably built on the nature of man's need for—and satisfaction in—tragedy? Stating this as a theorem, I claim that pessimism and tragedy do not mix and that this is the prime error committed in twentieth-century tragic writing. We ought to be quite down-to-earth about what man gets from the eventual optimism of authentic tragic art.

TRAGEDY: PESSIMISTIC OR OPTIMISTIC?

The main scholarly investigation of this book, therefore, will deal with the appropriateness of pessimism or optimism as the philosophical bias of real tragedy. This battle has been hinted at for centuries, but never studied. As something mentioned by critics, it is a modern matter; but any fireworks roughly akin to the central question have sputtered at best. The most representative display dates back some forty years.

In 1929, Joseph Wood Krutch wrote his now well-known essay, "The Tragic Fallacy," pointing out that modern dramas were too "mean and depressing" to be called tragedies. His argument is now so familiar as to be trite: the depression that the modern versions produced, Krutch believed, was the very opposite of the uplifting emotion inspired by a Shakespeare rising above the calamity he described. This essay (appearing in *The Modern Temper*, a book notorious to some in succeeding generations for its apparent fogyism) was one of the key focal points in the question of pessimism or optimism being the more suitable belief of tragedy. Krutch's impatience with modern attempts at tragedy was echoed by many other critics—but there were still others who, although not happy with the quality of modern tragedy, could not accept the idea that the significant fault lay in the changing philosophical disposition. The Shakespearean scholar E. E. Stoll, for example, completely denied the Krutch thesis in his *Shakespeare and Other Masters*. Mark Harris wrote a whole book, *The Case for Tragedy*, just in indignant answer to "The Tragic Fallacy" and Krutch's suggestion that tragedy could not exist in the modern world.

I wish that Krutch (who, for the rest of his long life, continued to sing the same tune in the *Saturday Review* and his regular *American Scholar* column[1]) had counter-replied with some thorough proofs and systematic analyses of the "depressing" plays and their nontragic results. True, numerous successive writers have theorized about our failure to produce tragedy in this century (or, for that matter, in the last three centuries): George Steiner in *The Death of Tragedy*, Herbert Muller in *The Spirit of Tragedy*, and John Gassner in *The Theatre in Our Times* have made some of the better points. Yet their lamentations, too, have largely tended only to identify nontragedy and posit the general contrasts between successful tragedy and the modern attempts.[2] They, and several others, have

1. For example, there is his article: "Must Writers Hate the Universe?" *Saturday Review*, 6 May 1967. *The American Scholar* column was aptly titled "If You Don't Mind My Saying So. . . ."

2. Surprisingly (considering the title of his book), Muller is ambiguous on the question of attitude. He says, first, "the tragic spirit is more or less pessimistic." This might be accepted as part of the paradox of the tragic statement, but how is it reconciled with the assertions which follow? ". . . pessimism itself is proud, for it implies that man deserves a better fate"; and then, "tragic spirit is essentially humanistic"; and, finally, "the tragic spirit is an affirmation of positive values." (*The Spirit of*

done a good job of reminding us of the nature of effective tragedy—always the tragedy of long ago. And of course the professional philosophers have regularly been fascinated by the concept and attitude of tragedy, particularly so (witness Hegel, Nietzsche, Schopenhauer, and de Unamuno) in the ages when it was least in evidence. It is redundant to suggest that tragedy is dead or decrepit; that grumble has become a literary obsession, and the dread day may come when books and articles on tragedy rival in number those on Shakespeare. Ironically, however, no one has followed up on the pessimism-optimism conflict.

I had better set my semantics straight now—in a preliminary way, at least—on this argument of "pessimism" versus "optimism." Most playwrights being popular rather than professional philosophers, I cannot expect that modern tragedies will contain formal statements of existence-value as made by a Plato, Hobbes, Russell, or any other trained philosopher. If I talk about a writer's outlook on life, that will have to be identified in somewhat more popular and less pedagogical terms. Pessimism and optimism are not even bona fide philosophies: they remain, chiefly, personal attitudes and predispositions of response. But I would hardly go so far as Walter Kaufmann, in his *Tragedy and Philosophy*, who decides: "Optimism and pessimism are simplistic categories, and Nietzsche did us a disservice when . . . he introduced them into the discussion of tragedy."[3] I find this kind of offhand dismissal amazing. Simplistic or not, the two alternatives of thought are utterly basic. Men discuss them, and even base their lives on the result. Artists choose them. Critics must deal with them too.

Tragedy [New York, 1956]) All this occurs within the space of three pages. Muller's qualifications of the positions do not wholly erase the feeling that he has confused pessimism and "positive values," even if he were taking pessimism in the bold sense of a Spengler or a von Hartmann. And the bulk of the book, in criticism of the modern drama as nontragic, amounts to a support of optimism.

3. Walter Kaufmann, *Tragedy and Philosophy* (New York, 1969), p. 214. The phrases theorizing that "tragedy is pessimistic" or "tragedy is optimistic," or a mixture of both, can be found moderately often in essays on tragedy. But they get brushed aside, as Kaufmann would have it, or receive little elaborated defense. In *Tragedy: A View of Life* (Ithaca, N.Y., 1956), p. 4, Henry A. Myers writes: "The tragic attitude is not optimism, for it does not represent the little that is evil in the world as rapidly diminishing, and it is not pessimism, for it does not represent that inevitable obliteration of good which leads one away from the unyielding persistence of the tragic hero and toward the resignation and acceptance of forgetfulness." From this, Myers is content to accept tragedy as "two-sided always."

Optimisme first appears, as that term, in France in 1737; the word "pessimism" does not occur to anyone until 1795. The dictionary says that pessimism is the "doctrine or belief that the evil in life outweighs the good" and is also the "tendency to expect misfortune or the worst outcome in any circumstance." This is a clear enough base, but it can be enriched by the more descriptive definition made by Albert Schweitzer: "Pessimism is depreciated will-to-live, and is found wherever man and society are no longer under the pressure of all those ideals of progress which must be thought out by a will-to-live that is consistent with itself, but have sunk to the level of letting actuality be, over wide stretches of life, nothing but actuality."[4] Optimism, of course, is not simply the absence or the reverse of pessimism. Again, Schweitzer's delineation of optimism—in its battle with pessimism—is particularly enlightening with reference to the credo that real tragedy is affirmative and optimistic:

> True optimism . . . consists in contemplating and willing the ideal in the light of a deep and self-consistent affirmation of life and the world. Because the spirit which is so directed proceeds with clear vision and impartial judgment in the valuing of all that is given, it wears to ordinary people the appearance of pessimism. [But] it wishes to pull down the old temples *in order to build them again more magnificently*[5] (my italics).

Such a type of optimism is akin to the healthy skepticism, as well as the fundamental optimism, of genuine tragedy. At any rate, pessimism and optimism are semantically and operatively quite *definite* outlooks. There need be little if any hedging about identifying their presence within a tragic statement.

Much more difficult is the comparative evaluation of their rationales —and, in fact, most of this book will have to grapple with that task. But let me make some introductory cases for each one against the other.

Doubt is clearly not new. It is probably much older than optimism, for primitive man must have had a very dark view of the terrors around him. In drama, some of the greatest ancient tragedies, such as Aeschylus's *Prometheus Bound*, are skeptical of the worth of existence. Formal cyni-

4. Albert Schweitzer, *The Philosophy of Civilization*, trans. C. T. Campion (New York, 1960), pp. 97–98.
5. Ibid., p. 99.

cism begins with Diogenes in fourth-century B.C. Athens,[6] and endures as a major force (though many of its antics were irrelevant to the tragedy question) throughout the whole Greek and Roman dramatic primacy. Homer experienced at least one period when he cursed existence. Yet all ancient and classical thought encompassed the reality of good as well as evil, and doubt, cynicism, or skepticism definitely did not then have to extend to pessimism. A *fully pessimistic* view of existence is quite new to tragedy—as this book intends to show.

The difference is in degree and goals. The skepticism of traditional tragedy does not categorically negate existence, and the goal of its doubting is ultimate truth. It doubts that knowledge is very attainable, in order to gain greater certainties in whatever knowledge *is* acceptable. It is anti-dogmatism, but not antilife. Classical cynicism preached the reduction of man's desires and appetites to limit outside influences that brought evil and unhappiness. Life could be virtuous, and happy, if thus "intelligently" lived. Doubt in other forms does not presuppose the whole world to be evil and meaningless; it attacks or challenges existing conditions to produce enlightenment and greater meaning. Pessimism, however, as expressed in modern drama, assumes that evil or meaninglessness is in irrevocable command of the universe. It shares that attitude Pierre Teilhard de Chardin talks against in fighting for his belief in the progress of man and the actuality of a future: the attitude that we are dejected because man and nature seem not to have progressed over the span of history, that although the subhuman became human, no such easily seen change has been evident since that first dramatic evolution. This is also the eschatological pessimism syndrome of "what can possibly be left for us?" Teilhard insists we *are* moving as a species. His essential man should be a seer: "Gazing upward, towards the space held in readiness for new creation, he dedicates himself body and soul, with faith reaffirmed, to a Progress which will bear with it or else sweep away all those who will not hear."[7] And God is the center, God will be "all in all." Tellingly, however, Teilhard is aware that this is laughable to what is now the majority

6. Not Antisthenes, as in the traditional view. The bohemian asceticism, indifferent to life, became a real "school" only with Diogenes. But it still was not pessimistic. See Donald R. Dudley, *A History of Cynicism* (London, 1937), chap. 1.

7. Pierre Teilhard de Chardin, *The Future of Man* (New York, 1964), p. 24; also chap. 22.

of consciousnesses: the pessimistic facts of life frown on its seeming mysticism.

In *The Birth of Tragedy*, Nietzsche shows that the problem of whether tragedy springs from pessimism or optimism goes back at least as far as Socrates' contributions to poetic theory—although pessimism as a formal system of thought did not then exist. Nietzsche held that the cynicism of Socrates and his pupil Plato was "naïve"—as well as a source of pessimism—in that it found the arts to be seductive in giving pleasure rather than utility. (A puzzling idea: did he mean a search for pleasure posits the nonpleasure of existing?) But he believed Socratism to be ultimately optimistic, the Socratic-Platonic dialectics celebrating "a jubilee in every conclusion," and he equated the optimism of its maxims—"virtue is knowledge; man only sins from ignorance; he who is virtuous is happy"— with the "death of tragedy." This seems a large confusion, and Morse Peckham complements it in his discussion of Nietzsche in *Beyond the Tragic Vision*.[8] He decides that Nietzsche's concept today would hold that both tragedy and comedy are sentimentalities which man has outgrown, and that the position has been substantiated and refined by the existentialists, logical positivists, et al. Perhaps so; this probably means the Nietzschean superman, like the existentialist, can transcend or dispense with such an "art of metaphysical comfort," as Nietzsche defined tragedy. A bad confusion follows from this, however. Peckham, seemingly with Nietzsche and on the optimism side in saying we leave the theatre in comfort, states that "tragedy reconciles us to life by persuading us to submit to it."[9] Now what? Is it optimism or pessimism which is nontragic? The suggested "adjustment syndrome" in the above quotation seriously neglects the basic arrogance of enacting tragic art and rather lustfully witnessing it: we *affirm* our lives by escaping, partially, their mortal conformity and by stretching their normal limits. We learn and see nothing in submission; with such stasis, why witness any further tragic art at all? This mistaken view is one result of the surprising critical silence on the whole pessimism-optimism question. In *The Birth of Tragedy*, at least, Nietzsche showed the difference between Greek optimism and the modern tragic attitude by suggesting "Apollonian" (dreamlike, therefore hopeful) and "Dionysian" (drunken, remoter from mind and

8. Morse Peckham, *Beyond the Tragic Vision* (New York, 1962), p. 369.
9. Ibid.

ideal) states in the poetic illusion of life, pointedly subtitling his book *Hellenism or Pessimism*. I think these terms are a bit more useful than Nietzsche's more rarified philosophical discussion.

Whether or not addressing themselves to the question of tragedy so much as did Nietzsche, the pessimistic philosophers have had the best of the Leibnizian optimists in modern times. Hobbes, Montaigne, Pascal, Schopenhauer—all have found man's desires to be a preponderant and eternal frustration of pleasure or life-affirmation because of the destructive evil inherent in their satisfaction. Schopenhauer particularly influenced the case for pessimism in elaborating on the Brahmanic notion of desire leading to evil. Eduard von Hartmann made pessimism actually popular. The sum of evil was so obviously greater than the sum of good in his time, he said, that one could get enthusiastically involved in the brave and "energetic" tasks of facing up to the trial of existence. And it must be admitted that they—the philosophical pessimists—did a better job of relating to the facts of existence than Leibniz. Finding reasonableness and rationality in this, "the best of all possible worlds," Leibniz did not exactly account for physical, historical proofs to the contrary. The optimism position—like the Teilhard de Chardin credo—does seem to rest more on subjective "evidence." But thereby hangs a great tale, which I presume to tell later in this book. For now I want to illustrate what this debate means to tragic drama in more practical terms.

The following is an argument between two important theatre men of today. Arthur Miller, whose own work perhaps disproves his public position on the subject, writes:

> There is a misconception of tragedy with which I have been struck in review after review, and in many conversations with writers and readers alike. It is the idea that tragedy is of necessity allied to pessimism. Even the dictionary says nothing more about the word than that it means a story with a sad or unhappy ending. This impression is so firmly fixed that I almost hesitate to claim that in truth tragedy implies more optimism in its author than does comedy, and that its final result ought to be the reinforcement of the onlooker's brightest opinions of the human animal.[10]

10. Quoted in Tom F. Driver, "Strength and Weakness in Arthur Miller," *Tulane Drama Review* 4 (May 1960): 50.

But director Harold Clurman finds no evil in pessimism in the theatre, suspecting that "our optimism . . . is often dread in disguise." He implies that serious plays have a right to more pessimism than optimism: "Good pessimism may be an intelligent confrontation of what life is. There is more vitality in classical pessimism than there is gaiety or uplift in our 'optimistic' comedies. . . . What is in dispute now is the implication that a play is bad when it is pessimistic—a hypothesis I believe to be pernicious as well as false."[11]

The debate between Miller and Clurman is very illustrative and less definitive. With the possible exception of *The Crucible*, Miller's own plays do not carry out his wise instructions for the proper tragic outlook. And, significantly, Clurman cites standards of vitality in *classical* pessimism, not the modern, while what he calls pessimism in classic drama is much more likely to be skepticism, if only because his argument is semantically incomplete. (As already stated, pessimism is a modern-day "philosophy.") He, and others, may assume too angrily and easily that people who object to pessimism in the theatre are addicted to rose-colored glasses or mass soporifics, while those who accept pessimism are feet-on-the-dirty-ground realists who boldly recognize evil and meanness as inevitable facts of life. Whether or not the hypothesis is "pernicious," I am convinced that—while a pessimistic play can sometimes be perfectly good ordinary drama—a tragedy *is* bad (that is, nontragic) when it is pessimistic. As Walter Kaufmann has admitted, though (like all other philosophers) he does not elaborate: "We have been told that tragedy is dead, that it died of optimism, faith in reason, confidence in progress. Tragedy is not dead, but what estranges us from it is just the opposite: despair."[12]

What helps to make this so serious is today's solidarity in extreme pessimism. An analysis of modern plays[13] does reveal that deep pessimism occurs far more often now than ever before. It is the wrong *Weltanschauung* compared to that optimistic vision Krutch described in 1929:

> [Tragedy] must gratify or at least reconcile the desires of the
> beholder, not necessarily, as the naïver exponents of Freudian
> psychology maintain, by gratifying individual and often ec-

11. Harold Clurman, "Pessimism in Drama," *Nation*, 9 May 1953, p. 402.
12. *Tragedy and Philosophy*, p. xviii.
13. See Appendixes.

centric wishes, but at least by satisfying the universally human desire to find in the world some justice, some meaning, or, at the very least, some recognizable order. Hence it is that every real tragedy, however tremendous it may be, is an affirmation of faith in life, a declaration that even if God is not in his Heaven, then at least Man is in his world. We accept gladly the outward defeats which it describes for the sake of the inward victories which it reveals.[14]

THE CONCEPT OF MODERN TRAGEDY

What do I mean by "modern tragedies?" What plays am I going to talk about? If pessimism and optimism are rather subjective labels to some critics, still more find "modern tragedy" a complete will-o'-the-wisp.

Are "new" tragedies self-defining, and thus self-validating—regardless of their vision? How do you identify the modern play intended as a tragedy, let alone decide whether or not it achieves the tragic standard of quality? The playwrights themselves have been schizophrenic on the point. I have already referred to Arthur Miller's self-contradiction. Or witness Maxwell Anderson, author of "The Essence of Tragedy."[15] That essay is mistitled since Anderson offers nothing more than a brief defense of two ingredients of tragedy, with barely a paragraph on its more spiritual "essence." But, as far as he goes, he is old party-line Aristotle: tragedy must show discovery which improves the hero as human being, for the benefit of audience enlightenment. It should be like "religious affirmation, an age-old rite restating and reassuring man's belief in his own destiny and his ultimate hope." That's fine, but then read or see Anderson's plays.

I don't intend to start a comprehensive discussion of the problem of definition. For that, one should turn to Oscar Mandel, F. L. Lucas,[16]

14. Joseph Wood Krutch, "The Tragic Fallacy," in *European Theories of the Drama*, ed. Barrett Clark (New York, 1947), pp. 520–21.

15. It appears in his book *Off-Broadway* (New York, 1947).

16. See Oscar Mandel, *A Definition of Tragedy* (New York, 1961) and F. L. Lucas, *Tragedy in Relation to Aristotle's Poetics* (London, 1927; rev. ed., New York, 1957). Walter Kaufmann in *Tragedy and Philosophy* offers his own "new" definition but it is not presented as a thoroughly worked-out fresh contribution.

or several others who have made good, up-to-date, studies of the formula of tragedy. Nevertheless, some peace needs to be made with the familiar controversy if I am to talk about a body of American tragedies. A strict Aristotelian definition, of course, entirely wipes out a notion of "modern tragedy." Also, producing a tragedy today which fits exact classic requirements such as the Aristotelian would really mean begetting an anachronism. If our critics persist in quoting *The Poetics* during their lamentations over the "death" of tragedy, all they can say with any reasonable accuracy is that modern plays failing to be tragic in the Aristotelian sense are: first, not Aristotelian tragedies; and second, not tragic according to some private, subjective estimate. Neither is a conclusive statement. On the other hand, if we adjust our definition of what is successful tragedy according to the peculiar psyche of our time, then hundreds of neurosis-chronicling melodramas might have to be admitted for discussion. The main point here is that there can be no fully brand-new standard of tragedy because one cannot ignore its long, rich, and *tested* tradition; we must give the traditionalists that much. Unless some playwright wishes to claim he has invented a new genre (such as the special tragi-comedy of the absurdists) any attempt to write "a tragedy" is at least partly based on producing the essential satisfactions which were present in past, successful tragedies. And we know something about these essential satisfactions from our knowledge of present productions, and the production history, of the best traditional works. That is, we have a fair idea of what happened when tragedy really worked. Our grasp has to be a bit intuitive.

I want to show this fairly systematically, however. I think the most useful standard for my purpose is a compromise—to work out the common denominators of the most respected (*production*-oriented) traditional and modern theories, most of which after all were based on noting what best led to tragic effect. What is the minimum agreement among Aristotle, Hegel, A. C. Bradley, Herbert Muller, and their like? Such a consensus would of necessity be understrict and general, and thus open the door to a fair sample of plays which have any claim at all to the tragic. We would have some sort of "definition" for argument's sake.

As I work it out, this middle ground among the Aristotelian, Shakespearean, and contemporary practices or definitions of tragedy come down to these requirements: 1. The central character or protagonist, if not always virtuous, must at least be seen as the center of theatrical attention and thus be in a position to enact something about whatever meaning-of-existence thought is involved in his crisis. 2. The crisis of the play, therefore, must center on the suffering of the central character. 3. His suffering must be in the form of emotional or spritual destruction as a minimum outcome; otherwise it is his complete physical destruction. 4. There must be a serious theme to the play in that thought is applied to the value (better yet, the meaning) of life, and some attempt at universal relevance in that the actions concern a broader section of humanity than an obviously localized ethnic, occupational, or other group. 5. The action should be at least slightly fictionalized beyond unembellished documentation of actual misfortune in real life. 6. The level of the spoken text must make some attempt, by commenting on as well as reporting the facts, at expressing the tragedy in terms of the fate of man.

Thus armed, I think it would be fair to talk about several dozen American plays as attempts at tragedy. Eventually, we will see nearly all of them as "different" tragedies—in that they depart from the traditional or satisfying tragedy not in these more tangible matters of ingredient or structure but in their tragic vision: the underlying attitude which influences all the ingredients. That, finally, is the most vital means to tragic pleasure, something about which an audience can and must be more intuitive than in the use of a crossly defended and scholarly list of literary-dramatic components.

A METHOD OF STUDY

Now, what to do with the working definition? Spotting "modern tragedies" aside, how can I insist on a particular kind of tragic vision? Is this only another "your 'beauty' versus my 'beauty'" argument? There is some merit in Walter Kaufmann's observation: "What is odd is not that nobody in the twentieth century writes Greek or Elizabethan tragedies, but rather that so many writers think this calls for comment and regret. After all, critics do not moan that nobody today writes music very similar to Palestrina's or Monteverdi's, or that the novel has replaced, after a fashion, epic poetry."[17] A nice *riposte*, on the surface, but Kaufmann mixes his logical supports badly. Missing Palestrina is not the same as

17. *Tragedy and Philosophy*, p. 374.

missing a basic musical genre of universal significance (were music to have an analog for tragedy); missing the epic poem is not missing a literary form which has a particular vision of life which has been curiously satisfying since the beginning of Western civilization. The epic poem is largely a structural phenomenon, Palestrina's and Monteverdi's music only a stylistic excellence of a single era.

I do accept the logic that I can only begin by saying that what tragedy is written for the twentieth century is merely different from that of Sophocles or Shakespeare or the ancient ritualists. It is not thereby faulty. On the other hand, it is viscerally clear in the act of going to the theatre (and, to a lesser degree, in reading modern serious plays) that the old sensations constituting a tragic pleasure simply aren't there. There is decline and it's time to explain it without a problematical subjectivity. While there have been, say, analyses of the Freudian touches or the Nietzschean influences in O'Neill, Williams, and Miller—or the nihilism in nonobjective theatre—there has been little relating of the practical meaning of such supposed influences on modern playwrights, and on them as a whole group. What do the influences do to a tragedian's dramaturgy, meaning, language, insight? As for the "fear" influence I see, it will not be enough to demonstrate that modern writers are more pessimistic than the Greek, Elizabethan, or neoclassic French paragons. Is the pessimism really the cause of weakened tragedy?

Those critical of our modern tragedians have mentioned several possible causal shortcomings. The first, dramatic technique, really can't be considered a significant difference between the modern and the classicist. Was Euripides that much more "talented" than Tennessee Williams? Racine than Miller? Or, is there something wrong with the modern's choice of material? Sometimes, perhaps: but this cannot be a fundamental cause. Especially today a writer is free to take his situations and his characters from nearly any source he chooses. He is not forced to dramatize a common salesman instead of a king. He is not forced to chronicle sexual trauma in a squalid neighborhood instead of a struggle for power in a royal court. We'll go along with practically anything sincere—and even sometimes when it is not. The same goes for stylistic range. Nor is there mitigation in intent. Modern authors have left all kinds of clues to the effect that they were most definitely trying to write *tragedy*. The one remaining significant difference should be obvious. It is the playwright's *attitude* which must be analyzed, and in tragedy that means his philosophical disposition.

Once I have picked out our modern tragedies, I am more concerned with "tragic vision," which is not necessarily the same as "tragedy"—in other words, more concerned with what they *do* than what they *are*. Within that concern, I will discuss features of tragedy only as they pertain to the debate between pessimistic and optimistic vision. I want to do this by seeing what has happened to the major features of dramatic-tragic experience in our time and how significantly the results derive from pessimistic impetus. The evaluation of this philosophy—if you allow that term to describe any individual playwright's outlook on life—must be in terms of its bearing on tragedy *as* tragedy, and as effective theatre. The method, from which I report only results, includes this investigative sequence: identification of the relevant plays; content-analysis of each play's premise or theme; identification of the resulting tragic vision; and, qualitative analysis of any effects of theme on plot, shape of plot, ease of dramatugy, characterization, language, nature and timing of the climax, and the like.

In brief, what must be done with the "fear" problem is to examine the change in the delicate interaction between the actual perception and the artistic conception of tragedy. The bond between tragedy and fear today is too governed, I believe, by the playwright's own dread of his world. In contrast, the "fear" that Aristotle mentioned in his unshakable yet ambiguous definition of tragedy is a temporary fear to be produced *in the audience*—not in the playwright as well—separated by some aesthetic distance from the play. Confronting that together, we then move on. The old forward-looking awe of great tragedy has given way to a futureless dread hardly at all removed from the playwright's dreadful perception of modern reality.

Part One:

FROM OPTIMISM to PESSIMISM

1. *BETWEEN OPTIMISM and PESSIMISM*

This should be an age of beautiful tragedies. After all, it is an age of hugely tragic events.

For a while, we are doing without. I sit in the theatre, watching the new plays—all those partial searches and attempts. I am not alone; the theatres are not emptying these days. Too often, however, the reconceived revivals as well as the new dramas do not spark a serious pleasure—akin to the tragic. The very latest "serious" work is obligatory conformist cynicism or some mindless homage to the icons of revolution. Eventually I sense around me that familiar and tangible frustration, unease, and impatience. I share it, but the most human of our complaints we keep as a dialogue with ourselves. The words for it are old: *Accidie*: "My spirit is drowsy; help me not to mark time." *Pathema*: "I fear death, and I fear for our life. Excite me: I want to dream and hero-worship and escape— *within the shape of understanding*. My outer life, so heavily reined, waits for justification; let this second life touch fancy. Are the two reconciled only with guilt?"

Neither the life of the world nor the life of the fancy needs to go this way. There are as many springs as winters. But our century's serious stories do not say so.

Thus burdened, we look to see the special sign of tragic art. In looking, we do find other kinds of beauty: man still survives himself. But the artists of our time cannot make tragedy—meaning—out of the tragic. They try—but there is something wrong with their thinking and how they see.

FEAR AS FLAW

Somewhere in his religious speculations, newly civilized man adorned his spirit; somewhere in the cynicism of his intellectual progress, his descendant chose to strip it. Having realized he possessed a soul, that impressionable early man had invented the tragic myth; discovering later that the myth was fiction, jaded modern man turned to the philosophies of fear and despair: pessimism, nihilism, and their kin.

Tragedy and pessimism (in the latter's various forms) have philosophical bases which, today, are especially intriguing to compare. The first is a magnificent expression of man's growth; the second, probably, a sign of his decline—at least where such intangibles as spirit are concerned. We needn't yet, however, believe the decline is universal or irreversible.

Tragedy predates pessimism as an organized system of thought by many centuries but now, in the twentieth century, pessimism has a great deal to do with attempting tragedy and tragedy has a great deal to say about the efficacy of pessimism. The paths of these two brands of thinking—and true tragedy is inherently a philosophy—cross first at the informal levels of individual world views, where a man makes his personal comparison between stating an equation for existence and noting the horrors and injustices of his world. In art and culture, the relationship is much more systematically and eloquently recorded: the paths cross again in any art forms where the artist's philosophy and psychological makeup have a strong effect on his work, where craft and technique are not enough. Tragedy is supremely such a creation but now, when we need it most, this normally instinctive genre is at one of its lowest ebbs. Tragic expression demands commenting on our humanity, betraying all the everyday concerns, credos, and reasons-for-being—privately repressed or publicly analyzed—which characterize our tenure with the conduct of life and our role in the destiny of our race. Today we *know* more of what is happening on our way to a tomorrow but *understand* correspondingly less of it. We are burdened with nonfulfilment even as we create a growing array of machinery and medicines of one kind or another for coping with the massive *angst* of the day. Through it all, there is one central sorrow: we could cry, almost uncontrollably, to think of the difference between man as he popularly behaves and man as he might have been by this time in his history. Hidden squarely in the middle of the gap, as in a mystery, is the essential emotional revelation of the artistically "tragic" creation.

Finally then, it is fear that impedes tragedy: how very many things we fear today. More than ever before, more acutely than in our primal memories (the species' *anamnesis*) of dark caves, puny fires, and the battle for subsistence, these lurking shadows—from vague uncertainties to outright terror—darken thought and affect not just literary debates or nice philosophical distinctions but the very manifestation of whatever opinions of existence we do have. Those who think at all can worry perpetually. We curse the ungovernability of man. We groan at the promise of democracy going sour while the majorities seem more often to embrace far less human systems. Aren't we really losing the battle against injustice? What about the galling increase in the compromise of man's concept of laws and order? Has education really dented the ignorant mob, or reached the people who cannot listen to reason? Man's physical life has improved, subpar though it may still be for some millions—why then does he seem spiritually less dignified and divine than in eras of plague, feudal tyranny, or universal slavery?

Far more than in formal artworks alone, other tensions reflect our exceptional struggle toward a world view. Camps of "either-or" proliferate; all those centuries before ours either wholly or relatively free of pessimism experienced significantly less militant calls of "if you're not all for it, you must be against it "—with particular regard to thought and action dependent in any way on faith. There are many such dilemmas, with most vocal majorities now on the negativist side. Which will you have: cynicism—or blind faith in "heritage" or "dogma?" Absurdism, with its "laudably" cold intellect and emotion—or the pleasure of objective meaning? Conservatism (in morals, politics, art, social rights)—or Liberalism? Church (and the integrity of its denominations)—or churchlessness, as the enlightened and inevitable late-twentieth-century step beyond ec-umenicism? The cult of youth—or the defensive fogyism of the adult?

These simplistic alternatives increasingly intrude upon our life-style—partly, it is true, because the dangers to our existence are excessively real and ironically seem more beyond our control. It is no time for fuzzy faith and embroidered mottoes on the wall. But it is also the legacy of a natural if haphazard evolution toward becoming the Jaded Society, or the An-archic Society. This evolution features a kind of education (formal in the classroom, but also now popularized through the fashion of dissent) which superencourages questioning, counterpointed by the facts of ex-istence which answer those questions in terms which seem to make faith laughable. The appropriate end, like Schopenhauer's "Nothing," is our "New Hedonism": we want only to live for now, some say, and we live corruptedly free of myth. Further, there is more powerlessness and more submission, the former justifying the latter or the latter creating the former. Regardless of which came first—though I will draw my own conclusions later—our estimate of ourselves is dim, and the literary-artistic manifestation of this is certainly relevant to the manner in which we think, live, and relate to our image of man today.

Thus—obsessed with phenomena and against the essential posture of myth, creativity, fable, allegory, creed, morality, archetype, and other nonphenomenal products of the mind—we people history's most *afraid* age. (An important corollary to this is that we cannot trust; whatever the justification, the fact remains that inability to trust fellow man is the operative factor in all of the era's most plaguing crises.) The curious thing is that—for all the objective evidence of our suffering—we as yet show little wisdom in expressing the tragic sense of life in our art. Why? Because *this fear, as pessimism, is antitragic.* Great tragic art has always been synonymous with great humanism, where the best thinking and imagination of the age gladly pitted themselves against the challenge of life. The basic philosophical question, best dramatized as a religious document in *The Book of Job,* has always been: "Does life make sense?" The manner in which this question is met or avoided inevitably char-acterizes man's various schools of philosophy, and the artistic dramatiza-tion of the question and its attempted answer is the reason for tragedy. It seems to me that there can be no tragic art which is ultimately an ex-pression of pessimistic belief.

THE MARKET FOR TRAGEDY

I don't want to sound the indignant alarm at a dearth of tragic drama; that is, after all, only a historical norm. I am thankful for the near-tragedies which I can comfortably call "great plays": *The Glass Menagerie, Death of a Salesman,* and *A Streetcar Named Desire*—to name only American works. There are several others, including some which had no ambition toward tragedy whatsoever. Furthermore, tragedy still lives; the only way it can truly die is for all people to utterly reject the revival of the old tragedies at the same time the playwrights are unable to make tragedy that is new. So my task is one of explanation rather than damnation. Tragedy, right now passing its own special milestone, contains many of the symbolic tensions of the real philosophical-aesthetic problems I've been listing.

One aspect of what's happening shows up in a more recent play that I admire very much. In Edward Albee's *A Delicate Balance* we have the most significant representation of the essence, and the effective treatment, of a world view of the 1960s or 1970s. The catalytic characters Harry and Edna bring what they call "the terror" into the house of Tobias and Agnes: a house of better-than-average wealth, education, sophistication—and completely typical spiritual desolation. While they insist, as old friends, on their right to "succor," they infect Tobias's family with their "plague." They move in.

The dramatization and description of this almost ludicrously blunt action is poetic in its moderate abstraction; Albee's insights are indirectly revealed but enormously suggestive to the point of near-universality. The play acts out a response to "the terror" as a very true dramatic metaphor for mid-twentieth-century fear, and the insights are brutal exposures of our perhaps unique loneliness based on our perception of figurative and literal death. That last is "the terror." A parallel metaphoric action might be to wear a sandwich-board to your next cocktail party—one which read, "Love me! I am afraid!" This forces our consideration: *can* we, any of us, spare concern from our own self-directed supply? "Dying," in this substitute-tragedy, is the passage of time in lives which have no hope of accomplishing what was once intended. Each moment is an opportunity lost for submitting to the ultimate cure of human exchange, but the characters cannot resist their selfish (i.e., mortal and very human) demons which, in turn, can't let them forget their own need for a distraction away from the vision of their mortality. The audience is confronted with a pesssimistic, poetic enactment: we are all dying and to some degree failing, and we know it so well that we cannot keep our minds on the more faithful job of human intercourse. Agnes touches on the theme:

> Time.
> Time happens, I suppose.
> To people. Everything becomes . . .
> too late, finally.

Could Albee have made a tragedy from this material? No. And his choice not to was perfectly right: he was writing in the 1960s. Theme isn't the point, because his theme is old. The play is a kind of drawing-room melodrama whose real contribution is exposure of The Truth, and there is something interesting in this with regard to the position of the playwright writing in the age of fear. By contrast, tragedy's job would be to consider the means and meanings of "the terror's" conquest. Tragedy would not be *against* meaninglessness—exposing that "truth"—but *for* something more: the attempted overthrow of evils which contribute to the "false" notion that life has no meaning.

And yet Albee convinces me *while I watch his play*. I can't really fault the pessimism. I think that if the play had aimed for tragedy, however, its pessimism would have made the attempt completely false. At least in terms of my illustration, *A Delicate Balance* emerges as an excellent philosophical image of our time precisely *because* it does not attempt the formula of tragedy—as perhaps *Tiny Alice* did. And if our other major twentieth-century playwrights (Williams, Miller, O'Neill, and a few others) had been at their full powers in the 1960s, I think we would have seen them avoiding the repetition of their old attempts at the genre. (Although you can find people who claim that Miller's 1964 play *After the Fall* is tragedy.)

This is the epochal turning point, then, because the decade of the sixties marks the end of a major quest for modern tragedy. No one has really attempted tragedy since the late 1950s, and when the genre is dusted off again—as it certainly will be—playwrights will have learned much from the implications of the stoppage. Thus we happen to have a neatly isolated era, 1920 to 1960, which contains virtually all of our weak tries at a twentieth-century tragic drama. There is a reason for the weakness and for the moratorium and, while we are in this waiting-period of experiment, we have a timely opportunity to examine the record.

Added to the "reason" in its perennial pessimism, modern tragedy is now also too conventional a proposition and therefore too risky a thing in a serious theatre which has gone heavily over to the vogue of the ephemeral in search of new sensation and surface form—to the vogue of newness for its own sake, categorical revolt, and taboo-breaking. All the influences since absurdism have magnified the theatre leaders' current fear of the "square" (though many musicals and comedies do maintain the old tried patterns)—and there is a minimum standard for the tragic formula which does indeed give it a relative "squareness."

Still, the thought behind the semitragedies remains with us in the newer nontragic styles. More than ever, the playwright finds progress an inconceivable idea. Now, it is more and more difficult to find a substantial serious play in each passing theatre season—let alone a tragedy. The dark comedies of cruelty and ritual are our current concerns. Nonetheless, the mocking new plays do pretend relevance to our life-meaning. Pessimism can share some of the blame (or credit) for this, too. Perhaps when you push pessimism to its limit long enough it must come full circle and find its form in a kind of comic vision. Perhaps many new writers are defended in Schiller's observation that comedy could have higher aims than tragedy, and make tragedy superfluous, its ultimate end being "to attribute more to chance than to destiny, and rather to laugh at inconsequence than to rage or weep at wickedness." Long Live the New Young Cynics, then, and good-bye to any neo-Shakespeares? The seeming vote for absurdism and its descendants is tempered by Schiller's added condition that this would be the case only when comedy was perfected. We haven't gotten there yet. When it comes to new work, in any case, most important Western theatre now rates stylistic fashions and intermedia experimentation more highly than theme and content. Tragedy is dormant because it does not look viable against the great pressure wave of salable cant, fad, and experimentalism. Our standards are staggeringly insecure right now. Even the word "standards" sounds repressive when permissiveness is the approach of the day. Motifs of cruelty, neoabsurdism, slander, and scatology are here because we either accept a serious (or serious-comic) theatre as a reminder of our guilts, or want a kind of catharsis via its blunt "honesty." Some of the new work is necessary and good but, in taking it all in, it is interesting how much we allow ourselves to be led more and more by the theatre prophets and visionaries. Those people used to have a terrible time with our dragging feet and scolding voices. Whatever the new theatre, anyway, deep pessimism still reigns; the message of the playwrights, wherever they comment on us, is hardly more hopeful and gives man nothing new to go on. Man is seen as ugly or mindless. The new black comedy is only another way of showing "what it's like"—as in the New American Exposés dreamed up by Megan Terry, Rochelle Owens, or Sam Shepard. A *Delicate Balance*, on the other hand, just happens to be a particularly thoughtful and meaningful presentation of an existence problem of today, though set into an already dated container.

But it is easy to be critical in this un-golden age. We ought to consider what it is like for the twentieth-century playwright. Can he make any easy choice between disgust and affirmation in commenting on our situation? Perhaps he has no choice. We should also remember that he has a much tougher audience to write for compared to the more insulated or less informed and sated audiences of any previous centuries. We believe in just as little as he does.

Let's look at it this way: is the modern serious playwright ever a happy man? Think of the radicals now, then of Genet, Beckett, Albee, Osborne, Miller, Williams, and then back to O'Neill, Anderson, Sherwood, and the others. (Here I might well have Euripides, or Tasso, or Oliver Goldsmith, or a few hundred more unhappies of yesterday thrown back at me —but was what they did with their "unhappiness" the same?) True, one definition of the artist is that he is a man dissatisfied; if he were totally happy, there would be nothing to write about. How can he be happy today when one of his gifts is to have better eyes than we do? Does he see actual triumph anywhere? How many people does he love, including himself, and how many love him? Does that really matter? In tragedy, it just might.

Here I think our playwright is somewhat like Colin Wilson's "Outsider" (although Wilson believed this could never be a possible identity for the artist). That is, he is a man who is "never alive in what he does," who is "not himself," but "a pipe through which life flows" because he can "never stop thinking."[1] He lacks appetite for life, partly because his vision denies him self-expression. This last symptom would seem to show that the contemporary playwright is not an Outsider—Wilson's conception of the central sick man of this age. Writing tragedy from fear, however, puts "self-expression" in a less healthy or curative light. The serious playwright of today is also an Admonitor. He speaks for us and himself much more in the sense of warning or chastisement—and, at the least, he does not love us. Sometimes he hates us.

The Outsider can't help what he sees and thinks and the playwright as Outsider-Admonitor is, in that respect, not to blame for mixing tragedy and fear. But that doesn't stop us from knowing in our bones that this is not what we need or want.

THE LAW OF HOPE

What *do* we need? Can we suppose extreme pessimism was acceptable when the "constitution" for tragedy was first written? The evidence is against it; instead, there is ample tradition for the optimism position in the ancient ritual tragedies. I'll briefly sketch in this alternative for tragic art before getting into the specifics of my main study.

While the rough outlines of these archaic stories are fairly familiar, that familiarity is also deceptive. It has special effect. Here is a preliminary suggestion about the ideal of tragic vision: the stories *are* immediately the form, content, and essence of "tragedy" as man invented it for himself—art without the window-dressing of art theory. Their simple essence reaffirms the possibility of an innate, universal "tragic pleasure" motif outside of later philosophic complexities.

1. These are general concepts from Wilson's *The Outsider* (New York, 1956). Selden Rodman, in his criticism of the aesthetic and philosophical intentions of modern artists, is one who specifically objects to Wilson's concept of the Outsider, whether artist or not. He says that Wilson misreads certain artists' spiritual dilemmas. I think Rodman, in turn, misreads Wilson—the latter using his imagined psychic recreations of certain archetypal Outsiders as a vehicle for defining a contemporary philosophical sickness as against writing traditional criticism. In any case, Rodman prefers to think of worthwhile artists of our time as aspiring Insiders—humanists who will dare to put man right back in the center of art again. See Selden Rodman, *The Insiders: Rejection and Rediscovery of Man in the Arts of Our Time* (Baton Rouge, La., 1960). But he's talking about what they ought to be; I'll stay with Outsiders as what they are.

It would be an excessive diversion to summarize the plots and "points" of all the old tragic ritual-myths, but such a summary would spotlight a striking feature: their similarity to one another. Tammuz, Dionysus, Osiris, Adonis: their rituals, which are always *quests*, are alike in a way that goes beyond the possibility of coincidence. This is the "monomyth" theory at work.[2] Long before the birth of Christ, the natural religion of tragedy was invented—simply because man needed it. In ancient and widely separated civilizations such as those of Egypt, Mexico, and Tibet— where no exchange of ideas could have existed among societies because of obvious geographical, not to mention chronological, barriers—great dramatic mysteries were contrived along common lines, toward a common purpose. From the earliest of these inventings, the basic religious and poetic experience of tragedy has remained essentially the same, for it sprang from a hunger that is little different in man of 3000 B.C., A.D. 1600, or of the twentieth century.

As tragedy should do today—difficult as this is to accept—the great tragic legends of ancient times always asked the same questions in the *hope* of discovery: "What is man, and what determines his fate? To what can man aspire?" Even then, the partnership of tragedy and philosophy was cemented. The resulting answer was a contrived, *promising* suggestion. The stories were made to show that progress and improvement just might be possible, through a mixture of superb effort and faith. The Osiris story (of the good king who was destroyed by evil only to be resurrected), like others, even exploited the downright simple-mindedness of its peasant audience: *you* may not rise far, but *some* men *do* become gods. Well, why not? Even today, we do not and should not insist on utter facticity for the calming or the challenging of our spirits. As Erik Erikson writes in *Insight and Responsibility*: ". . . there is something in the anatomy even of mature hope which suggests that it is the most child-like of all ego-qualities, and the most dependent for its verification on the charity of fate; thus religious sentiment induces adults to restore their hopefulness in periodic petitionary prayer, assuming a measure of childlikeness toward unseen, omnipotent popwers."[3] What may be that vague hope in the case of prayerful religion is in tragedy a more dis-

2. That is, a central pattern and commonality in all mythic ritual. See Lord Raglan, *The Hero* (Oxford, 1937).
3. Erik Erikson, *Insight and Responsibility* (London, 1964), p. 116.

ciplined expectation—because of the catastrophe which showers benefits on the witnesses.

In all the old rituals, then, the hero's "tragic flaw" was necessary so that the superman the people created would not become completely godlike. Otherwise, he could avoid suffering entirely—serving no scapegoat function and learning nothing from an embattled discovery of man's capacities in extremis, and of the outer limits of mortality. As he was, he had a greater capacity for suffering than ordinary man. Men died through him, and then experienced a rebirth which paralleled his own. His assumption of risk in carrying the fight to its conclusion enabled man to gather data on himself prior to the reality of his own death—and this resulted in hope. In much ancient ritual, the hope actually invited an expectation of transcending death. Later on, it at least meant the greater data afforded continuing possibilities for progress in the business of seeking the meaningful life. In the tragic passions, hope was always deliberately preordained by man's own creation: it was, in fact, a kind of dramaturgical-religious *law*. As Erikson says: "Hope is both the earliest and the most indispensable virtue inherent in the state of being alive."[4]

4. Ibid., p. 115.

2. NEW TRAGEDIES, NEW VISIONS

Emphasizing American theatre as the most active proving ground for the pessimism-optimism contest, I will now move to the specifics of a systematic study of the problem.

In America, the affair with tragedy started with O'Neill. It was a fairly clean beginning. In the rest of the world it was a turning point, toward the beginning of the end. In all cases, however, the early part of the twentieth century saw the development of or the transition to a tragic drama which was motivated by significantly changed personal outlooks in the playwrights. In several senses, our century has been the epoch of "new" tragedies.

This was the time when the American serious play (what there was of it) made an abrupt switch from optimism to pessimism. I suppose it was doubly understandable. Before the First World War, even our few attempts at a thoughtful, critical social realism had to have happy endings. Well into the century, producers still upheld the "average theatregoing taste" by insisting on a ban on pessimism and other kinds of offensive nastiness. In those days, in short, we were rather far to the right—and we should admit, as penance, that categorical outlawing of any feature of art is foolish. Let things fail uncensored: that's good politics, if nothing else.

Especially at first, the American tragedians ran hard with the ball they had just thrown themselves. Susan Glaspell and Eugene O'Neill started working on unhappy endings in laboratory-like theatres in Provincetown and Washington Square. And the twenties and thirties saw a good deal of theorizing on and criticism of tragedy; it was on our minds, as if we were heeding Shelley's warning about the equation between an absence of tragedy and a third-rate culture. Quantitatively, we did get to be Number One. Of course, the War and the general social tensions of a nation growing too fast in too many directions and going suddenly internationalist provided an overobvious supply of tragic topics. In general, the state of our tragedy then was overinfluenced, overimpressionable, and overhasty in achievement—but it did have the stereotyped American virtue of ambitious do-it-nowism. In America, tragedy was a novelty.

No such clear-cut epochs of modern tragedy evolved in England, France, Germany, or the other Western theatre cultures. In fact England in the same period fell behind the others in developing any kind of original playwriting. Content with Shaw's continuity and longevity, Galsworthy's *Justice* and other Edwardian reform-tragedies, English playwrights did not even match the social-problem-drama vitality of America's 1930s until John Osborne and a few other spokesmen of the working class broke the fusty monopoly of West End "entertainments" in the late 1950s. Their subjects were socially real and the modes new enough to show lack of dust, but still there was little to pretend to the title of tragedy. In Europe generally, there was understandable and laudable emphasis on following through with the producing and writing freedoms of the still peaking "ism" explosion and the free theatre movement. Attempts at tragedy were very rare; tragedy was not experimental. Except for the lonely pretensions and perhaps isolated successes of Ibsen, Tolstoy, Strindberg, Hauptmann, and a few others, tragedy had not developed the kind of nineteenth-century momentum to attract the twentieth-century playwright away from the lure and excitement of new styles, if not new themes. In terms of practical ambition, Europe's feet were more on the ground. On the other hand, the massive work and all the amateur psychology and philosophy expended in cultivating expressionism, impressionism, symbolism, and lingering naturalism and social realism did play a considerable role in influencing those later playwrights, European or otherwise, who *did* aspire to Melpomene's song.

And so perhaps typically brash and inexperienced American theatre has been the chief source of tragic writing in this century—but with the spirit apropos of the time. The despairing themes were not unique to America—really *echtig* German expressionism, for example, is among the most relentlessly black of dramatic portraits of man one can find—but it was the American who tried to create definite tragedy of, say, the war or dehumanization theme. And the Americans, like most beginning playwrights, were especially aware of formulas—of the general theory and structure of tragedy. They tended to see their themes in a tragic shape, and the usual distinction we make between a country's "serious" and "tragic" theatre was less often necessary.

Certainly the American theatre had a meagre tragic tradition on which to build. But if this fact was no help, it was also no hindrance. After the imitative formula tragedies had their day, the slate was clean of any old lessons for mating a *Weltanschauung* and a dramatic form. America, furthermore, had no Shakespeare against whom all national standards of tragic art, as in England, were inevitably measured. This too was both blessing and barrier. On balance, the only direction to go was upward. In the last century, there were scores of "tragedies" with such titles as *Oralloossa, The Gladiator, Brutus,* and *Francesca da Rimini,* written by such play-mechanics as G. H. Boker, Robert Montgomery Bird, and John Howard Payne—all manner of romantic-heroic-exotic-adventure tragedies which in fact were all formula vehicles, tragic only in their outer dressing. In this heyday of romantic tragedy—1830 to 1860—there was certainly no question of finding any native expression of the slightest originality confronting the problem of existence. Then came a steady diet of light comedy and musical shows, until O'Neill's 1920 tragedy, *Beyond the Horizon.* This was preceded by less than five years of experimentation with a few one-act tragedies, also mostly by O'Neill. From this date forward, however, some genuine serious theatre was to get an annual New York showing.

If their visions went "awry," what shaped the playwrights' new outlooks on life? Realistically, we must recognize really new influences which modern tragedians have been unable to escape. The most unique one, compared to those affecting writers of any other century, is the development of global war followed by acquisition of the means for instant doomsday. Perhaps here alone is a reason why we could never return to optimistic tragedy—but I think such a defense ignores basic conditions under which man's thought survives, as long as he himself survives. And notice that extreme pessimism began before this influence came about. World war has not been worldwide war. It was a relatively small fraction of the globe which was actively involved in the 1914–18 war, and there were still sizable areas of the world which did not feel war in the second "global" conflict. It is only today that we all feel, emotionally, liable to global involvement—because of nuclear weaponry. The pessimism has had other sources.

Other influences are in intellectual, scientific, and philosophical movements—part of a mushrooming thrust of knowledge and theory of the era. Modern communication, with the rapid growth of education and idea exchange, makes these influences more available and more prone to interinfluence. And thus the alienated intellectual who can spend a career devouring books, articles, symposia, works of art, and conversation regarding theology, psychology, sociology, political and social history, and the like—and get nary a morsel of brain food for a positive thought and hope. The evidence in the influences appears to be for the negative. Many of our playwrights have gone out of their way to show us that they have done their homework (in general serious playwrights in America can now be recognized as bona fide intellectuals if they wish) and that the wisdom of twentieth-century despair can be thoroughly documented. Several specific influences leave their traces most often.

First there is social Darwinism and some pure Darwinism: a hopeless awareness of the fallibility of heredity, the quixotic progress of natural evolution, and a consciousness of man's biological vulnerability. The key Darwin tenets read like some play premises: variations in offspring are governed by chance; in the struggle for existence, organisms whose chance variations are least fitted for adaptation to prevailing conditions are destroyed; man's presence on earth is an accident of nature in that he happened to develop those variations which allowed his survival. In practice, the influence becomes a kind of selective or weighted Darwinism —because most playwrights essentially state that man is not going to improve, that he does not evolve better species to cope with the changes in his environment.

Psychology is more than obviously a central influence. There is vast proof of man's psychological helplessness and irresponsibility, and many authors base a story of man's general limitedness on Freudianism and other popular sources of psychological theory. Oversimplifications of such material are particularly useful to the pessimist. Determinism, as with naturalism throughout the art world, got plenty of exercise. Notice, for example, how O'Neill kept coming up with his idea of the *tragic cycle*. As in his uncompleted chain of plays ended with *More Stately Mansions*, the central form is pure determinism: the evolution of the American dynasty of tragic families.

Other writings in social science add to the "facts" of human weakness. Cutthroat domestic and international economics (mixed with politics) are typical of man in society. This is partly more determinism. The playwright and the people generally are certain that a given economic system causes just one kind of culture and thus the future is cut and dried. If totalitarianism looms somewhere ahead, this is accepted as the direct result of a present brand of economics, political disease, or an indulgence in militarism.

Another key influence, widely acknowledged, is the marked change in attitude toward God and church in what Mircea Eliade has called our "desacralized age." Agnosticism and atheism, in a playwright's intellectual surroundings if not in himself, play large roles in his conception of tragic goals and the nature of modern ideals and justice. Death-of-God theory and associated Nietzscheanisms were involved at the beginning of the modern tragedy epoch in O'Neill's earliest work. Certain individual outlooks on the world are specifically aided by formal nihilist and negativist teachings. Conscious influence is of course difficult to locate and prove, as when some plays turn out to be good demonstrations of an existential viewpoint, and that detective work may be left to the doctoral dissertations. In general, however, the representative modern tragedian cannot be unfamiliar with the gist of major philosophical and theological credos leaning to agnostic or theologically pragmatic despair. For example, in today's intellectual climate, just where and how often are you going to get into a good discussion on "man as spiritual," "man made in God's image," "life as morality," "the rewards of existence," and the like?

Further possibilities are in artistic-literary style, as in naturalism's teaching of man's smallness and weakness or the existential position of absurdism. Expressionism, for another example, insists on dehumanization in characterization. Style can have a fashion and power which is hard to resist. Style and content can intertwine. Whether by means of style, science, or the general intellectual mood of his time (or a good pair of eyes), the playwright can defend a statement that we have made no discernible progress with love, and that man alone or in society hasn't the wherewithal to put a bit more divinity into his existence. I can't refute this. Somehow the writer learns to be pessimistic, and then uses certain influences deliberately to support a thesis. This I do regret. Without question, pessimistic tragedians are sometimes ill-equipped to interpret these scientific, philosophical, or other theories the way they do. But they read into them what they need.

THE ATTEMPTS

It is time I turned to specific examples in plays. According to the public and private critics, perhaps no American playwright succeeded with tragedy. According to minimum requirements (see my working definition of modern tragic drama in the introduction), quite a number attempted it. Quantity is finally unimporant, but I happen to find some sixty plays written for our representative national theatre (Broadway, like it or not) which qualify as "tragic."[1] The major voices of the movement have been O'Neill (a case can be made for seeing fifteen of his plays as attempts at modern tragedy); Maxwell Anderson (eleven plays); Tennessee Williams (at least five); and Arthur Miller, Clifford Odets, and Elmer Rice (at least three each). Within the overall body of our drama, some of the better-known tragic plays are O'Neill's *The Hairy Ape, Mourning Becomes Electra, and Strange Interlude;* Anderson's

1. For the complete list, see Appendix A.

Elizabeth the Queen, Mary of Scotland, Key Largo, and *Winterset;* Miller's *All My Sons,* plus of course *Death of a Salesman* and *The Crucible;* Williams's *Summer and Smoke, Orpheus Descending,* and *A Streetcar Named Desire;* Odets's *Golden Boy;* John Steinbeck's *Of Mice and Men;* Robert Sherwood's *The Petrified Forest;* Paul Green's *In Abraham's Bosom;* Rice's *The Adding Machine;* and Lillian Hellman's *The Children's Hour.* Among newer dramatists, Edward Albee might be seen as part-time tragedian in *Who's Afraid of Virginia Woolf?* or *Tiny Alice.*

There are many borderline "tragedies," as well as plays which meet most of the requirements of my fairly permissive modern-traditional consensus without ever intending to be tragic.[2] Whatever the best candidates are, the general picture is unlikely to change—of our twentieth-century conception of tragedy (or even "where are we going" commentary plays) based almost without exception on a new depth of pessimism. I find just three would-be tragedies which talk optimism. These are Robert Sherwood's *There Shall Be No Night,* Arthur Miller's *The Crucible,* and Archibald MacLeish's *J. B.* (Interestingly, none of these is now regarded as "sophisticated" drama.) For me, *The Crucible* is the closest the American theatre has come to authentic tragedy, though it does not rank as one of our great plays.

THE NEW VISIONS

The playwrights produced, consciously or not, several basically new visions of how man may see the "tragedy" of his world. Under each vision, a curious new thing happens: the audience is pressured by the *playwright's* role in, and attitude toward, the tragic situation. Overall, I have already tentatively named the contemporary tragedian Outsider-Admonitor. Now, more specifically, the playwright can be seen as having a special role in each contemporary outlook. To identify and discuss these is to begin to note major departures from a successful concept of the tragic.

First come the premises—the dynamics on which the plays are built, or the logical remains after a boiling-down. It may not be unfair to call

2. Oscar Mandel's term "paratragedy" would serve. He uses it to refer to plays which are serious intrigues or commentaries but lack final tragic ingredients such as tragic destruction. See *A Definition of Tragedy,* chap. 5.

them the authors' favorite obsessions. Sample premises include: Dreams and aspirations destroy the right to survive (in a world where "the cards are stacked against you"); Life is a sexual and/or psychological hell; Life is a meaningless treadmill; Life is an inescapable treadmill of sin and guilt; Man has neither the right nor the ability to climb out of his low station; Man is not responsible for his aberration; The sensitive are always destroyed by the insensitive majority; Man is incapable of justice and humanity; and, Social complexity destroys humanity and selflessness.[3] These premises are extrapolated from our tragic drama; they state what the given play acts out. How they are emphasized is a question of tragic vision.

The new visions are most clearly and meaningfully delineated when they are made to name the source of destruction in the tragedy. Thus I see the following major types: a Tragedy of Illusory Identity; of Irresponsibility; of Martyrdom; of Sensitivity; of Social Disintegration; of Imprisonment; and, of Inheritance. Some of my classifications, of course, seem little different from certain traditional types in Greek or Elizabethan models—the "Tragedy of Inheritance," for example. But these differ underneath, in the modern author's special attitude toward his concept. In the end, his treatment and its pessimistic emphasis make the resulting tragedy very unlike the old. Other visions, such as the Tragedy of Irresponsibility, are uniquely modern because they were suggested entirely by modern discovery or thought. Or they are from the very first, as in the

3. Plays built on these premises include: For "dreams and aspirations," etc., see (in the Appendix) *Beyond the Horizon, The Emperor Jones, Gold, Dynamo, Golden Boy, All My Sons,* and *Sweet Bird of Youth.* For "life is a sexual and/or psychological hell," see *Diff'rent, John Hawthorne, The Hand of the Potter, White Desert, Desire Under the Elms, Wild Birds, Out of the Sea, Machinal, Gypsy, Night Over Taos, The Children's Hour, Clash By Night, Cream in the Well, A Streetcar Named Desire, Summer and Smoke,* and *The Lovers.* For "life is a meaningless treadmill," see *The Adding Machine* and *Street Scene.* For ". . . treadmill of sin and guilt," see *Anna Christie, The Verge, Shame Woman, Gypsy, Ethan Frome,* and *Long Day's Journey into Night.* For "man has neither the right," etc., see *The Hairy Ape.* For "man is not responsible," etc., see *The Hand of the Potter* or *Of Mice and Men.* For "the sensitive. . . ," etc., see *The Right to Dream, The Great God Brown, The Petrified Forest, The Iceman Cometh, The Glass Menagerie,* and *A Streetcar Named Desire.* For "man incapable of justice," etc., see *Winterset* or *Incident at Vichy.* For "social complexity," etc., see *Death of a Salesman* or *Panic.* This, of course, is only a partial list and—as seen in the fact some plays are listed twice—a suggested point of departure.

Tragedy of Martyrdom, structurally contrary to the needs of tragic statement of whatever era.

There could be other categories as well as, perhaps, better names for them. I also know the classifications sometimes overlap, when certain attempts have auxiliary or subordinate themes. They do, however, indicate the primary source of the tragedy in the plays of each type and I believe the seven categories do describe all the *major* tragic visions developed by our twentieth-century playwrights.[4] While labels should not be sacred, the philosophical intents have been neither isolated nor hidden and the kinship of certain kinds of attempts at tragedy thus more clearly seen does reveal a lot about the view of life which the given plays attempt to express. I will now give brief descriptions of what these modern pessimistic visions appear to say to us.

The Tragedy of Illusory Identity

Problems of illusion regarding identity go back at least as far as Oedipus, but their pessimistic application in a complete tragic vision begins with O'Neill. O'Neill is still the chief user of the vision, and he depended heavily on giving his victims a "touch of the poet." It is a touch which beckons man to drug himself, and the tragedy finds the writer serving as a kind of Anesthetist-figure. The resulting protagonist is an inebriated or drugged type, or a "mad" visionary, and he lives a lie in terms of his life situation. He generates despair and learns nothing while he pits an impractical ideal against grim reality. The developed concept of the tragedy of illusory identity occurs where the protagonist suffers because of a disastrous inability to know himself. Either he has a false idea of his identity in life or cannot identify himself at all. The problem nearly always involves an excess of illusion or delusion. His confusion of the real versus the ideal amounts to a monomania whose only resolution is a pessimistic generalization about the impossibility of living; consequently the death wish is common and the usual end of the play is the hero's quasi- or actual suicide.

There is serious disorientation in this type of hopeless tragedy, and it is caused by the characters' leading a life of escape through dreams, hallucinations, and excessive role-playing. "Who wants to see life as it is?" says Edmund in *Long Day's Journey Into Night*—an "inheritance" trag-

4. For listing by categories, see the Appendix.

edy which also employs "illusory identity" motifs. Freud's conception of psychosexual intoxication is relevant: the hero knows the tensions of not being at home in his environment and is not known in return by his universe or existence. He lives a lie, he is uprooted. As distinct from the tragedy of sensitivity, however, this disorientation exists in terms of the dramatic situation—not the upheaval of the protagonist's senses.

The archetypes, too, are all from O'Neill. In *Beyond the Horizon,* for example, Robert Mayo's insistence on playing the role of the dreamer and poet is disastrous in the face of the demands that farm work and real life make on him. His senses are jarred by physical challenge, but he lives his lie mainly in the light of the situation—having the position of a farmer with an unimaginative, nagging wife and yet the soul of a poet. Each role destroys the other. *The Emperor Jones* tells a story of an ex-convict living the illusion of royal might at the expense of the gullible subjects who eventually kill him. The illusion in *The Hairy Ape* is concerned with the impossibility of exchanging roles in different social strata of a class-conscious society. O'Neill returned to this "tragedy" in his later plays, and *A Touch of the Poet* is the chronological climax of O'Neill's tragedies of illusory identity. This play is intended as a tragi-comic tale of an old soldier forced to give up living in his illusory past grandeur at the same time he realizes that he hasn't any present. Faced with a threat to his ideal role, he chooses the illusion above everything else. The play is obviously not a "tragedy," but it is the beginning of O'Neill's last "tragic cycle." Edward Albee's semi-tragedy *Who's Afraid of Virginia Woolf?* is in part another exercise in the necessity for illusion. In all these cases, the underlying attitude is that life is so unjust and so fruitless that illusion is called for. Then, when man tries that, life destroys him for it. The vision does not bother to depict the *worth* of the protagonist coreacting with the worth of the struggle.

Tennessee Williams's *Sweet Bird of Youth* is another tragedy of illusory identity. Williams shows the attempt to recapture that "sweet bird of youth" in the persons of two fading idols whose occupations depend on the illusion of their attractiveness. The gigolo Chance and the movie-star Princess live the lies of success in conflict with the ideal of youthfulness. The difficulty, as far as tragedy is concerned, is typical: theme and vision exist before the fact of the play, and the play is enforced to enact the vision.

Dreams and fantasies are acceptable and even healthy in real life, or in artistic experience—but only up to a point. The point is met in tragedy. Extreme illusion is basically the weak or sick man's escape from his impotence, and that is why the ideals in question are often so meagre. Given both a world so unbeatable and a personal flesh so weak, certain versions of modern man can dream of being other things or other men, or confuse the original identity to avoid responsibility for its destiny. For some, this will be an involuntary shift—as in insanity; for others it will be more voluntary—the application of a neurotic disguise. "Who am I? I don't really know. Am I something 'else'?" In any case the operative feature is always escape, an avoidance of the fight and the pain. It can become the sick fantasy of the un-hero who becomes a greater figure in his own imagination but without any substantiating conquest for the audience to see. Our blunt subjective response can be to find him a "sissy" or a "weakling."

For all the characters of this pessimistic vision, their illusion is their weakness and also their supposed tragic flaw. The author finds the necessity for "illusory identity" a tragic source of destruction. We can see the main difficulties with this in the later chapters dealing with perspective or distance, the stature of character, effort, and enlightenment.

The Tragedy of Irresponsibility

I'd like to illustrate this next concept (more thoroughly later on) through the approach Theodore Dreiser took in 1921 in *The Hand of the Potter,* the story of a sexual psychopath "tragically" destroyed by his "natural" weakness and society's laws and lack of understanding. It is interesting that Dreiser took his title from the famous line in the *Rubaiyat.* The full quatrain, No. 86, reads:

> After a momentary silence spake
> Some vessel of a more ungainly make;
>   "They sneer at me for leaning all awry:
> What! did the Hand then of the Potter shake?"

Fitzgerald's translation of the Persian hedonist poem is a strong pessimistic reaction against a bewildering universe. The exact context of the line, furthermore, suggests the idea of Providential unconcern in producing man so imperfect in his ability to control himself and his destiny. It expresses the basic premise of the "tragedy of irresponsibility."

Dreiser was the first major writer to attempt scientific naturalistic tragedy in America, and most of his anomie fed on pessimistic Darwinism. He carried the Darwinian and scientistic rationales of naturalism further than any other American playwright, to show the pathetic irresponsibility of man according to the psychological, biological, and "chemic" facts of his imperfection. This vision also occurs in Susan Glaspell's *The Verge* and John Steinbeck's *Of Mice and Men*. The pseudo-tragic biogenetic motifs also have some influence on such dramas as Sidney Howard's *The Silver Cord* and Lillian Hellman's *The Children's Hour*. More recently, it plays a somewhat less direct role in the thinking of Tennessee Williams. Arthur Miller's *After the Fall* analyzes a helpless guilt in the will-to-power and will-to-success. The typical idée fixe of this very modern tragic vision is: "It's no use; that's the way we are made."

It tends to be a researched outlook, making the most of or overinterpreting Freudian psychology, the theory of evolution, determinism, predestination, and the actual and symbolic impact of nature erring. Man cannot control his destiny by will and talent and life is primarily a struggle for survival, with the fittest organisms succeeding. The "fittest" are not necessarily the morally or ethically most fit members of the species and instead such success as there is is due to arbitrary fortunes, a chance nod from Nature. (Dreiser always spelled it with a capital "N.") Man's tragedy is simply that he is born, that he is man—and therefore likely to make grave mistakes or get into pitiable difficulties that will not be his fault. Even if he escapes serious trouble, there is certainly nothing he can do to ensure triumph or conquest in the name of mankind. Dreiser is the spokesman in an essay, when he says: "Is life worth living? Is there any use? . . . In so far as one may judge by chemistry and physics man appears to be in the grip of a blind force or process which cannot help itself and from which man can derive no power to help himself save by accident or peradventure."[5] Later writers have avoided the kind of hysterical and sweeping generalizations one finds in Dreiser's defenses of his pessimism, but those employing this particular tragic vision still have no brighter opinion of human potential.

5. Theodore Dreiser, *Hey Rub-a-Dub-Dub: A Book of the Mystery and Wonder and Terror of Life* (New York, 1920), p. 123.

The antitragic weakness of "irresponsibility" relates mostly to the necessity for moral statement, and I will discuss this in chapter 8.

The Tragedy of Martyrdom

The modern martyr figures are generally the more intellectual of our protagonists, their mental sensitivity leading them to see the value in giving up. They specialize in inactivity while living, and believe what Krutch bemoans: "Intelligence can no longer believe in anything, not even in itself. It can only stand idly by with refinements and gallantry and perception while the world is taken over by the apes once more."[6] This time the playwright is acting as Sacrificial Priest, urging his characters and all thinking men over the brink into Tammuz' death-pit. The program is euthanasia, and the plays say: "Don't keep suffering with this hopeless life; let your death be an ironic token of its stupidity."

The "tragedy of martyrdom" begins with Maxwell Anderson, who was its chief exponent. This type of world view results in a play which insists on the conclusion of willing and open submission to death as an end in itself—an escape from a life pessimistically prejudged. Fulfillment comes from the act of martyrdom ("See what you made me do?" the hero's action implies) rather than from enlightenment that might result from struggling against tragic catastrophe. Perception does not come with the intelligence, and the only "heroism" is in acting on something like Schopenhauer's praise of suicide as a denial of will.

This martyrdom is the primary tragic action of many of Anderson's important plays: Winterset, Elizabeth the Queen, Mary of Scotland, The Wingless Victory, The Masque of Kings, Key Largo, and Anne of the Thousand Days. Another American example is Robert Sherwood's The Petrified Forest, and aspects of the vision help to weaken Tiny Alice by Edward Albee.

The mere act of self-destruction would not point to a "bad" tragic vision—what of Cassius, Brutus, Othello, and the many other suicides in traditional tragedy? The issue is in what the protagonist thinks of it and when he decides in its favor. For the moderns, it is neither a sudden nor a painful decision; the play is largely a means of confirming the

6. Review of The Petrified Forest, Nation, 23 January 1935, p. 111.

necessity for quitting the struggle. Anderson's plays lead to the sacrifice of royal people who cannot submit to ignoble demands or of ordinary people who wish to purge themselves of guilt and avoid further contact with human weakness and injustice. The former plan would seem to evoke no inherent pessimistic martyrdom, until one sees what Anderson stresses, neglecting what human potential is being intolerably cut off with those execution axes. *Winterset*, in the second group, insists on the blackest possible picture of existence. Perhaps the least passive martyr, in the accordingly least pessimistic play, is found in Essex in *Elizabeth the Queen*. His choice of death, at least, is preceded by some very active struggles to attain fulfillment in love and power—on earth. Sherwood's *The Petrified Forest* dramatizes the difficulty in being too thoughtful in a chaotic, inhuman world: civilized values are dead and economic collapse and fascism run loose. In the play, the weakness of the hero, Alan Squier, and the theme of martyrdom are interdependent.

It is very characteristic of this vision that the protagonist involved will not take action to save himself from harm. Sometimes it is a wish for death or punishment inspired by guilt. In effect, it is almost as if the hero had the same religious intent as a martyr of the church meeting death at the hands of pagans. He feels that death is the beginning of life, or preferable to a worthless life on earth. The argument over the "tragic saint" is a familiar one: can a story of martyrdom ever be tragic? Once again, I think it depends on the lateness of the decision—whether death follows a struggle which is affirmation. And it is decided in playwright attitude. Becket in Eliot's *Murder in the Cathedral* is definitely a martyr, but we must note that Eliot says—through his treatment of this *crusading* martyr and victim—that "suffering is action." The modern martyrdom-minded playwrights do not attempt to work this out boldly. Through them, life is given no chance to prove itself and their heroes simply pre-judge existence—saying, with Mio in *Winterset*, that "the rats will inherit the earth."

This is a distortion because it must be the *cause* that creates the martyr—not the victim's mere self or "image." Victimization, however unjust, is not sufficient. The characters enacting the "tragedy of martyrdom" are not working for any constituency but rather for themselves in the vaguest kinds of escapes. My main illustrations of this are in chapter 6.

The Tragedy of Sensitivity

This conception of tragedy has two divisions, in which the source of destruction is either a general and more symbolic "sensitivity" or the end-product of an extremist passion.[7] The role the playwright shares with his key character is that of the Casualty, the Injured One.

According to the first vision, the oversensitive protagonist is bound to suffer because the *rest* of the world is so insensitive. The resulting disorientation forces him to live a life which is in constant conflict with the animalism of the majority. The only adjustment a thus-deranged hero can offer is a pathetic and disastrous role-playing which to him preserves the illusions he prefers as values, but which in reality are long dead in the ruthlessly changing—that is, regressing—world. The role-playing here is dangerous in terms of the situation to be faced, as in illusory identity, but its most serious conflict with "accepted" life is in the disorientation of the senses—chiefly a mixture of aesthetic and sexual sensitivity. This vision is the home of our most delicate protagonists.

A few examples of the type are Eugene O'Neill's *The Great God Brown, Strange Interlude,* and *The Iceman Cometh* (plus in the partial use of the vision in practically all of his other plays) as well as Tennessee Williams's *The Glass Menagerie, A Streetcar Named Desire,* and the minor work *Slapstick Tragedy.* The characters of such dramas are often actual or emotional "artist" types, enacting the well-worn theme of the sensitive mistreated artist attempting to express his creative humanity in a basically insensitive world. The playwright himself is personally intimate with the theme. As in *The Iceman Cometh* and *Strange Interlude,* the characters can barely hang on to their original romantic-artistic-sexual ideals; reality simply keeps on revealing the ideal as target. O'Neill may have denied actual death in such plays through the role-playing of his people, but he clearly denied life as well. Mixing disgust with life and a dread of death, his idea of existence came to be suspended animation—what he was later to call the necessary life of the "fog" people.

The Glass Menagerie and *A Streetcar Named Desire* are, respectively, lyric and violent dramatizations of sensitive women who lead lives of repressed desperation or neurotic dreaming because their senses are too

7. A term suggested in Doris Falk's study, *Eugene O'Neill and the Tragic Tension* (New Brunswick, N.J., 1958).

thinly armored for dealing with the coarse world around them. In the former play, their sensual delicacy ensures their continual failure in a social atmosphere which has traded gentility for brutality, and the idea also carries over to Tom, the central figure. As to the latter, Williams said that *Streetcar*'s theme is that "the apes will inherit the earth." This variation of Anderson's expression of human destiny emphasizes a vision of man's anthropological regression, with animalism and loveless sensuality seen as throttling reason, compassion, and morality. Williams's sensitive protagonists cannot make successful adjustments to this kind of life-problem without becoming animals themselves and, failing this, they are destroyed. Finding most men savage, Williams sympathizes with the delicately built person whose soul is revolted by crass life. The insensitive prosper because they are insensitive: they copulate, they survive, they increase their number. Because the Blanche-like souls are so overwhelmingly outnumbered, Williams has little hope for us.

The related type of tragedy is an expansion of hypersensitivity as a tragic flaw in the wholly sexual sense. This vision of extremist passion is far less allegorical than the usual straight tragedy of sensitivity. And how can "passion" equate with "sensitivity"? Because the playwright in some way sympathizes with it as a sensitivity or human vulnerability. Dramas such as Williams's *Summer and Smoke* and Sophie Treadwell's *Machinal* see destruction in sexual maladjustment: frigidity is tragic weakness. Erring libido is also the basis for O'Neill's *Desire Under the Elms* and *Diff'rent*; Anderson's *Night Over Taos* and *White Desert*; Dan Totheroh's classic rural tragedy, *Wild Birds*; and Lillian Hellman's *The Children's Hour*. The vision is a primary or secondary force in many other modern American would-be tragedies, e.g., *A View from the Bridge*. Errant passion would seem to duplicate the conception of the tragedy of irresponsibility, but the plays of this outlook are not concerned with pseudoscientific persuasion for a rethinking of man's responsibility. Here the ungoverned passion is used as a theatrical vehicle for pessimism which is especially conscious of how people find ways to be cruel.

Either tragedy of hypersensitivity, in conclusion, serves to make its spokesmen-characters "tragically" suspect in a society which has become crudely jaded and which lives life as an animal struggle and ritual of bestial expression and gratification. To be tragic is to be different: i.e., sensitive. A fairly common alternative is to seek out equally disoriented souls and be confined with them in a den of despair such as that in *The Iceman Cometh*. In any case, the values are upside down and those who realize this are in the minority and cannot be heard. The protagonist's implied pleas, "Where am I?" "Who am I?" and "What kind of world is this?" are asked in sensual context.

The most usual antitragic problem with the vision is the playwright's tendency to choose up his sides too simplistically. Rather full of minority feelings himself, he has trouble with the tragic perspective discussed in the next chapter.

The Tragedy of Social Disintegration

This pessimistic vision indulges in too much social criticism to have time for a tragic expresson. The issues are socio-political and they reduce to an overanxious desire to contrast gigantic, wrong, impersonal society with causally minute men. It is protest rather than proclamation, and major difficulties arise with protagonist-stature. Sentimentalism can result, philosophically, rather than exaltation and enlargement. The playwright is Critic.

The role of society as antagonist in tragedy is as old as Greek drama, as in Euripides' *The Trojan Women*. But angry concentration on specific institutional society as an impersonal yet personified destructive force worthy of the villain's role is a much more modern development. What I call the "tragedy of social disintegration" uses this as a support for pessimism, and also doubles as a thesis play.

This vision usually calls for an understanding of society's individual members by society as a whole. It is never the story of great men momentarily downtrodden: *all* men are the slaves of society. The hero is consistently small because he must serve the purpose of irony in the picture of man as individual evilly overpowered by the gargantuan anonymity of men abstractly together. This "social" tragedy, like bourgeois tragedy of the eighteenth century, is unwittingly not far from satirical caricature in its depiction of the weak character or characteristic evolved by a wrong-headed social structure.

Representative plays are Arthur Miller's *Death of a Salesman* and perhaps *Incident at Vichy*, Maxwell Anderson's *Gods of the Lightning*, (with Harold Hickerson), Paul Green's *In Abraham's Bosom*, and Archibald MacLeish's *Panic*. Also characteristic of the vision are two plays which nonetheless avoid pessimistic conclusions: Miller's *The Crucible*, and Robert Sherwood's *There Shall Be No Night*. It is significant how these plays escaped.

The Crucible tells the story of the Salem witch trials in a way that makes man stand above the bigotry and evil of the society that perpetrated the purges. The persecuted Proctors, who have the power to end the hysterical torture, are doomed *by their own tremendous struggles*. The characters do act out their drives and try to act upon their fates. Their single sins mesh with their strengths to trap them against any possibility of nontragic escape, despite their great effort. John and Elizabeth love and affirm life, but his adulterous act and her lie—in being nobly confronted—enforce a tragic inevitability on the outcome in connection with the perfectly designed timing of their accusation by Salem society. Proctor knows what he is doing and does not go to his death as a martyr. He is afraid, but it is not a little man's dread. His action produces insight in the society that will be stricken with shame and *knowledge* after his death. As for *There Shall Be No Night*, although history proves him wrong, the hero of Sherwood's drama of the Russo-Finnish war believes that war will exhaust man's bestiality and actually serve as his first great awakening. In the face of doom, he manages to enact St. Paul's teaching, used by Sherwood, that "we glory in tribulation; knowing that tribulation worketh patience; and patience, experience; and experience, hope."

Other tragedies of social disintegration, however, present a black picture of society's treatment of the individual without giving any cause for future hope. Some, such as *Gods of the Lightning* in its condemnation of society's treatment of Sacco and Vanzetti, are quite specifically related to social evils of the day—and go no farther than a message for reform.

Somewhat sentimentally and wistfully, the ultimate plea in the tragedy of social disintegration is that society must pay attention to the forgotten little man who serves the whole—and this is familiar as the message of *Death of a Salesman*. The man pays his taxes, he goes to war, he dutifully feeds the economy, and he does his full day's work without fail. Then, rather than our admiring a team or a social class or a nation of people, it should be this individual who is worthy of our respect. The whole is the sum of all its parts, the vision recalls, but nobody regards the parts any more. The conclusion for this tragedy is the conclusion of the streets: we are allowed to pass on with our eyes callously shut because the man in trouble is "nobody important."

The Tragedy of Imprisonment

Here we have a view where life is regarded as a spiritual or physical trap; evil routine or the isolation of true soul destroys any ability for survival. Human identity and richness of character are supposedly negated in a pessimistic conception of locales—where people are cut off from the full range of experience. The playwright becomes a kind of neurotic Icarus: he is chiefly concerned with abandoning existence but also knows there is no other place to go.

As with sensitivity, there are two subtypes; *imprisonment* as the tragic fact of the world, or *environment*, wherein the playwright stresses specific physical surroundings directly producing defeated men. Tennessee Williams's *Orpheus Descending* and Elmer Rice's *Adding Machine* exemplify the former. Rice's *Street Scene* shows the more physical side of imprisonment-through-locale. The first kind of vision is the abstraction, the second the "photograph."

The imprisoned characters are victims of routine that is the standard life of an isolated world. The world is not open, and they actually *lack* society. As in the nineteenth-century rural tragedies of the German and Russian theatres (Tolstoy's *Power of Darkness* is one example), provincialism can be tragic. Symbolically, in the modern "imprisonment" tragedy, the entire world can be nothing but provinces.

It is difficult to identify with the characters presented under this outlook. They are often freak mutations found in a part of the world conceived as if forgotten by passing time, or they are the specialized characters of some strange version of existence. They are likely to be "specialized" in the clinical-psychological sense and thus hard to get to know universally. Our world is corrupt, they will say, but that is the limit of their insight because the playwright does not wish to picture them as having any contact with an "outside," balanced world.

The theme of Williams's view of imprisonment is expressed by the Orpheus, Val Xavier:

> Nobody ever gets to know *nobody*! We're all of
> us sentenced to solitary confinement inside our
> own skins for life!

And Val insistently wears a snakeskin jacket. As Williams has frankly described himself, these people are strangers to the world. "Corruption rots men's hearts. . . ," and man has made his world a prison of prejudice, bigotry, and hateful distrust. Williams's prisoners, Val, Vee, Carol, and Lady, wish to flee from the corruption and Val says it for all of them when he describes the bird they would have to emulate:

> You know they's a kind of bird that don't have
> legs so it can't light on nothing but has to stay
> all its life on its wings in the sky?

That, and its camouflage, allows the bird to avoid corrupting contact with the earth—and it is Williams's ultimate poetic symbol of this branch of his pessimism. His Orpheus descends into hell on earth, and Williams goes out of his way to make his end violent: a shut case of how yearning, compassionate people are burnt out if they break prison rules. Their wings are even less effective than those of Icarus.

The Adding Machine sees existence as a trap of conformity, with a similar conclusion that man cannot be allowed to exceed or escape it. Rice's later play, *Street Scene,* is a naturalistic study of "imprisonment" supported by environmentalist psychology and sociology.

Street Scene's characters are tied to responsibilities which no one "outside" will share, and they are hopelessly cut off from a knowledge of a happier world which might equip them with the independence (and, to a point, the selfishness) that could save them from their treadmill existence. It is the tragedy of the ghetto, but Rice's text gives no sign the playwright would reject pessimism in any other kind of environment. The ghetto just enlarges the destructive power of the human environment, and Rice nowhere qualifies the conclusion of his street's most educated character:

> That's all there is in life—nothing but pain.
> From before we're born, until we die! Everywhere
> you look, oppression and cruelty! If it doesn't
> come from Nature, it comes from humanity—humanity

> trampling on itself and tearing at its own throat.
> The whole world is nothing but a blood-stained arena,
> filled with misery and suffering. It's too high
> a price to pay for life—life isn't worth it!

The environment means people are living in confined quarters in too great numbers, and when their varied backgrounds, beliefs, and characteristics are mixed indiscriminately they are unable to live with the privacy necessary to human dignity or achieve what they want without someone knowing their every weakness and thereby interfering. Their conglomeration produces a compound that eats at man psychologically, sociologically, spiritually, and physically. The sum total of the surroundings infects the unfortunate prisoner beyond the effect produced by succumbing to these influences one at a time. The characters have no room to breathe, or to live. The surroundings are below a human standard, but they are man-made—so we can expect their malignant infecting power to endure.

In the typical "environment" or "imprisonment" tragedy, characters cannot act upon life and thus cannot make any tragic revelations for an audience regarding what that life does to them. The play, rather than building a tragic structure, *assumes* the structure of dismal reality and stands as an episode with variations more than a monumental conclusion.

The Tragedy of Inheritance

A key argument in O'Neill's *Long Day's Journey into Night* boils down to:

> TYRONE: Mary! For God's sake, forget the past!
> MARY: Why? How can I? The past is the present,
>   isn't it? It's the future, too. We all try
>   to lie out of that but life won't let us.

This is the problem of the character placed in the world of this tragic vision: he lives under the *curse* of the cycle of weakness and sin that man perpetuates. He inherits empty time. Here we have a more mythic version of a personal despair which will dictate the structure of the tragedy. It is not the dramatization of a terrible "fact," but a metaphor based on pessimistic response to the fact as seen through the playwright's life. This time the playwright takes on the role of The Accursed One.

More specifically, in the related plays, the protagonist knows he springs from corrupt *seed*—not corrupt environment. His job is to passively accept the curse of birth, enduring the sentence of life stemming from helpless "original" sins. This situation can be found most often in O'Neill's dramas and heroes, the latter having very clear-cut cases of Kierkegaard's "sickness unto death" and void-feelings (which will be considered in detail in chapters 6 and 8). The play's crisis, if any, is hardly more pleasurably terrible than the beginning. Contrasts, such as the reversal of fortune, are especially unlikely because they are contrary to the endless-sentence metaphor.

The outlook is the basis for *Anna Christie, Mourning Becomes Electra, Long Day's Journey, A Moon for the Misbegotten, More Stately Mansions*, MacLeish's *J. B.*, and other plays. "Inheritance" overtones are part of more recent plays, such as Albee's *Who's Afraid of Virginia Woolf?* (though it would still be primarily a vision of "illusory identity"). The typical feature throughout is the drawn-out legacy of waiting for something—and nothing, with the pessimistic credo that that is the perennial human task. In the O'Neill plays there is a vast suspenselessness because we are told so often in so many ways that the future will be the same as the past. A convenient "curse" always relates to this; as morphine-addicted Mary Tyrone says: "We can't forget." The inheritance is not some brand of biogenetic "irresponsibility," but rather the consistent spiritual imperfectibility of man.

Thus human weaknesses that may have little scientific chance of being passed on through the genes are passed on by poetic license: alcoholic sons come from alcoholic fathers, or a crime of passion committed long ago lives on to curse all the criminal's progeny. These are old themes, but the modern vision's use of them imbues them with pessimistically prejudged conclusions. The characters of this tragedy are not allowed to develop independent personalities that might have the necessary characteristics to lift them up and out of their helplessness. They are only mirrors of antecedent personalities or "sins." Any departure from this would wreck the unconscious formula of the inheritance-minded playwright.

Anna Christie displays an interesting symbol of the tragedy of inheritance. It tells another O'Neill sailor story, with an ironic fate personified in "that ole davil sea." The playwright relates the characters' misfortunes through the destructive effect the sea has upon them from generation to generation. Thus the mythic curse of the sea passes from Anna's father to Anna and, although she is reunited with her last-chance lover as the play ends, their future is very cloudy. This continuing effect shows that death cannot remove the curses of the past.[8]

Mourning Becomes Electra, with heavily psychological interpretations, restages the endless legacy of the curse of the house of Atreus—as passed on by the crimes of modern counterparts of Agamemnon and Clytemnaestra. The semiautobiographical plays, *A Moon for the Misbegotten* and *Long Day's Journey*, depict the aftermath and the continuing helplessness of the curse of despair and human failing (alcoholism, penury, and addiction) on the "haunted" Tyrone family. Archibald MacLeish's verse dramatization of the trials of Job, *J. B.*, however, manages to end on a more hopeful note than the other modern tragedies of inheritance. In this play, the twentieth-century Job is afflicted with various contemporary blights and is offered solace by contemporary pseudocomforters. The curse he inherits is the primal one of original sin and the hypothesis that God is vindictive. J. B. is able to reject this at the end of his torture and find meaning in both life and God.

The effect of the vision, then, is a matter of how the playwright wishes to treat it, depending most heavily on his perspective on subject and subject matter. Otherwise, its main problems will show up in language attitude, character-effort, and dramaturgical structure,

Now, in the following chapters, I want to indicate and analyze the various key effects of pessimism upon modern tragedy, mostly by recalling the practical results in the better-known dramas of the epoch. These

---

8. O'Neill's elaboration on the ending of *Anna Christie* reflects the mystic nature of the inherited doom idea, and the way he himself sees all outcomes: "My ending seems to have a false definiteness about it that is misleading—a happy-ever-after which I did not intend. I rely on the father's last speech of superstitious uncertainty to let my theme flow through and on. . . . In short, all of them at the end have a vague foreboding that, although they have had their moment, the decision still rests with the sea which has achieved the conquest of Anna." Quoted in Frank O'Hara, *Today in American Drama* (Chicago, 1939), p. 20.

effects—the legacy of pessimism—include the production of an ingrown attitude in the playwright as part of his work, the enervating effect on dramaturgy and entertaining action, the lowered stature of the hero and other characters, the spiritless struggle, the despairing tone of the language, the lack of enlightenment, and the vague modern attitudes toward evil and sin which comprise contemporary moral statement. Why do these characteristics negate tragic art?

Part Two:

THE LEGACY of FEAR

3. *THE DISTANCE of DESPAIR*

OVERVIEW

Contemporary man takes himself very seriously, and contemporary playwrights seem to take themselves even more seriously. Many playwrights attempting tragedy in our time have gone so far in this attitude as to be dangerously defensive about their vision of the tragic. One imagines them, at least as far as we can tell from their plays, very unable to laugh, to see things whole—and very unwilling to see themselves, their topics, and their worries from any but their own biased vantage point of the moment. (This applies all the more to the young writers of the current, posttragic, scene.) Those wanting to create tragedy either have started out inherently ingrown about their thematic aims, or else have grown so in attempting to communicate material with which they have deep personal involvement. The result is something more than a case of old romantic melancholy and fashionable Weltschmerz; more than a style, it is often a blanket conviction.

Personalized pessimism brings the writer too close to his work. Why does this weaken the ability to "see" tragically? For one thing, the ingrown attitude of pessimistic tragedy reduces the perspective necessary to perceive the contrast basic to ideal tragic vision. For another, a relatively large incidence of autobiographical or semiautobiographical stories tends to give modern tragic drama a skewed and embittered point of view that is too lacking in control and universality to be artfully tragic.

INTROSPECTION

All the problems related to the modern tragedian's closeness to his "tragedy" come down to a matter of perspective. Somehow he can't quite look at what happens to his protagonist with the right sort of sight, at the right distance from the despair. In many modern tragedies, an associated quality is excessive introspection, and the playwright really does appear to suffer those symptoms Kierkegaard describes as The Sickness Unto Death, or he believes with de Unamuno that "consciousness is a disease." The big preoccupation is the playwright-protagonist's self-pity over personal pain, or else his brooding indignation over how contemporary man frustrates his alleged humanity.

Consider making an artistic tragedy that genuinely comes from and speaks to our present situation. We seem to have the perfect subject: in recent years, the whole world has been profoundly shocked by the violent destruction of three very real hero-figures in John Kennedy, Martin Luther King, and Robert Kennedy. What classical threnodies can have surpassed the keening of the millions reacting to the fact and implication of the loss of these men? In each case, we talked of "martyrdom" and "tragedy" and even of "purgation" through their proxy-death via our dark and violent sides. Who can doubt that the careers and quests of the slain had a deep significant relation to the hopes of large sections of contemporary mankind, thus meeting the test of a crucial goal—as in Oedipus's importance to all Thebes, or the cleansing of Hamlet's state through the Prince's battle against corruption?

Urgent material; and yet it takes a very balanced and special attitude to adapt such losses and real pain to the ends of artistic tragedy. Further into this book, in fact, I want to support the point that as soon as such stories "prove" themselves by happening, they are toxic to tragic art. (The familiar art *vs.* nature truisms aid only a fraction of the concept.) But imagine the mid-twentieth-century playwright or poet so moved by these events, by this monstrous new proof of man's inhumanity to man, this discouraging return-plunge into darkness, that he writes a tragedy about them. He broods, ashamed of his race, either wanting to shout out condemnation or poetically confront man with the image of his waning morality. Something like these emotions set Maxwell Anderson to writing *Winterset* and *Gods of the Lightning*, his point of reference being America's shameful handling of Sacco and Vanzetti. History is of course full of events about which man needs to be reminded. Then, too, there is the analysis of the playwright's personal history as the trigger for artistic tragedy, to which his natural artist's introspection will incline. It is his job, his right, to brood about the sufferings and wrongs he has seen. If he can express the meaning of the events in such a way that man might somehow avoid them in the future, might learn a little more of what is required of his humanity, thus hoping to move on—well and good. That is what tragedy is all about.

But where must the introspection and the brooding stop? What happens when concentration on the evil referent leads the thinker to pessimism? What if the personal horror or personal guilt in effect cause the playwright to write his tragedy *for* himself or *against* his audience? Usually it is a matter of seeing trees instead of forests, or seeing a forest too illusory for tragedy.

"Who wants to see life as it is, if they can help it?" wrote O'Neill, and he and most of the other modern tragedians, in their pessimism, have turned out plays which either preach for or display an exceptional, dark, and escapist subjectivity about life. *The Iceman Cometh* would be just one example, and we can all name our own further instances. The common denominator throughout is an introspection that doesn't do much for the world. When Colin Wilson wrote about this very problem in his book *The Stature of Man*[1] he based much of his discussion on the sociology of Reisman and Whyte: that is, on the inherent emptiness of the "other-directed" or the "organization" man. For him, negativist modern playwrights helped shape a correspondingly negative culture by writing in their spirit of retreat. Here was a case of inwardness which had the

1. One of Wilson's major conclusions about the negativism in current culture (particularly the American) is that "the chief necessity of our age is to dare to be inner-directed." This of course contrasts with the usual conformity which seeks to imitate values decreed outside the self. Wilson hopes for a return to intuitions, not merely to escape, but as a "first step in regaining detachment and, eventually, the control that comes with detachment." See *The Stature of Man* (New York, 1959), p. 170.

very opposite effect as "innerdirectedness." The inner-directed man, a real rarity, would have an inner strength based on positive, expanding convictions: independence. Typically, the contemporary serious play-wright shows an introspection which is nothing as bad as mindless "other-directedness" but hardly as good as this self-reliant "inner-directedness"; he has gone inside himself and gotten stuck, too much inside his theme and catastrophe. This does not necessarily corrupt the possibility of strong emotions making for some captivating theatre, but an author with such a spiritual myopia does dodge real tragedy in being too concerned with himself as metaphorically the most tragic victim of his times, or too doubtful about mankind's chances since he decides these odds by extending his own despair. He cannot, as all tragic poets of stature have done (accidentally?—well, certainly not because of any rules), permit humor and joy in the midst of tragedy because he is re-lentlessly reliving his own attitudinal development or proving a one-sided point.

His protagonist, and probably his other major spokesman-characters, looks only within or back. He cannot have anything like the broad *Weltanschauung*, as Albert Schweitzer exemplified it, required for an outlook on the world which can see misfortune and evil in perspective—in contrast with their opposites across the full scope of human experience. Schweitzer's delineation of the world-affirming outlook suggests what the artist needs to study the sense *or* the senselessness of universal life:

> Deepened world- and life-affirmation consists in this: that we have the will to maintain our own life and every kind of ex-istence that we can in any way influence, and to bring them to their highest value. It demands from us that we think out all ideals of the material and spiritual perfecting of individual men, of society, and of mankind as a whole, and let ourselves be de-termined by them to steady activity and constant hope. *It does not allow us to withdraw into ourselves* [Italics mine].[2]

This position seems implicit in just about every successful tragic drama of our history; the real tragedian does have to be a bit of a philosophical

2. *The Philosophy of Civilization*, trans. C. T. Campion, (New York, 1960), p. 278.

brawler. He must directly enjoy fighting for positive ideas advancing over present imperfection.

A point about objectivity is illustrated in the response to *Death of a Salesman*, regarding how much the author's outlook was under his control. Miller writes in the introduction to his collected plays that he was surprised to see how audiences wept over Willy Loman's story, since he had written the play "half in laughter and joy."[3] He adds: "I am convinced the play is not a document of pessimism, a philosophy in which I do not believe." But later in the same volume he offers this contradiction: "I did not realize while writing the play that so many people in the world do not see as clearly, or would admit, as I thought they must, how futile most lives are; so there could be no hope of consoling the audience for the death of this man."[4] The last statement is a truer one, in terms of what happens in *Death of a Salesman*. How Miller felt originally does not necessarily determine audience response. His characters express despair and confusion, and Miller loads on the pathos in their behalf. The logical conclusion would be that Miller *unconsciously* wants pessimism. An optimistic vision applied to the play as Miller created it would have reduced the "weeping" and thereby much of the drama's popular emotional appeal.

A case of the playwright playing his referents off against himself and his vision is Tennessee Williams's relation to *Orpheus Descending*. Williams himself said he worked harder, in a more personal way, on *Orpheus* than on any of his other plays. Through the seventeen years since the play's appearance in its original form, as *Battle of Angels*, he drew even closer to the theme and his perspective decreased rather than grew. He was accordingly alarmed when it again failed to meet with approval. As far as the play shows, Williams's misery and horror remain isolated phenomena. Val, Lady, Vee, and Carol, however sad and unfortunate, are specialized and symbolicized victims who cannot struggle grandly enough to represent the tragic end of a life that means something to men at large. The dreadful locale corrupts and destroys the characters—but largely on the evidence of Williams's personal philosophy more than on any open, universal insight.

Williams is terribly *inside* this work. Tentatively we can ask: is the

3. Arthur Miller, *Collected Plays* (New York, 1957), p. 38.
4. Ibid., p. 34.

author's fixed idea of the pathetic psychosis (at the least, Val, Vee, and Carol have distinct psychosexual wounds) as the central product of life too introspective and bitterly ingrown for tragedy? Is it too "untrue"? Eric Bentley wrote in *The Dramatic Event* that "the new psychological drama, school of Williams . . . springs from fear of . . . society, of the world, and from pre-occupation with the self. Now art that doesn't spring from the whole man but from one side of him tends, I think, not to become art at all but to remain neurotic or quasi-neurotic fantasy."[5] To deny the label "art" to Williams's work is to ignore the presence of a real poetry, whatever its subjects, as art in the theatre. But the criticism does tell the story of Williams's inability to make tragedy, though he succeeds brilliantly otherwise, out of his characters' final degradation. At this point it might be said that *Orpheus* is not aimed at tragedy, but there is only one other alternative: would Williams allow us to call it a melo-drama? No, make no mistake about it, this is a much mulled-over state-ment of a vision of existence, shaped to suggest a "tragic" statement. And perhaps its faults as tragic art might be reflected in Williams's own words on life: "There is a horror in things, a horror at heart of the meaningless-ness of existence. Some people cling to a certain philosophy that is handed down to them and which they accept. Life has a meaning if you're bucking for heaven. But if heaven is a fantasy, we are in this jungle with whatever we can work out for ourselves. It seems to me that the cards are stacked against us."[6] This is also the underlying message brooding within his plays.

I am now on the fringes of that shaky business of psychoanalyzing the artist. The Bentley remark above has already hinted at something like maladjusted, antisocial writing. The dangers in this kind of innuendo are well known. Freud himself was badly mistaken in his analysis of Leonardo da Vinci's psyche through the study of Leonardo's work. Then there was the pseudoscientific work of Lombroso, Kretschmer, and others who tried, for example, to equate genius and mental disease or implied that certain artistic tendencies corresponded with certain physiological traits. Even today, I doubt that the professionals are far behind the man on the street in assuming that the artist is neurotic. And yet history is fairly full of examples of great and loving art produced by the psychologically,

5. *The Dramatic Event* (Boston, 1954), p. 259.
6. "The Angel of the Odd," *Time*, 9 March 1962, p. 53.

sexually, or criminally abnormal personality. But could we make some educated guesses where psychology relates to philosophy? For instance, is introversion negative or positive? Where alienation is the fashion, what range in *Weltanschauung* can be expected? To illustrate, I suspect that our representative pessimistic playwright *is* less social in his being able to handle and enjoy relationship with socety in general, and with his audience. The contemporary artist's difficulties with personal social expression are so much more acceptable or understandable in today's world that a writer need no longer feel and act as a minority, as "other," in this regard. In a fair amount of the latest drama, after all, the expression that goes with a pathological, homosexual, or criminal ethic is openly exploited.

Amplifying this with modest clinical accuracy, I will point out that enough introspection begets introversion, where a negative relation of the subject to the object is expressed and all interest generated in thinking refers back to the subject. This may be direct or abstract, but the path leads to the same narrow gate; it is ingrowing. Psychiatric evidence might mention an ego- or fantasy-cathexis here, a condition in which psychic energy is overconcentrated on a given object, namely, the ego of self or the subject's wish-formation. The latter would be especially possible in the writing of what I have called the tragedy of illusory identity. In any case, responses to outside objects and events would have clearly questionable objectivity or accuracy. Chronic brooding appears to lead to a defensive philosophical set and the lack of self-love implied appears to make that set habitually negative: that is, some variation of the view that "the world does not improve."

All right: so some modern obsessive thinking is self-centered and introspective. Isn't Hamlet also introspective to a dangerous degree? It might be enough to answer that Hamlet isn't Shakespeare, and Shakespeare isn't Hamlet. But more specifically, Hamlet's withdrawal into himself is not continual, and is self-centered only in a few scenes; the rest of the time he thinks of Denmark and a kingdom with justice first. The play he dominates is concerned, through him, with more universal implications of his problem than its mere contribution to his pain. Unlike the contemporary tragic figure, Hamlet does not want to "lose the name of action," because wrongs must be corrected for the sake of a whole nation, for a better life for Hamlet and those after him. The ingrown

protagonist of our day is more unrelentingly and unidimensionally maladjusted. The familiar characterization is that of the case-history type
who stays that way because it is the natural and only reaction of being
a thinking and feeling man. Electra, Phédre, Oedipus, and Richard III
are also "case-histories," but they act out their complexes as the grand
drive of the plays to which they each give life. For the moderns, the
play is a vehicle for their clinical observation and not the end-product
forced by their natures. Too many of our would-be tragedians do not
wish to give up their brooding whereas in classical tragedy the playwright
is objectively aware of both character and himself, able to move all his
contrived people—despite such long stretches of subjectivity as the soliloquy—more as if they were really on their own. There is a place where
white is white, where values are oriented again after the void of despair
and where we know that what happens to the protagonist is not a condemnation of the whole life-struggle. Without such considerable objectivity there is triviality and mere pathos.

Psychological introversion is an understandable condition of the central
character in any tragedy, post-Freudian or not, but when the playwright
does his storytelling only on the level of the psychological he falls short
of tragedy and the logical law which says that destruction follows when
fate is tempted nobly enough by a noble (and obviously *inner-directed*,
not *introverted*) error—in search of something better rather than acceptance of an infinite bad.

APOLOGIA

Self-pitying pessimism is usually most clearly evident in the
openly autobiographical tragedy, where the playwright in effect apologizes
for or explains himself. When the author uses components of his own
life story to make tragedy, it is usual that his central characters become
unique, rather naturalistic, and too special figures—actual instead of more
universal people. He knows these people so well he gives them psychological rather than human fullness because in deciding their (his) story is
tragic, he is trying to make an analytical point about them instead of making them perform according to the requirements of an artistic genre. And
he is ever so sure about seeing the whole business as "a tragedy." Here the

playwright moves inward again, but often with the special destination of Freud's "paradisal time," childhood.

Premodern tragedies are anything but autobiographical, and the characters are fictional (even when historical) and thus exist fundamentally to serve the needs of the tragic pattern. The author's personal or family pessimism is irrelevant. By contrast, lacking great perspective on any artistic identity of the people with whom he has suffered through life so intimately, the modern author simply recreates his personal hell as he experienced it, examining it as an amateur psychologist instead of *creating* it as a statement of fate. Logically, this cannot be a tragic hell for everyone else unless he is able to transcend himself as a lone individual case history and prove he is universal and representative. And for that, again, perspective is essential. He seems to say: "Look at what this particular life has done to the protagonist (a symbol for myself): isn't it unjust that he was never allowed real happiness in life, or that he should be so misunderstood?" This risks very sour grapes.

O'Neill's *Long Day's Journey into Night,* for example, serves as personal apologia for the dramatist's life and an explication of his family story. His last wife, Carlotta Monterey O'Neill, very significantly described his approach to writing the play:

> He explained to me that he had to write this play about his youth and his family. It was a thing that haunted him. He was bedeviled into writing it, it was something that came from his very guts, he had to get it out of his system, he had to forgive whatever it was that caused this tragedy between himself and his mother and father.
>
> When he started *Long Day's Journey,* it was a most strange experience to watch that man being tortured every day by his own writing. He would come out of his study at the end of the day gaunt and sometimes weeping. His eyes would be all red and he looked ten years older than when he went in in the morning. I think he felt freer when he got it out of his system. It was his way of making peace with his family—and himself.[7]

7. Seymour Peck, "A Talk with Mrs. O'Neill," reprinted in Oscar Cargill et al., *O'Neill and His Plays* (New York, 1961), p. 93.

Such punitive closeness to his tragedy suggests that the playwright is more interested in writing psychodrama, where the patients enact their guilts in a vague hope of adjusting to them—with the ironic twist that the session-leader knows a cure is impossible, since he writes of a past whose hopeless conclusion is already known to him. True, *Long Day's Journey* is intense and gripping, and it shows that O'Neill finally got some perspective on his unfortunate family—but not on where the family misfortune stood in relation to a meaning revealed in the whole of existence. The Tyrones' life on stage is merely the enduring of the curse of the weaknesses they all pass on to each other, and the play's length is sustained by verbal torture, suffering, and all the biographical proof of O'Neill's right to the nonperspective of the congenital pessimist. The attempt may stand as an impressive catharsis for him, but *katharsis* does not lead to *anagnorisis* this time, and it remains for us to pretend that the other prerequisites of tragedy can be found in an anticlimactic tearing of victims whose mortal wounds were inflicted long ago. He tried to do on paper what he could not do in actual communication with his people, and the writing was penance. His haunted view can only plead for pity and absolution for the Tyrone weakness and, against all hope of tragedy, for himself.

O'Neill's other plays are hardly free of autobiographical workings-out, such as the sanatorium love affair in *The Straw*. In fact the plays are usually the story of the Sensitive Dreamer in a Materialistic, Insensitive, and Unjust World: therein, at least, the standard tragedy of the second-year playwriting student. (The first year is for experiment with forms and effects.) O'Neill never really changed this emphasis from *Beyond the Horizon* to *Long Day's Journey*. Does this matter? Surely there are people who go to *Long Day's Journey* not knowing it is autobiographical and (bless them) who could not care less if they did. It still seems to me they must see the effects of introspective apology. Take any moderately successful commercial tragedy for comparison: Robert Bolt's *A Man for All Seasons* is a good tragic story. Notice what makes it "play?" The hero has accomplished something which earns him a tragic *ethos*, and the playwright has no reason to take a biased view of him or his existence: Sir Thomas More is neither Bolt's father, nor Bolt himself.

Another apologia is in Miller's *After the Fall*, even though a few have (briefly) called this Miller's greatest play and a true tragedy. The playwright himself said the play's technique is the confession—to get at the theme equating success and inhumanity. Quentin spills all to The Listener. Quentin is Miller, pressing to analyze his ability to hurt. This is man after the Fall, facing the legacy of his imperfection so that, after recognizing it, he can love. Quentin is intended finally to walk offstage tall and straight with Holga (who represents Miller's third wife). He has learned that all men are dangerous but he is going to hope. This slightly avoids pessimism—but only by saying so, and only on the last two pages. The whole process certainly does not avoid an intellectual self-indulgence on Miller's part in dwelling on his self-analysis, enjoying the fact of his self-perceptions. (His more recent *The Price* does better as statement by avoiding any pretense of form or "meaning of life" study—things which cloud *After the Fall*. It even reveals Miller the humorist.) Quentin tries to fight back his acquired despair and sometimes feels a hope he cannot justify, but then he thinks of the pointlessness of his life: "Whatever I look at, I seem to see its death. . . . Why can't I weep? Why do I feel an understanding with this slaughterhouse? I don't understand what I'm supposed to be to anyone." The body of the play does not substantiate the hint of possibility through the alliance with Holga. There *is* no real play or active discovery, but rather endless rhetorical questioning and introspection.

A few years ago there was a critical vogue for saying *A Streetcar Named Desire* was one of Tennessee Williams's most objective and nonpersonalized plays. Some of this may have been impatience with irrelevant public worries ("Gosh, Williams's life is certainly full of sick people") very like the idiotic criticism of Miller for putting Marilyn Monroe too obviously under scrutiny in *After the Fall* ("Wow, *that* must have been a weird marriage"). But if *Streetcar* is not strictly autobiographical, like most Williams plays it *is* extremely personal. It grew from the author's stay in the French Quarter in New Orleans, and seems his finest statement of the life he experienced there and in his other southern haunts. As Randolph Goodman points out, "it was in New Orleans that Williams discovered that all his material as a writer would henceforth be cut from the fabric of his own life."[8] Williams's characters—Alma, Laura, Blanche, Old Nonno, Amanda, and others—are largely products of his

8. *Drama on Stage* (New York, 1961), p. 275.

own observation of members of his family or other intimates. Their adaptation to his thematic purposes is partly meant to *reemphasize* the indignity of a failure; for all their poetic beauty as broken or dusty artifacts of a past or a beaten sensibility they serve a definite allegorical function. Of course all writers draw on what they know and live, and there is no intrinsic crime in a personal statement. Personal experience in our modern tragedians, however, seems to have bred pessimism, and the result twists the view. It is interesting, for example, that Williams's most autobiographical play, *The Glass Menagerie,* is one of his least pessimistic and most successful. In it he does not make a closed statement of fate, and he writes of a central character *in transition.*

Williams knows that the best symbol of his standard theme of the ironic corruption and destruction of the sensitive lies in his own life. But he is repelled by life and he is a confirmed pessimist. He has openly stated several times that literary creation is for him partly a retreat from a world he finds frightening and rapacious. As *tragedy,* some of his writing feels like a justification or symbolic explanation of his relationship with a personally traumatic past, perhaps even more than in O'Neill: "At the age of fourteen, I discovered writing as an escape from a world of reality in which I felt acutely uncomfortable. It immediately became my place of retreat, my cave, my refuge. From what? From being called a sissy by the neighborhood kids, and Miss Nancy by my father, because I would rather read books . . . than play marbles and baseball and other normal kid games."[9] Williams has been hurt, just as many other artists of long ago were hurt, embittered, and frightened by their world. Yet it is not apparent that any successful tragedian—at least when he composed acceptable tragic art—leaned more to hate and distrust of his world than to their opposite attitudes. While too much love may blind the artist to his subject's faults, hate and dread blot out all the attributes that have to be acknowledged to say that life goes usefully on—the premise on which tragedy, as praise of striving, is based. The more a tragic hero knows and appreciates the good, the more tellingly he can suffer from evil. Williams survives well materially, but he has more than intimated that life has not allowed him love and freedom from continuing fear. A good view of his nearness to his thematic work is afforded by his self-interview:

9. Quoted in Goodman, *Drama on Stage,* p. 274.

ANSWER: I think, without planning to do so, I have followed the developing tension and anger and violence of the world and time that I live in through my own steadily increasing tension as a writer and person.

QUESTION: Then you admit that this "developing tension," as you call it, is a reflection of a condition in yourself?

ANSWER: Yes.

QUESTION: A morbid condition?

ANSWER: Yes.

QUESTION: Perhaps verging on the psychotic?

ANSWER: I guess my work has always been a kind of psychotherapy for me.[10]

The question in such an admission is whether his psychological infirmity makes him labor points relevant to his own torture and not to the experience of his audience. In *Streetcar*, he is never serene enough about the central symbolic problem of the play to fully understand that there are other alternatives for the sick and the sensitive than brutal suppression or destruction. His brooding does not appear to let him see things whole, even though he does see things which are rich and peculiar in their drama:

> All my life I have been haunted by the obsession that to desire a thing or to love a thing intensely is to place yourself in a vulnerable position, to be a possible, if not a probable, loser of what you most want. . . . Having always to contend with this adversary of fear, which was sometimes terror, gave me a certain tendency toward an atmosphere of hysteria and violence in my writing, an atmosphere that has existed in it since the beginning.[11]

The question we ask of apologia as tragedy is, where is *illusion* in the autobiography (as artful transcendance, not illusory escapism)? The same thing is missing when the playwright becomes too close to a cause in his tragedy, when he writes a kind of admonitory tragedy, but this is better discussed in the next chapter as its chief difficulties are in terms of the tragic plot structure.

10. Ibid., p. 293.
11. Ibid., p. 277.

DISTANCE AND PERSPECTIVE

The goal of aesthetic distancing in tragedy is to achieve audience perspective on action and emotion in order to universalize a meaning of representative man's action or emotion. That is why a harmony exists within the tragic disorder. Personal pain, despair—i.e., actual man—is never enough. In traditional tragedy, it seems clearer that the playwright has considered his work first as art, even as entertainment, and much later a part of himself. It is not insignificant that the Greek tragedians wrote to compete for prizes, and that Shakespeare turned out plays to keep his company flourishing (and delivering maximum production). Aeschylus, Sophocles, and Euripides must have been almost automatically distanced by the very form of tragedy they created—a precise, objectively reasoned structure conforming to the production capacities and exigencies of their theatre. Aeschylus was a soldier, but there his equation with Agamemnon ends. Despair could not make the tragedy; only the tragedy could shape the despair, and then deny it. Euripides was more psychologically oriented and more complex than Aeschylus or Sophocles, but his psychology affected the Euripidean art *as* art (chopping down the chorus, reducing *stasimon*, and the like) more than it created private and closed involvement with a tragic theory. Aesthetic distance in the tragedy would suggest that the playwright is not psychoanalyzing himself, rationalizing his own history, or indignantly cursing his audience for a specific evil it has condoned. Loss of perspective regarding a belief is one seed of insanity, which is an extreme parallel except for what it says about balance in producing such an extreme story as a tragedy. As Goethe noted, tragedy must be "conceived by a man whose spirit is harmonious and educated"[12]—educated in the sense of a wider knowledge of his world.

Edward Bullough originated the concept, calling it "psychical distance," and the aspect of that which is useful to enriching the tragic perspective is that it denotes a somewhat disinterested attitude, less geared to the *utility* of the art object's relevance. This ideal would also be suggested in the *rasa* concept of Hindu aesthetics (the tasting or savoring of the thing indirectly from its portrayal) or Schiller's *schein* (the semblance of a thing as artistically more desirable than its reality). At such

12. Johann W. von Goethe, "Concerning Truth and the Appearance of Truth in Works of Art," trans. J. Evarts, in *Seven Arts* (Indian Hills, Colo., 1955), p. 224.

proper distance, the spectator will suspend his own *specific* practical, moral, ethical, and utilitarian concerns.

In traditional tragedy, there is a healthy distinction between fear of the particular, as in Othello's fear of losing Desdemona, and dread of the whole—the latter mood almost never occurring even in the darkest of classical visions, such as in *Timon* or *Prometheus* or *The Trojan Women*. When despair appears in, say, a Timon or a Hecuba, it is not total and it is counterpointed with contrasts which show that hope might be more generalized than despair for man left behind. Modern tragedy, when it grows too introspective, is incapable of this more balanced attitude; there is a literary-philosophical-artistic impasse, as reflected in Kierkegaard's warning about despair: "The despairing person's condition of despair can be directly described, as the poet does in fact by attributing to him the appropriate lines. But to describe despair is possible only by its opposite; and if the lines are to have poetic value, they must contain in their coloring a reflection of the dialectical opposite."[13] Finally, the question of a necessary creativity is raised in Ronald Peacock's pertinent criticism of the "eccentric tragedy." Such work is self-destroying because its despair is the actuality of the playwright's view and not the conclusion of his imagined and created characters:

> There are eccentric books and poems and paintings, which attract and repel tastes with equal violence. They are creations of individuals, and even those who are repelled cannot always deny their imaginative power. But eccentric tragedy is a contradiction in terms. The poet here works not in the material of personal fantasy but of human life. The actions, passions, suffering of men in their relations with one another bind him to *their* laws and suppress *his* fancy; and the highest function of his imagination in this case is the illumnation of the world outside himself. A poet trying to create his own tragic values enters the arena of opinion; his audience loses its cohesion and emotional unity; we disagree with his opinion and are insensible to his tragedy. All subjects that deal with the exceptional or the pathological case—the subjects of Kleist, for instance, and

13. Søren Kierkegaard, *Fear and Trembling: The Sickness Unto Death*, trans. Walter Lowrie (Garden City, N.Y., 1954), p. 163.

some of Strindberg—lose their tragic power; at the most they
arouse the curiosity and pathos that characterize the bystander
and not the participant.[14]

I am afraid this criticism applies all too frequently to the tragedies since
Strindberg. Against them, it is through distance fostered by "fancy" that
we might interpretatively contribute more meaning to the witnessing of
the tragedy.

In summary, then, total implication and meaning on a more universal
and timeless level are too important to sacrifice for an intense but isolated
apologia, and tragic playwrights must necessarily campaign against ex-
clusivity in any world-view. With perspective the artist can connect an
intellectual and emotional depiction of misery with a similar regard for
giving us the sense and feeling of why tragic events are tragic next to what
might have been—and, next to the loss of whatever is *good* and *worthwhile*, suggest what we might imagine or extrapolate about man at the
suprareal level of ourselves. Here the protagonist-playwright is not bi-
ographically and individually small, but collectively and representatively
large.

14. Ronald Peacock, *The Poet in the Theatre* (New York, 1960), pp. 156–57.

4. STORIES and STRUCTURE

Some of the time, the stories of the modern tragedies turn out like O'Neill's description of the pattern of existence in *Long Day's Journey*:

> Then the hand lets the veil fall and you are alone, lost in the fog again, and you stumble on toward nowhere, for no good reason!

Perhaps this is not a scrupulously fair superscription for this chapter, except when you think of the plays' movement and progress through a tragic plot—a vantage point we have forgotten to frequent. The stories often do lead nowhere, and the continuum suggested in successful conceptions of dramaturgy becomes a major nemesis for the pessimistic author. Here, probably, is the best symbol of his constitutional incompatibility with tragedy: he cannot believe there is progress, a future suggested by the passage of time, an up as well as a down to the rhythm of life.

The black outlook works against tragic story and structure in three essential ways. First, the pessimistic attitude causes the author to overload his play with the negative aspects and expressions of a propagandistic view of the world—in order to support a case for despair. Next, his dramaturgy becomes evident in and of itself because of the pressure he applies toward reaching a pessimistic conclusion; thus what happens in his plot can lack credibility. Finally, because pessimism decrees that fortune is always low, there is rarely a tragic reversal of fortune; the play structure tends to be monotonous, like a straight line downhill. The story can be simply boring.

With this, I am inviting debate. Contrary to Croce and others who caution against formulas of generic boundary and attendant pigeonholing, a basic tenet of my argument *is* that tragedy is a definite and specialized genre (as art or even as philosophy). Kaufmann says that "the difference between tragedy and comedy is not in essence one of subject matter, but depends upon our point of view. The same action, involving the same people, can be represented as tragic or comic."[1] True, but the shape of that subject matter comes from point of view and the shape affects generic response. There is no argument over the fact that x plays of the past were tragedies, and that they all have a fairly common effect. Why not then accept the deduction that they achieved this through a certain like definiteness of form? Northrop Frye reminds us, "the source of tragic effect must be sought, as Aristotle pointed out, in the tragic *mythos* or plot-structure,"[2] and it seems to me that the modern tragedy lacks emphasis on *mythos* because of its prevailing attitude. What happens and how it is put together do matter, and—recalling how O'Neill was no better off when cribbing the Oresteia plot—the attitude toward the use of story is most important of all. Kaufmann is still not quite right when he says: "What makes a tragedy a tragedy is not *what* is presented but *how* it is presented, and it is all-important to distinguish the story used by a playwright from his handling of it, the ancient myth from the play's plot."[3] I think the "what" and the "how" are inherently joined in tragedy, and that their precise joint handling is made or unmade by the writer's attitude toward the outcome.

1. *Tragedy and Philosophy*, p. 45.
2. Northrop Frye, *Anatomy of Criticism* (New York, 1966), p. 207.
3. *Tragedy and Philosophy*, p. 89.

LOADED PLOTS

I have already discussed the problem of one-sided viewing, coming from the introspective attitude; but such lack of perspective is only one possible aspect of the difficulty. There is a more tangible and simple effect of the predisposition, whether from introspection, critical indignation, or just general pessimism: a lack of enthusiasm for and about plotting or the burdening of it with elements which work against dramatic story. It may be said that optimism is also a preconception, or is one-sided, but optimism can include skepticism, cynicism, and pure naïve faith—while pessimism is innately narrower. Most important for now, optimism admits the possibility of *drama*.

Aristotle and countless others have always held that good plot must come from character: dramatis personae must evolve their lives rather than biased and meddling playwright-attitudes. The modern pessimist playwright often stacks his plot in order to have the "right" things happen to his characters—it cannot occur to him that glorious contrast can be plausible—so that in the end they (he) and we may conclude what the characters had already concluded at the plot's beginning. This is the accepted agenda of the playwright as Critic or as Casualty. He understands his characters' defeat too soon, right from the opening curtain, and looks ahead to how we will be doing the same. Why is this wrong? John Gassner, in discussing this quality in the modern drama, answers:

> [The playwright] fails chiefly because in striving so arduously for an element of "enlightenment," or for the conversion of his characters and the audience to his point of view, he so often substitutes statement for dramatic process. . . . The unsupported frontal assault soon crumbles, since there is no effective tragic enlightenment when the play lacks compelling human reality. Emotions deeply rooted in character being absent, no rapport has been established between the observer . . . and the actor . . . except on a basis of superficial agreement or partisanship more or less extraneous to art.[4]

Let us say instead, "extraneous to tragedy," for the best of our playwrights

4. John Gassner, *The Theatre in Our Times* (New York, 1954), p. 63.

do not always fail to create human emotion—even if it is usually pathos—through conflicts implied in the character study they favor over situation-molding.

Already I may appear to risk self-contradiction, because I do want very much to emphasize that tragedy is a contrived fiction, an *entertainment*. But manipulation of plot and other dramatic components is not in itself wrong—excepting always that basic rule that good dramaturgy ought never to call attention to itself as such. The question is where the manipulation is led by attitude. In the archetypal myth of old tragedy, the plot is indeed very "canned," but precisely that nature (the creator knowing its whole shape and content) enabled man to control outcomes. As Mircea Eliade writes in *Myth and Reality*, ". . . in one way or another one 'lives' the myth, in the sense that one is seized by the sacred, exalting power of the events recollected or reenacted."[5] This is still no guarantee of a workable tragic context, however. Mythic ritual can be a bore in itself for an audience when insistence on it is too evident, or when content leads nowhere. "Temporal progress towards X or Y or Z"—like it or not, that is still the rudimentary story-shape to which man relates. Today we hear too much about experimenting with a "theatre of ritual." Admittedly, it is correct that, as Alfred North Whitehead says, "mankind became artists in ritual," but the usual dramatic ritual of our day (*a la* Peter Brook, the Genet people, and the cults of Cruelty or Rock and Revolution) means a ritual of effects as production values—masks, "primal" costuming, symbolic properties, chanting, ritual "signs," icons, gestures, and so forth. What is overlooked in this easy novelty of going back to our racial and psychological childhood is that one must have a story beneath it all, a story that works. Ritual is eventually *story*.

And tragedy is *creation*. We need misfortunes created for their deliberate fictive attractiveness and revelatory possibilities. The order lost in quest then becomes an order reestablished through artistic control: yes, manipulation. And it is in the nature of the good story that attitude about outcomes can fluctuate until very late.

If you believe your hero is an already beaten person, it is going to be incongruous to write scenes depicting good fortune or varied mood. That is the limitation which the pessimistic playwright accepts. Several of the

5. Mircea Eliade, *Myth and Reality* (New York, 1963), p. 19.

playwrights can produce good melodrama. When they try to elevate this to tragedy, however, the need to point the way seems to shove variety and excitement to the rear as if such matters are too unsophisticated for the task of tragedy. We can almost hear them say: "Plot is just something I need to tell my gloomy story or to contain my argument for pessimism." Then how much can really *happen*? It may be more a matter of citation and documentation. Hence the use of episodic flashback technique in Miller's *Death of a Salesman* and *After the Fall*: "Here's how he got that way, see?" *Machinal* has to be planned as "a tragedy in ten episodes." The pessimist's episode, further, is rarely a playlet in itself (not being intrinsically plotted and dramatic) because it is an ex post facto cause of the present despair.

It's partly naturalism and verisimilitude: modern life itself is not varied and exciting, full of triumph as well as tragedy—therefore why expect anything different of tragedy on the stage? Naturalism as a dramaturgical means is an effective style, as an extreme reaction to the pressure of past and present reality, used to persuade the audience that "this is how it really is." By definition, naturalism demands more attention to faults than attributes in an environment or situation and interest-through-contrast is beside the point. Otherwise, why use a style aimed at a compressed verisimilitude and the detailing of the life of the body? Thus the spectator is drawn into a critical attitude about "failings" and "limitations" and the author chooses to direct this negative response at a less-than-broad canvas of life. The necessary clutter of naturalism—valid and useful though it may be in many a work of art—is nonetheless inappropriate for commenting on the spirit, via the intangible nondetails which are the framework of tragedy.

There are two main kinds of this modern denial of plot. In the first, the story will be full of drawn-out reasons and traumas which motivate the pessimistic conclusion. This can be a "loaded" or a simply boring plot, or both, to show that the world is meaningless and fulfillment impossible. O'Neill, for example, particularly tries to show the *long* process of mere endurance and empty and painful monotony. Ordinary loading occurs in plots which set down the circumstances which, uninterestingly, posit a given failure.

I think it will be useful to sketch the outlines of some plays of the circumstantial or drawn-out type. In O'Neill's *Diff'rent* (1920), heroine

Emma Crosby is a victim of her Puritanism. She rejects a faithful suitor, the sea captain Caleb, because she learns he was once seduced by a native girl in the south seas. *Years later,* she falls in love with a worthless young man while Caleb remains true and waits hopelessly for Emma's softening. When Emma succumbs to the young man, Caleb hangs himself; and when Emma discovers the young man only wants her money, she too commits suicide. (The plot imitates the action of the certainly decreasing possibility.) Another O'Neill play, *Gold* (1921), does this with an inevitability theme, recounting the long chain of events stemming from a greed for a treasure of gold which bit by bit destroys the family of ship captain Bartlett. Other dreary stackings of misfortune and hopeless passions (which do not relate to a meaningful fight against the life-problem) are basic to the "sex tragedies" and "farm tragedies" which almost became genres in their own right in the twenties and thirties. The basic story and attitude are nearly always the same: love is doomed by libido and man is doomed from the first by harsh existence. Sophie Treadwell's *Machinal* (1928) employed a kind of expressionism to reflect a mechanistic world closing in on the Young Woman's hopeless dream for a love the world has rejected as out of its style. Her sexual frigidity, a product of her upbringing, makes her marriage a torture and childbirth a nightmare. Rejecting her crass husband, she eventually becomes involved with a murderous young man who gives her the idea of killing her husband. When she does so, she is betrayed by her lover, caught, tried, and executed. Partly based on a contemporary murder trial, the play was nonetheless presented as the author's own conception of a contemporary "tragedy." Owen and Donald Davis's dramatization of Edith Wharton's novel, *Ethan Frome* (1936), was pure straight-line-down hopeless tragedy. Ethan is trapped by his farm work and responsibilities to his helpless women, then condemned by an impossible love affair and related attempt at lovers' suicide to an existence which is the punishment for an obviously unreasonable dream. In Dan Totheroh's *Wild Birds* (1925), orphan Mazie lives on a farm where she is enslaved by the brutal Slag. Her chance for love comes in the form of a boy escaped from reform school who becomes Slag's bond-slave in return for secrecy. When Slag discovers Mazie pregnant, he whips the boy to death and Mazie kills herself. Maxwell Anderson's *White Desert* (1924) pictures two couples becoming sexually entangled in their barren North Dakota homestead setting. Jealousy, promiscuity, and guilt follow on one another until the erring wife is killed by a crazed husband. In Lynn Riggs's *Cream in the Well* (1940), the Sawter family live on an Oklahoma farm, plagued by a helpless tendency for incest and perversion. One daughter sadistically goads her brother's fiancé into suicide. The disgusted brother comes home after sexually debasing himself. The two perverts are drawn together, but this ends in the girl's suicide. In Clifford Odets's *Clash By Night* (1941), Mae Wilenski is disappointed with life and her stupid but honest husband Jerry. When a more attractive man comes to board with the Wilenskis, Mae, after a short struggle, decides to submit to his advances. Jerry slowly comprehends the situation, then stalks down his wife's lover and kills him. David Liebovitz' *John Hawthorne* (1921), modestly admired in its time as an honest attempt at tragedy, tells the story of Laura, a lonely mountain girl who marries a rich but stern old farmer. Inevitably she falls in love with the farmhand John Hawthorne. When discovered, John kills the old man in an argument. John and Laura try to run away, but Laura—who has always been obsessed with questions of salvation—becomes fanatic about John's sin (for which she is mostly responsible). Since she cannot convert him, Laura betrays him to the sheriff with the idea she is saving his soul. It is obvious that most of these plays I have described are actually melodramas, but we should not overlook the fact that they were often regarded by their authors as expressions of fate, as tragedies of the times. Nor should we ignore the consistency with which the hopelessly structured story occurs to the playwright. In the case of the "farm tragedies," a fascination with Freud clearly affected the preoccupation with sexual tension as a "tragic" aspect of the contemporary obstacle to any happiness.

Other stories of how one cannot succeed in this century favor (like *Machinal*) episodic plotting to document the environmental outlook. Rice's *Street Scene* (1929) is an example, in which Anna Maurrant is persecuted by her brutal and unloving husband and her neighbors are equally oppressed by other evils, all fostered by the ghetto. Trying to find some tenderness and kindness in this existence, Anna allows herself to become involved with an opportunistic milkman. Maurrant sets a trap for her and, confirming his suspicions about her infidelity, he kills her lover and mortally wounds her. He himself is pursued and killed after the murder, as the tenement people around him go on with their complaints about capitalism, the unions, and racial and social conflict. Like the "farm" tragediennes, Anna is doomed as the one person foolish enough to have wanted love and warmth in this unjust and cruel life.

The simplistic tragedy of sensitivity also loads its plot with "evidence" that the rest of the world is all Hobbesian compared to the innocent little hopes of the lonely poet visionary. In Irving Kaye Davis's *The Right to Dream* (1923), defensiveness is obvious. Against her family's wishes, a rich girl marries a young writer and starves with him in a tenement while he tries to fulfill himself. When their life becomes too wretched, the girl's mother interferes, and the writer takes a degrading job as editor of a mystery magazine. Soon he is rich but artistically destroyed. He kills himself. I am afraid today's artist-figures still see themselves in this way when they work in the context of tragedy, where the cards are stacked against them by life. There are many more plays deliberately emphasizing lengthy suffering more than the "stacked" plot, and O'Neill's *The Iceman Cometh, Mourning Becomes Electra,* and *Long Day's Journey* come most immediately to mind.

The other type of plot denial is in what I will call the admonitory tragedy, which features a pressured, violent conclusion or otherwise somewhat incredible scenario meant to confirm pessimism. This is where the soap box comes in. The improbability of *The Petrified Forest,* for instance, is certainly affected by the great need for pessimistic philosophizing and pushing the melodrama for editorial ends. In *Winterset,* Anderson—working in an atmosphere of social unrest and topical criticism which keeps him deep in an ingrown 1930s context—heavy-handedly makes Mio Romagna enact a martyrdom which supposedly proves how unjust and unimprovable life is today. Under Anderson's pushing, all symbols of antagonism to this "son" of a Sacco or Vanzetti are unidimensionally reinforcing the clichés that society is mindless, government arbitrary, triumph of human spirit laughable, so that "the rats will inherit the earth." If it is not tenement poverty which crushes these people, it is the heartless minion of the law, or the carnivorous force of crime, or that unjust Boston judge with his prejudice against anarchists—all things we have allowed our society to develop. Most of the characters have reason, according to the bleak life Anderson generalizes in the play, to shout with

Garth, "Oh, God damn the world.!" The persuasion is difficult to keep under control. For example, the playwright must make sure we see there is no point in taking an injustice to a court. By chance the court might be fair. It is a forced case of *Winter-set*, as Samuel Selden uses the ideas of Summer and Winter as the antipodes of tragedy.[6]

In *Gods of the Lightning*, the social cause is far more specifically brandished. Macready and Capraro (again, read Sacco and Vanzetti), the former a fiery leader of the strikers in a mill town walkout, the latter a passive but fervent anarchist, are arrested for the murder of a payroll messenger. Their trial is unjust, and they are "framed" and sent to electrocution while their comrades mourn their passing and all that is politically related to it.

Paul Green's *In Abraham's Bosom* (1926) and DuBose Heyward's *Brass Ankle* (1932) speak out on prejudice against the Negro, and quite obviously spend dramaturgical energy enacting the effect of prejudice. Abraham tries to educate his people and lift them out of their despair in a white world, but is flawed by his mulatto identity and perverse arrogance. When Abe whips a Negro pupil, he loses his school. Years later he is still trying to help the Negroes but his own pride and an errant son betray him to vindictive white people. In the Heyward play, Ruth Leamer discovers with the birth of her second child that she has Negro blood and her husband, a champion of the whites, is crushed. Ruth attempts to save them from their society's ostracism by announcing she had a Negro lover who fathered the black child. Her husband, in rage, kills both Ruth and the infant. The "moral" of these plays is worthy, the drama is often there, and the white converts may sometimes be made. But as expressions of a tragedy of their time, their conclusions are pessimistic. If nothing else, this ironically lets a guilty audience go free by implying that nothing would change the situation, which is only an essential evil of existence corrupted by societal imperfection.

The thrust of indignation against man's society is basically the same in *Death of a Salesman*. The pathos is all there, irresistibly so, and aiming for that was Miller's main effort. But persuasion again skews things if we expect to take with us the insight of a tragedy. As another writer has noticed: "Willy Loman's personal values are ultimately so

6. Samuel Selden, *Man in His Theatre* (Chapel Hill, N.C., 1957), chap. 3.

confused with those of the enemy Society that when their praises are sung at the end of the play, its whole intellectual structure collapses into meaninglessness."[7]

In short, the pessimist as Critic may be inclined to "message tragedy." The complaining spirit involved, however, holds too narrow a view of the whole to comment on something so universal as the life-problem. As Professor Stoll put it, "poetry is not a gospel, tragedy not a play with a 'message,' no answer to the riddle of existence in either ever [being] satisfied."[8] The intellectual, moral, or other worth of the tragedian's statement is not an end in itself in the tragedy, but must coexist with story and structure contrived so as to *shape* the facts about our society and our existence. Pessimistic thought does not shape facts of life so much as it overreacts to life's disorganization. It is indignation, not exaltation,

A final example on this point is the pessimist's ability to force the victimization of his victim to ensure that his tragic structure completely fits his thematic bias. In the conclusion of *Orpheus Descending*, the sympathetic characters suddenly and too obediently (to Williams's plan) go out of their way to open themselves to destruction. Lady must step in front of Val, must take the bullet meant for him from Jabe's gun, must take it in her stomach where Val's baby has just been formed. And all that Val and Lady have possessed must go to doom with them in the confectionery fire. The play is not without beauty, interest, and thoughtful images of man's coldness. It made a rather haunting film as *The Fugitive Kind*. But we must ask that a tragic story not persuade so transparently. Of course a violent end is no problem in itself, but I refer to a violent shoving of a large generalization into a small closed specificity. This is no new theorem convenient to the epoch; remember that *Titus Andronicus*, for example, is also bad tragedy (and drama) because Shakespeare pushed so hard and self-consciously for unmotivated violence and gore.

EMPTY CRISES

Lear starts his play emotionally and chronologically "late." He is in "winter" in nearly every sense, save for the fact that he is a king with

---

7. Richard Foster, "Comedy Before Tragedy," *Nation*, 31 December 1960, p. 527.
8. E. E. Stoll, *Shakespeare and Other Masters* (Cambridge, Mass., 1940), p. 81.

power. Let us be frank and admit that this is probably a flaw in *King Lear*. By the time of the storm we wish him well enough but in the first scenes we could prefer to see him closer to a moment of *spritual* "high fortune." Instead we see a mean minded old bastard. This timing comes from the playwright's "point of attack"; that is, when should he open the curtain or bring up the lights on the spectator's first glimpse of his character's story—within the overall continuum of antecedent and anticipated material? Many a tragedy begins late in the sense that harbingers of coming doom are already evident in the first few pages of text. But what of the space between the point of attack and the location of the play's real crisis? Here I think we can see a significant difference between modern and traditional tragedy. The typical contemporary work (especially the tragedies of illusory identity and inheritance) starts either after the true causal crisis or unusually close before it,[9] so that little is left of the play except aftermath or seeing how our man is going to take it. One obvious consequence of this is lost contrast. Even more immediately for theatre, how can monotony (at least of moods) be avoided?

Northrop Frye has pictured the career of the tragic character as a quite definite structure of seven phases, growing from the heroic to the ironic. To paraphrase him freely, they depict: the aristocratic glory of the hero, as in myth, through his innocence or purity or excusable extremism which makes him susceptible to the problem; then the confrontation of this quality with its opposite to begin the main battle; the low point where entrapment vitiates the former breadth of vision; next moving to the shock of destruction; and finally to the phase of meaning, as in demonic ritual, where vision arises out of the necessary and violent fate of the hero.[10] The number of phases notwithstanding, I believe we should accept the fact that the tragic structure is definitely programmed. The timing and the nature of the crisis is one crucial part of the form. Tragedy displays poles of extremes and the development between them incites a strong linear structure, because the movement of the tragedy is *toward* events which *can never recur*. Life and its choices, says tragedy, are never quite the same again as each additional experience with life accumulates, but the linear progression is full of variety and even of turns

9. See Appendix C for data on this subject.
10. In *Anatomy of Criticism*, pp. 219–23.

despite the fact they never form a circle.[11] Without this exciting linearity, the battle is over before begun. With it, the playwright can capture the form of an ideal life. There is an as yet unknown crisis to build toward. Pessimism denies such a crisis. In his article, "A Metaphor for Dramatic Form," Marvin Rosenberg finds the basis for drama in linear form. Its sequential tension-release pattern produces catharsis. He quotes Susanne Langer stating that "movement toward destiny" is the *only* proper dramatic form. Langer continues: "It is only a present filled with its own future that is really dramatic. A sheer immediacy, an imperishable direct experience without the ominous forward movement of consequential forward action, would not be so. . . . This tension between past and future is what gives to acts, situations, and even such constituent elements as gestures and attitudes and tones the peculiar intensity known as dramatic quality. . . ." For Rosenberg, this means linearity. It is interesting that he finds the time in *Death of a Salesman,* for example, to be "interior." He says "it moves from a central situation back and forth in fantasy and memory to widen and deepen a present emotional moment. A linear ending is tagged on to the play, but it is neither necessary nor inevitable." He concludes that the modern drama's form is "flux." Its conception of time merely states that "life is," not that "life is X or Y or Z."[12]

Notice the basic story occurring to O'Neill, Rice, and the others who arrange the play as a treadmill. Look at the plot of *Beyond the Horizon.* On a New England farm, two brothers love the same girl, Ruth Atkins. Robert Mayo is a frail dreamer who wants to go on a voyage to satisfy a longing to go "beyond the horizon." Andrew Mayo is satisfied with being a very good farmer. Robert assumes Ruth loves his more vigorous brother but, as he is about to leave, he discovers that Ruth loves him—or so she says. Robert stays on the farm and Andrew goes on the voyage. The reversal of roles makes everyone almost immediately wretched. Rob-

11. See the treadmill form of much modern tragedy (indicated in Appendix), plus Harold H. Watts, "Myth and Drama," in *Tragedy: Modern Essays in Criticism,* ed. L. Michel and R. B. Sewall (Englewood Cliffs, N.J., 1963), p. 83 ff. Watts offers a good discussion of the relative possibilities of the cyclic and linear myths.

12. Marvin Rosenberg, "A Metaphor for Dramatic Form," *Journal of Aesthetics and Art Criticism,* 17 (December 1958): 174–80. Rosenberg continues the idea in a later article, "Drama is Arousal," *JAAC,* 27 (Summer 1969): 425–31. The aspect of suspense is specially emphasized.

ert's incompetence on the farm incites his father's hatred. Ruth quickly realizes she loved Andrew after all. The farm goes to ruin. After years of wandering, Andrew returns to the farm. Overwork and the hopelessness of his situation aggravate Robert's frail health into tuberculosis and he dies speaking of the places he never got to see.

The crisis of *Beyond the Horizon* is in the first of the play's three acts, when poet Robert decides to stay home from the sea. After that, there are developments but no crises. His recognition of Ruth as a shrew might be some sort of crisis later in the play if their sex duel were the point of the tragedy and the source of the real catastrophe, such as that is. Yet all further bits of plot are only follow-ups, part of the sentence of a two-and-a-half act denouement. The play spans thirteen years. After their years of punishment, Robert, Ruth, and Andrew discuss a reexchange of roles—but only after all new movement is proven useless, as by the arbitrary device of Robert's fatal illness. When Ruth tells Andrew she loved him after all, he must shatter her for her sacrilege in the face of Robert's dying. And she admits: "I wouldn't know how to feel love, even if I tried, any more." When Andrew asks Ruth to make peace with Robert, she can only say, "I'll go. But it won't do any good." After another five years of waiting, the end is (we hope) near. Now another typical O'Neill device appears in the nemesis-form of the "quack doctor" who is to take on symbolic responsibility for Robert's death. In the only semblance of struggle he has mustered, Robert blames the doctor for the death of his mother, father, and daughter—just as the hero of *Long Day's Journey* fights against the aftereffects of his miserly father's habitual patronage of the inept doctor who contributes to Edmund's terminal tuberculosis. Robert's death, of course, is only a medical inevitability and has nothing to do with his character or the doctor's. Pessimist Robert has known his fate all along, as against any hope in better medical care: "I don't believe in miracles—in my case. Besides, I know more than any doctor on earth *could* know—because I *feel* what's coming." The structure and the disease enact the same process of decay.

The pattern, therefore, is proof upon proof of the appropriateness of despair. It is so unrelieved we must assume it is O'Neill's own, and that this was his intention. In good classic tragedy, the protagonist is not convinced about the outcome until quite late in the play and therefore has some hope. The true crisis is late, and the characters retain enough strength to act their way to an uncertain consequence. They recognize out of action, not predestined revelation.

Death of a Salesman starts extremely late in the protagonist's career. Decay is years old when Willy's story opens, and the play will add to aspects of a crisis already in progress. We do not know a great deal about the history of Willy's decay except through Miller's expressionistic recollections of certain traumatic scenes from the past. That means we take it on faith that there were some *good* moments back there for Willy, that he was once personable, honest, worthy of love, and so on—for he is *not* any of these things during all the scenes of the past and present shown on the stage.

The play begins on a low level of fortune and goes lower. Willy is already semidemented and physically fading fast. Miller says in the stage directions: "A few moments ago as he was taking his cases out of his car, he was probably thinking how wonderfully safe and warm the sight of Linda would be. But this was a few moments ago and for Willy Loman at this stage of his life, a moment can die at birth or linger for a very long time; a remark heard years ago can return to him now and hold him fast so that he is not aware of happenings around him."[13] A character who *starts* his story with us while out of touch with reality can offer little in the way of comment on his situation, through experience with variables and a perspective of things. We can't trust his spiritual sight now or at any later phase, and it is possible to decide that his situation is inconsequentially unique. Curiously, Miller comments elsewhere: "The effort to eliminate antecedent material has threatened to eliminate the past from many plays. We are impatient to get on with it—so much so that anyone making a study of some highly creditable plays of the moment would be hard put to imagine what their characters were like a month before their actions and stories begin."[14] Actually, the trend goes that one worse: it is safe to assume that the character of a month ago would be just about as badly off as at the point of attack. But Miller's statement is still a valid criticism of modern drama attempting tragedy, and he un-

13. *Death of a Salesman*, a reader's edition especially expanded by the author (New York, 1955), pp. 6–7.
14. Miller, *Collected Plays* (New York, 1957), p. 20.

wittingly elaborates further against *Death of a Salesman* in speaking of the effect he wants:

> Willy Loman does not merely suggest or hint that he is at the end of his strength and of his justifications, he is hardly on the stage for five minutes when he does so; he does not gradually imply a deadly conflict with his son, an implication dropped into the midst of serenity and surface calm, he is avowedly grappling with that conflict at the outset. The ultimate matter with which the play will close *is announced at the outset* and is the matter of its every moment from the first [Italics mine].[15]

That much false surety is possible only with pessimism, and the "ultimate matter" of the play is preordained defeat. We can therefore *watch* Willy with great pity, but there is no point in joining him.

Crisis is emasculated in *Winterset* because of *conscious* waiting as the form of the play. There is waiting for death, waiting for disease to vanquish the gangster Trock (significantly, nature is the only force that will bury this particular "blind worm"), waiting for Trock to murder Mio and Miriamne, and waiting for the world to show again that nothing has been accomplished by the act of living and nothing so fine as revenge for injustice could have been realized. As Esdras says:

> the ground we walk on is impacted down and hard
> with blood and bones of those who died unjustly.
> There's not one title to land or life, even your own,
> but was built on rape and murder, back a few years.
> It would take a fire indeed to burn out all this error.

The play is supposedly integrated by Mio's continuing quest for revenge, his single identity as the avenging angel:

> For my heritage
> they've left me one thing only, and that's to be
> my father's voice crying up out of the earth
> and quicklime where they stuck him.

15. Ibid., p. 25.

This might result in a structure aiming toward crisis, but even this drive pales in the fatal moment in which Mio's love for Miriamne gives him a new self-image and takes his mind off revenge. Anderson *avoids* confrontation. The balance is removed by the pessimistic necessity of having everyone suffer, making all lives meaningless, without allowing them their "day in court." Mad though the Judge is, he reasons the same way the "sane" characters do when he says:

> We were born too early. Even you who are young are not of the elect. In a hundred years man will put his finger on life itself, and then he will live as long as he likes. For you and me we shall die soon—one day, one year more or less, when or where, it's no matter. It's what we call an indeterminate sentence.

Until the sentence is terminated by a dramaturgical euthanasia, the characters submit to the ambiguity of their lives which, in turn, produces the ambiguity or meaninglessness of their deaths. The ever-closing structure is a drain. T. R. Henn speaks of the tragic structure through his image of the *net*[16]—the tangle circling tighter and tighter around the victim by means of specific stages. Significantly, though, Henn admits that the image is useful only up to the stage of enlightenment because there the spirit, at least, of the victim seems to "slash across the meshes" in finding a kind of new life in the meaning of the catastrophe.

ANTIPERIPETY

A slightly different aspect of the same problem comes up in mandatory lack of reversal.

What does it mean to reverse fortune? Loss—and contrast. The tragedy which depicts some such peripeteia at least incidentally admits the possibility of a good or hopeful status somewhere in time and the character's career. The audience is able to contrast present and past and see what former potential is being denied. Even if the reversal is to be "sudden" or not, as per the old dictum, most modern serious plays are committed to the single level of fortune in pure stasis of evil and fatalism.

16. T. R. Henn, *The Harvest of Tragedy* (London, 1956).

Aristotle saw part of the changeover as forming a passage from "ignorance to knowledge" and Maxwell Anderson advised tragedy to show a "reversal for the better." Perhaps seeing tragedy's form as a continuum of present to past to future clarifies the necessity for a shift. Stasis in time and development is meaningless. The present is the problem, the past is a reference to the "what might have been" or the "high fortune," and the future is the basic question of tragedy.

The idea that this means inevitability in the plot has been worked over a great deal. Mandel says at one point that "to obtain tragedy, the author must withdraw all doubt from the issue."[17] Morrell assumes that one can see a great tragedy again and again because suspense about its developments is never important; it is "always a rehearsal," and "never a performance." He states that "surprise is unimportant to tragedy."[18] In such positions, I think, the relationship of reversal to inevitability and suspense is misunderstood. We are told that the outcome of *Hamlet, Oedipus, Othello*, and other tragedies, is never in doubt and thus suspense does not figure in the tragic structure. Of course Othello's doom is inevitable—once he errs and allows himself to be manipulated in just that way he is most susceptible. *When* does inevitability assert itself? What must be understood is the timing and not the fact of it. Perhaps most of all, citing doom as the eradicator of suspense neglects the artistic status of the tragedy. Spontaneity, or "the illusion of the first time," is generated by the truly artistic tragic drama. Its structure appears flexible enough to allow dramatic irony and an increasing rather than decreasing array of meanings. Partly because of the depth of interpretable images and events, we can go to our fortieth *Hamlet* or twentieth *Lear* or *Othello*. Amid its and our subjectivity, seeing it move along on stage, it seems emotionally possible that events may take a new turn. We are unmoved by, in fact unable to concentrate on, advance knowledge of Act Five while experiencing Act Three.

Successful tragedy contains contrasts and actual or possible reversals— of fortune and development. *Romeo and Juliet* and *Hamlet*, to name two of dozens of examples, move up and down through the use of what could

17. *A Definition of Tragedy*, p. 39.
18. Roy Morrell, "The Psychology of Tragic Pleasure," in *Tragedy: Modern Essays in Criticism*, ed. L. Michel and R. B. Sewall, p. 278.

initially be regarded as irrelevant events and tones: street fights, comedy, new locales, the player's speech, and so forth. Then there is the comedy and relief of *Macbeth*'s porter scene, or the mixed burlesque and madness of the Pentheus-Tiresias exchanges in Euripides' *The Bacchae*. At least some of these moments are conscious attempts at entertainment and variety. They help to shift attitude, maintain possibility, and move the play out of two dimensions into three. Variety relieves—and maintains audience interest. In Greek tragedy, the chorus itself is an automatic relief and variation which breaks a straight line. Even so, a linear continuity still contains attempts to break above and below its trend. Suspense serves a function.

Another way to approach this is to consider how many tragedies connote the possibility of escape, even a subjective and illusory one. The true tragedy does posit doom; but our participation is based on the emotional response to the avenue of escape which *seems* to be open to the protagonist (and symbolically to us) well into the confrontation period. It is this hope which sustains the character's ability to act, and thus to mean. The pessimistic tragedy holds out no such illusion. We are informed early that later developments will be seen precisely for what they are: false alarms. This is the way *Strange Interlude* adds up its twenty-three years. *Ethan Frome* covers twenty years. Mattie, the long-ago hope, must be wheeled in in that final scene, to ask, "Ain't you ever goin' to die, Ethan Frome?" And Ethan says, "The Fromes're tough, I guess. The doctor was sayin' to me only the other day—Frome, he says, 'you'll likely touch a hundred." And that is just the point to be made in an epilogue of hopeless survival.

Or again consider *Death of a Salesman*. Far more pessimistically than optimistically, there is never any avenue of escape or hope which the Lomans are capable of using. There is no fortuitous development, and no characters enter the scene as saviors. The only development in the play to add suspense about the outcome is the illusion about the possibility of Biff and Happy going into the sporting-goods business together, sponsored by the big businessman, Bill Oliver. But the idea of Oliver's starting these two boys in business is only another of Willy's inventions. Willy rarely thinks: he concocts, dreams, imagines. When he does stop to think, it is a pessimism born of continuous defeat:

WILLY: Ben, nothing's working out. I don't know
what to do.

. . . .

I am building something with this firm, Ben,
and if a man is building something he must be
on the right track, mustn't he?

BEN: What are you building? Lay your hand on
it. Where is it?

WILLY: That's true . . . there's nothing.

Although Miller points out that Willy goes to his death happily, doing something he believes will really solve Biff 's problems and thereby those of the whole family, the effect is not one of hope for the audience or the rest of the people in the play. Biff does not change. The crowds in Willy's dream do not come to the funeral. Willy's family does not glorify him for what he has done, or rejoice over the $20,000 he has given them by his death. The cycle will only continue. The irony in Linda's conclusion, "We're free . . . we're free," is the source of the pessimistic reaction or, at the least, the pathetic response. Willy is only "happy" in suicide because he is deluded. The question is: is tragic structure a rehearsal or recall of factors leading to doom, or is it a *discovery* of factors leading to *either* doom or the ideal? The process, through art, should appear to be up to the hero, whereas the pessimistic playwright says it is up to life. And life's pattern and dimensionality are already known—in the metaphor of the Treadmill-as-Form. This is something like the Chekhovian story defended by Herbert Muller, but tragedy is *not* mere attrition.

If classical plot is only sometimes a case of high-to-low fortune, the modern pattern is well represented in O'Neill's *Long Day's Journey*: there is never a question of high fortune past or present, but rather low-to-low, or lower. This is a good instance of the antiperipety problem.

The impression of the play's past-to-present continuum makes this quite clear. Tyrone's miserliness is partly to blame for his wife's dope addiction and Edmund's advanced illness. Tyrone's preference for cut-rate medical care led to an irresponsible use of morphine during Mary's childbirth with Edmund, and permitted "quack" Doctor Hardy to make an improper and belated diagnosis of Edmund's disease. Then Tyrone's family can be a disappointment to him in its weakwilled retreat from life. What else can we expect from the conception? The story centers on the last stage of conflict over the Tyrones' mutual feelings of guilt in their mutual destruction. This means they voice their final expression of dread over what the past has done to them and confirm the fact that curses of this past cannot be lived down. The result, for the tragic theatre, is static homage to gloom. The characterization clearly portrays stupor, of people past hope. The action they create is then a series of jerks and false starts, skipping from one pseudo-clash to another without actually moving any development forward. For example, Tyrone and his sons can watch Mary in disgust as they see her sink deeper into addiction. Jamie discloses his animosity to the family: he resents Tyrone's ambition for him as an actor and hates Edmund as a sibling rival. Mary rails against Tyrone's failure to make a decent home for the family, especially in an emotional sense. But there is nothing to really learn or to await that is not determined from the first. The affected moments of peace when one Tyrone feigns ignorance or innocence of another's vice are at best idle contrasts for the tirades which follow. We are well aware that the characters know too much about each other, so there can be no charity over weakness. We are not surprised when they revert to scourging one another with characteristic O'Neill verbosity. Their anguish has no curative purpose and it is a conflict which resolves and impels nothing except a degree of sustained complaint which becomes a vehicle for virtuoso performance. The story line, and the characters, however, remain essentially inert because O'Neill refuses to see man as any finer than his recollection of these particular specimens. Will Mary go back to taking drugs after a temporary cure, and will Edmund's illness be fatal? Even these questions are answered by mood and attitude early in the play, and have little to do with the meaning of the story or the value of character. The effect is similar to that of *Beyond the Horizon* and many another "illusory-identity" or "inheritance" play—its bulk affirms the image of the sentence of waiting through an enduring hell on earth where the only blessing is death.

The antireversal approach of pessimism does not answer to the paradox of essential tragedy, of that "fortunate fall" wherein a destruction posits more good than evil. The unvaried slipping toward the indefinite end in the modern pessimistic tragedy is like that experienced by Eliot's intellectuals in *The Hollow Men*: "This is the way the world ends/ this is the way the world ends/ this is the way the world ends/ Not with a bang but a whimper." Hebbel put the lesson in a motto: content presents the task, form the solution in the drama.

5. MEN BORN to SORROW

How does "fear" weaken tragic character? I'll begin an answer with a happier example. In a recent and heavy dose of playgoing, digesting about forty London and provincial productions over a short time, a curious comparative impression occurred to me. In an especially comprehensive sampling of distinguished modern "tragedies," avant-garde sensations, and new plays of very serious comment—following upon a similar experience of New York's best—it was a shock to realize that the most tangible moment of audience inspiration had come in, of all things, an Abbey Theatre revival of Dion Boucicault's old warhorse of a melodrama, *The Shaughraun*. Such feelings defy reasoned substantiation, yet one knows them when they come and knows they are there.

And I am talking about the reaction of a sophisticated audience of "repeaters" represented at most of the productions of a given season. I do not mean that *The Shaughraun* simply provided the most measurable audience enjoyment, since, naturally, the melodrama is the most immediate crowd-pleaser and its technique openly forces the audience to cheer the hero and boo the villain. There *was* literal movement to the edge of the seats, but not only because of the thrills and surprises of the plot line. The audience was intellectually and emotionally involved with the characters, polarizing on hero and villain in a more substantial and charged way than we would admit—not unlike the excitement-through-character generated by the good production of *Hamlet*. Identification occurred because the characters were attempting to do something we could not attempt ourselves and, despite all the comic hokum, the melodrama was flirting with a serious illusion which seduced us into caring about the characters' success in battle, love, and intrigue to the point where it was *an inspiration to our spirit*. In this way the audience was "inspired." The central reaction was joy, moving to the edge of the seats to get closer to *people*—and two-dimensional people at that.[1] The gratitude felt in this all-but-forgotten experience after many a season of human coldness was almost physically tangible. The traditional tragedy is not unlike the classic melodrama in this optimistic regard, in that it invites a certain awe derived from the exceptionality of the characters' audacity, charm, representativeness, and importance to the given problem.

What people inhabit the modern tragedies? They seem to have been born according to strict rules of pessimistic belief. As we have heard in hundreds of books and articles, they must be limited, antiheroic, unsuccessful, and low-ranked. All pessimistic protagonists are losers. This is a problem for tragedy because such men's natures drastically cut down identification due to their highly specialized relation to life. We are not drawn to their power or spirit or potential because, by definition, they are not expected to be powerful or successful. Some more specific problems in this legacy: Where can we direct envy? We take little vicarious pleasure from following the adventure and the sense of their careers because they believe life to be purposeless and meaningless, assuming they cannot be fulfilled in the first place. They lack appetite for life. Because their rank and stature are admonitorially low, they do not "matter" to society at large. The three-dimensional characterization is too often avoided by the pessimistic playwright because the dark side and a dark-seeing nature must be emphasized. A whole man would upset the apple cart in at least occasionally seeing the balanced view of trauma or di-

---

1. For more on this, it is interesting to compare Eric Bentley's case for dramatic *types*—to which I refer in the third section of this chapter.

lemma. The pessimist's men are pathos-, not ethos-, oriented. Their natures and their records may even stand as our guilt.

THE MAKING OF THE MODERN HERO

Little-known theorist Eric Voegelin had the interesting idea that tragedy's decline began as early as Sophocles and Euripides, chiefly because their heroes were made too specific, shown too collapsed under fate, or because they submerged their worlds in the demonic, the hero becoming "incomprehensible" in a "sea of disorder."[2] At the very least, we can say to that that there are ameliorating qualities in Sophocles and Euripides which reestablish communication with tragedy's audience above the level of the necessary derangement and disorder. The speculation can be very appropriately applied, however, to the heroes of the modern tragedy. Their chief problem as heroes is the necessity of their a priori confusion—also a major influence on the question of enlightenment. And of course the contemporary playwright rejects the conception of making a hero in the first place. In Rice's *The Adding Machine*, representative pathetic man is Mr. Zero. When, after his sentencing, Zero is to be reincarnated, Charles, the police authority, at first tells him (Origin-of-Species-like) that he will go back to being a monkey. His own "retreading" describes the making of all modern little men:

> You'll be a baby again—a bald, red-faced little animal, and then you'll go through it all again. There'll be millions of others like you—all with their mouths open, squalling for food. And then when you get a little older you'll begin to learn things— and you'll learn all the wrong things and learn them all in the wrong way. You'll eat the wrong food and wear the wrong clothes and you'll live in swarming dens where there's no light and no air. You'll learn to be a liar and a bully and a braggart and a coward and a sneak. You'll learn to fear the sunlight and to hate beauty. By that time you'll be ready for school. There they'll tell you the truth about a great many things that you don't give a damn about and they'll tell you lies about all the

2. See Anselm Atkins, "Eric Voegelin and the Decline of Tragedy," *Drama Survey* (Winter 1966–67): 280–85.

> things you ought to know—and about all the things you want
> to know they'll tell you nothing at all. When you get through
> you'll be ready for your life-work. You'll be ready to take a job.

(On an adding machine, of course. And the officer's style of speech gives him away as the too-obvious spokesman for Rice, even allowing for expressionism's normal avoidance of three-dimensionality.) Charles continues:

> You're a failure, Zero, a failure. A waste product. . . . True, you
> move and eat and digest and excrete and reproduce. But any
> microscopic organism can do as much.

And so on. So Zero asks not to be sent back to earth. Charles sends a girl with him to help him forget what it's going to be like. Her name is Hope. Of course she's just a trick, she doesn't exist. Zero goes off like a fool looking for her.

True, Zero is a particularly simplistic device for a message play. Some of our playwrights have created great characters and great roles—in Blanche, Willy, and a few others—but almost never a portrait suitable to tragedy's heroism (I'll try to do something with this imprecise term shortly), where there should be change via learning and growth. About the only character conceived on heroic lines, John Proctor in *The Crucible*, lacks the greater depth of development we get in an unheroic Willy and others like him.

So we wish that our contemporary protagonists were more heroic and that everything that happened to them was more universally important and related to the great extremes of fortune and misfortune experienced nearer the dawn of man's religious consciousness. Yet our fact-facing and a democratic hesitation to create a "hero" class are in opposition to this more ideal tragic sense. As Krutch concludes: "If the plays and novels of today deal with littler people and less mighty emotions it is not because we have become interested in commonplace souls but because we have come, willy-nilly, to see the soul of man as commonplace and its emotions as mean."[3] Soul evolves when mind evolves. The hero ought to think, just as the playwright ought to be philosophical.

The modern hero *must* be a loser. He is selected from out of a series of

3. Krutch, "The Tragic Fallacy," in *European Theories of the Drama*, ed. Barrett Clark, p. 519.

traumas and unusually one-sided situations which have completely in-
doctrinated him in the methods of assuming the worst. O'Neill's sympathetic characters—"protagonist" is not technically appropriate—are
out of joint with the world far longer than the traditional tragic character,
and dissonance is for them the rule rather than the exception. This exceptional dissonance is what makes them obedient to the playwright's
outlook. But, for the dramatic needs of tragedy alone, their disorientation,
in being so natural a part of their self-images (think of the people of *The
Iceman Cometh*), precludes the sudden dramatic revelation of an obstacle
that dictates the structure of tragic developments. Others are given the
"touch of the poet"—in *Beyond the Horizon, Long Day's Journey, Dynamo, Desire Under the Elms, The Great God Brown,* and *A Touch of
the Poet* itself. The touch is calculatedly inapt in a world which always
turned out to be spoiled by godless fate, a world unable to assimilate such
dreamers unless it be by allowing them to ship off to some actual or illusory sea, where they will not be able to put down roots long enough to
upset anyone's practical, and therefore insensitive, equilibrium. The new
hero is not a decision-maker or proclaimer or prime mover. One feels he
resents the focus turned on him. In O'Neill he seeks the anonymity of a
vast "sea" or "jungle" or "dynamo," but is not even equipped to achieve
that.

Alan Squier in *The Petrified Forest* knows that the intellectual cannot
be the modern hero, for the intellectuals have failed their world. Still,
Squier the talky thinker is very definitely Sherwood's "hero." As Squier
analyzes it:

> ALAN: You see—the trouble with me is, I belong to a
>   vanishing race. I'm one of the intellectuals.
> GABBY: That means you've got brains. I can see you have.
> ALAN: Yes—brains without purpose. Noise without sound.
>   Shape without substance.

And he explains his failure in such a way as to make pessimistic complaint
that the thinking man was not allowed to survive:

> ALAN: It's nature hitting back. She's fighting back with
>   strange instruments called neuroses. She's deliberately
>   inflicting mankind with the jitters. Nature is proving

> that she can't be beaten—not by the likes of us. She's
> taking the world away from the intellectuals and
> giving it back to the apes.

In *Machinal*, the "heroine" is weak because the world is mechanistic
and the libido vulnerable. Much of her tragic problem is her terror at
having a baby because she didn't love her hubsand—in turn caused by
her frigidity and his mindlessness. In this stream-of-consciousness reaction we are to find her dramatic action: release. But so what?

> I was climing the golden stairs. . . . I met my baby coming
> down. . . . All the dead going up to Heaven to rest. . . . All the
> babies coming down to earth to be born. Dead going up . . .
> babies coming down. I can't go on. . . . Oh, let me alone . . . let
> me alone.

In *Abraham's Bosom*, the "hero" has a chip on his shoulder and a
sweeping generalization to lead him to his particular destruction. Voices
from the white world tell Abe that the only way for him to have peace is
death:

> God damn 'em to hell! Dey don't give me no chance. Dey
> stop every crack, nail up every do' and shet me in. Dey stomp
> on me, squash me, mash me in de ground lak a worm. Dey
> ain't no place for me. I lost, ain't no home, no 'biding place. . . .

The modern pessimistic hero is totally convinced that he is totally overpowered. The only variation in this heroic ingredient is the "peg" the
playwright finds on which to hang the defeat.

We are told it is healthy to relate to a realistic picture of man and his
limitedness, so we cannot expect heroes to be made in the old way. But,
even given the "usefulness" of the "honest" picture of man, how often is
this kind of characterization plausible, consistent, and motivated—when
pessimism is forcing twists of character to come to the surface while other
potentials are kept submerged? The king-figure can thus be more be-
lievable to me than the pessimistic hero. *Both* the spectator and the character must accept the importance of their self-interest and self-valuing.
We should accept the fact that man naturally speculates about the hero
and heroism, and that *this* is good for man too. Images of greatness and

a kind of exceptionality keep less heroic man operating and thus, bit by tiny bit, growing. Insisting that all men are Zeroes is false, but, more importantly, it is a position which cannot improve the lot of the true Zeroes of reality. This hints at the hero's *job*: to practice virtue and ambitious adventure. Remember that in the value of heroic leadership, Freud's "father" concept is indispensable, showing authority as exemplar. Or, as Sidney Hook[4] describes him, the hero is an event-making man who acts on Ifs, the man who can break through the confining web of contingent history to destroy old relativities and define the new limits of the possible. In *The Stature of Man* Colin Wilson argues against the "fallacy of insignificance" which appears to be the accepted antiheroic nature of modern man, both in art and reality. Wilson sees the hero as the man who has directed courage plus qualities most needed by his age. He does not want merely to fit in but wishes to expand his freedom.[5] Similarly, at the end of tragedy, the real hero's spirit seems greater than the physical strength and struggle which couldn't quite head off his destruction. Thus we are pleased at what he has done on our behalf. Technically and superficially, the hero is lost—as the pessimist's hero is automatically lost—but his assets of character allow us to know better. We treasure his memory and thus he lives on. He stood for something.

IDENTIFICATION

The very soul of tragedy is that it enables the beholder to experience vicariously the quest for personal and moral transcendence of commonness. It allows the ordinary mortal to identify with the tragic hero in the latter's tantalizingly near brush with Godlike dimensions, greatness, and the abstraction of immortality. Through an expanded concept of "character" which appears "noble" the spectator is presented with a simultaneous moral challenge and an ego-directed pleasure.

Certainly the identification is never total. Aesthetic distance exists to allow pleasure, for total identification would become pathological delusion. But the primitive principle is there psychologically and artistically: identify with strength. What we become, says Eric Bentley in *The Life of*

4. In *The Hero in History* (New York, 1943). See chap. 11, sec. 3.
5. In *The Stature of Man* (New York, 1959), p. 73.

the Drama, depends on "the people we model ourselves on."[6] There must be a certain amount of familiarity, but the traditional hero is also atypical of man. Identification occurs in part *because* of this appealing falsehood. The hero is entertainment, power, pride: he is creative, he generates things, he exudes possibility and potential—even as the physicists would define the word. We do not identify because we find him to be the character who is "just like me" but through his being better and stronger and more clever than we are at the same time he is not too unlike us. This has to be a position for an optimist.

The notion of his exceptionality therefore must be kept in balance, and it is a balance based on some very practical processes of art. I am speaking of the familiar generalization that the successful tragic hero is a true individual. Bentley brings us usefully down to earth on this matter by defending the *type* in good or high drama as against the upholding of the character as fully unique. He states that "first and foremost he is a force in the story." He *does*, he does not merely *exist*. (Notice how sorely we miss the old-time villain to make things hum.) Cognition is not the whole story, however. In reacting to archetype rather than individual, re-cognition is important because it can tell one something one knows and then make one realize. Bentley goes on to explain that the extreme individual is too likely to be exceptional—not on some heroic-moral-ethical ground, but in his psychological rationalization and analysis. Certainly this is true of the pessimistic tragedy of this century; the pessimist sides with his victim-protagonist through the too-total defense of his brokenness, along with its explanation. Further, Bentley notes that "character was never fate *all on its own*,"[7] that it is not wholly inside men, but also "in the air." In other words, character is largely an idea, an artistic construction. "We identify ourselves with a Shakespeare character less in the sense of 'I am this man, I have these traits of character' than in the sense of 'becoming this man, I know what it is to be alive.' "[8] It *is* a put-up job, hoping to move closer to an ideal. The playwright creates existences through characterization, so that they may act. This is also in line with the principle that the great character has a mystery about him, whereas pessimism too often overexplains. In fact, this is a consistent

6. Eric Bentley, *The Life of the Drama* (New York, 1967), p. 160.
7. Ibid., p. 57.
8. Ibid., p. 61.

difference between modern and traditional-successful tragedy. The old hero is not completely defined, and some room is left for us to understand him according to our own experience and comprehension. The modern pessimistic hero is inside a closed circle of wounded features.

Where to find the modern character with whom we identify? Tennessee Williams, for one, talks of the importance of understanding and loving other people rather than hating and fearing those "on the same little world that we live in." He asks: "Why don't we meet these people and get to know them as I try to meet and know people in my plays?" Well, there is a gap between Williams's belief and practice on this point. More eloquently than in the propaganda machines he abhors, most of his plays certainly do persuade us to "fear the other people on the same little world that we live in." And, although Williams does try to meet and know people in his plays, he hardly gives us a broad cross-section of humanity to befriend. The question concerns whom we are getting to know. Because of his vision, there are not many different kinds of people in Williams's world, and they are, moreover, highly specialized and even allegorical characters. The friendliness, hospitality, and gentility he envisions are things of the old, dying, southern tradition. The people of this tradition, by Williams's evidence, are destroyed and demented by the act of clinging to it. The plays themselves, particularly *Streetcar*, are testaments to the danger of maintaining the old friendship in a world which will not tolerate it. In what features do his characters represent our tragic ambitions? Perhaps in striving for allegorical natures, some of the combinations of traits, habits, and goals leave us well behind. Look at the major characters and their actions in *Orpheus Descending*. The pure-sexed, snakeskin-jacketed, guitar-fondling Val Xavier falls in love with a middle-aged Italian store proprietress whose father was cremated in his orchard by racist vigilantes. The two secondary characters, also oppressed by the bigotry- and prejudice-ridden southern surroundings, further exemplify the playwright's affinity for unique psychological cases and weird human types. One is a self-scourging nymphomaniac who derives pleasure from making love near the gates of Cypress Hill cemetery and the other is a sheriff's wife who, aided by visions, paints religious pictures which are actually Rorshachian expressions of her own sexual and religious obsessions. Bizarre as they are, these are the only "good" characters in the play, and they are the ones we must watch as they endure their trials. Their selection for such focus is a function of pessimism.

O'Neill finds his characters' tragic nature in their *lack* of character. What they actually do does not have a direct bearing on the vague depression that is their play's conclusion nearly as much as what they accept or do not do. In any case it is not a decision, and not based on character but on a peculiarity. Their original obstacles may have been no fault of their own, but each is not impossible to overcome (*a la* comedy) and passive acceptance we must equate with the inherently weak nature of each character. In *Long Day's Journey*, Tyrone sold himself for money and popular success, doing a mediocre play year after year that left him wealthy but artistically ruined. Jamie failed as an actor and as a human being because his will was exhausted just in negating what his father represented. Mary's drug addition originated beyond her own control, but her feeling for life made her allow it to consume her spirit. Edmund, cursed by his physical weakness, has rejected life in favor of constant retreat. His father is a symbol of the crassness he sees in the world, and he has become socialistic and anarchistic in addition to flouting his parents' religion and everything else they represent. Where do we connect with character in all this?

Let us take a longer look at the identification situation in the case of *Winterset*. Mio Romagna's life is dedicated to avenging his father's unjust execution. As a result, his drives are never geared to achieving personal fulfillment, and his life as Mio, the individual, has no meaning except as an extension of his father's life. He is his father's vengeance-minded ghost more than a human being in his own right. He is not his own man. Mio comes on the scene not grandly but with a history of resignation at his back. To his friend Carr, he says blankly: "This river bank's loaded with typhus rats, too. Might as well die one death as another." Then Carr asks, "Last time I saw you you couldn't think of anything you wanted to do except curse God and pass out. Still feeling low?" Mio replies that he is not feeling much different. Indeed, it is hard to imagine this young man with the outlook of a bitter old man ever feeling "different":

> Talk about the lost generation, I'm the only one fits that title.
> When the State executes your father, and your mother dies of
> grief, and you know damn well he was innocent, and the
> authorities of your home town politely inform you they'd

consider it a favor if you lived somewhere else—that cuts you off
from the world—with a meat-axe.

Mio is a strange mixture of characteristics (a bit like *Golden Boy's* Joe
Bonaparte.) He has an improbably pedantic and large vocabulary. He is
morose and suicidal almost to the point of melancholic affectation. Always ready with the obscure literary allusion to the blackness he sees
around him, he has somewhere picked up an affinity for, and competence
with, better literature. Such qualities suggest the heavy hand of the playwright, for they do not go together in the same body—that of a righteous
juvenile delinquent—without the result being illogical, strained, and
melodramatic. His literary ability, of course, is forced on him by Anderson
to produce the picture of a modern hero as a tragically displaced person
ironically living a life that is meaner than that of many a hedonist of far
less intellect. Such a hero is forced to find ideals in fiction and poetic
dreams. He can see concepts such as "honor" and "heroism" only in
books.

Mio's alter ego Carr has a pessimism which reflects back on the uni-
dimensionality of the protagonist. Carr theorizes that evidence is just
one of the many things that one can buy in the world:

> In fact, at the moment, I don't think of anything you can't buy,
> including life, honor, virtue, glory, public office, conjugal
> affection, and all kinds of justice, from the traffic court to the
> immortal nine.

It is possible to sympathize with such complaint, but it is not a contribution to character which spurs identification. Even a love theme turns
out to be a strange mutation of character under Anderson's pessimism.

Like O'Neill's characters, Anderson's are never allowed to achieve real
love. As an adaptation of *Romeo and Juliet* (plus *Hamlet* and others, for
all of that), *Winterset* shows Mio (Ro-mio) and Miriamne as "star
cross'd lovers" from the moment they meet. Their affection helps to
provide some raison d'être for the play's "poetry" but there is only weak
motivation for, and evidence of, love. Romeo and Juliet may fall in love
with incredible speed, but at least such love may be motivated as swift
physical attraction. The bitter emotional climate in *Winterset* does not
nourish such possibility and Mio and Miriamne spend most of their time

together explaining why no good can come from their relationship and how each is hopeless and worthless as a possible mate. Mio and the other little people of the play know that modern love is at best a function of "the glands."

Eventually, Mio's crucial indecision becomes an unmotivated denial of character except as the slavish necessity of his pessimism. As Eleanor Flexner observes: "For an act and a half, Anderson is writing a play about a boy whose sole purpose in life is to clear his father's name, if not to avenge him. Suddenly, however, he allows him to abandon the purpose which is the root action of the play, and, violating every principle of character which he has so carefully established in the first part, brings about a catastrophic denouement which he invests with a completely false aura of tragic inevitability."[9] The problem is that such drifting in the wind is caused by the lack of an anchor of being really alive. The characters are easily manipulated because they are not intended to care. Old Esdras, a man beaten by life more than the others simply because he has endured its disappointments longer, says:

> When we're young
> we have faith in what is seen, but when we're old
> we know that what is seen is traced in air
> and built on water. There's no guilt under heaven
> just as there's no heaven, till men believe it—
> no earth, till men have seen it, and have a word
> to say this is the earth.

Anderson's theoretical version of the great goal of mankind is a contradiction of the picture he gives through his own tragic heroes: "The dream of the race is that it may make itself better and wiser than it is, and every great philosopher or artist who has ever appeared among us has turned his face away from what man is toward whatever seems to him most god-like that man may become."[10] The vision which an Anderson play enacts, however, hasn't the slightest room for such speculation. That kind of participation with character is out of the question with the Mios and the McClouds. It is only Anderson who identifies with his martyrs, and that is part of the reason we cannot.

9. Flexner, *American Playwrights, 1918–1938* (New York, 1938), p. 106.
10. Quoted in Selden, *Man in His Theatre*, p. 103.

MODERN RANK AND STATURE

Reality says there are no heroes. Our politics says all men are created equal. Politics and expedient theology say that nobody ought to be far more important, far richer, or far more gifted than anyone else. We reject the superman as we reject Naziism's superrace. Democracy, unionism, socialism, and even Christianity have often made the "common" man the central character of contemporary education, religion, government, and culture. The contemporary hero would be a freak. These are today's realities, but they don't do away with continuing concerns about the size or importance of a protagonist.

Our epoch's classic case of the rank-stature problem as a facet of tragic character is of course *Death of a Salesman*. I will review some of Miller's theory on the tragedy of the common man.[11] Miller requests that we not confuse rank and stature, or pay more attention to a character because he assumes greater social rank. "So long as the hero may be said to have had alternatives of a magnitude to have materially changed the course of his life, it seems to me that in this respect at least, he cannot be debarred from the heroic role." To Miller it doesn't matter if the hero falls from a great or a small height, whether he is highly conscious or only dimly aware of what is going on, as long as there is intensity: "human passions to surpass his given bonds" and "the fanatic insistence upon his self-conceived role" (which defines Hitler and Nero as well as one possible Hamlet). Any play of character, says Miller, must show characters who are somewhat self-deluded or less than fully self-aware. Only in a play of "forces" like *Prometheus* can characters be fully aware. Then he contends that brave death makes his man more human; to Miller, Willy dies in joy. "In terms of his character, he has achieved a very powerful piece of knowledge," namely, that he is loved by his son and is forgiven. But is mere joy via delusion, in the manner of Robert Mayo, enough? Miller's answer: "It goes without saying that in a society where there is basic disagreement as to the right way to live, there can hardly be agreement as to the right way to die, and both life and death must be heavily weighted with meaningless futility." This logic is hard to follow. More-

---

11. Miller's comments on this subject have been published in a variety of sources. Some of the elaborations, which I paraphrase, are most conveniently found in his introduction to his *Collected Plays* (New York, 1957).

over, why accept this common-denominator approach? Aren't there men of stature who *know* something about best values of death—or life? Miller seems to dislike the stature concept as much as rank: "Our society—and I am speaking of every industrialized society in the world—is so complex, each person being so specialized an integer, that the moment any individual is dramatically characterized and set forth as a hero, our common sense reduces him to the size of a complainer, a misfit."[12] But nonhero Willy is also a complainer and misfit. The audience still must decide whether or not it cares about a "little man."

In the Brooklyn democracy of *Death of a Salesman*, the man of high stature is not only absent from the stage, he is not to be admired when he does exert his indirect force. It is the shadowy presence of the successful and rich man that incites Willy Loman to foolish quests for a false social stature. This call to Babbittry in the jungle of capitalism (and the seeming disgust with capitalism) is what allowed occasional Marxist interpretations of the play. It appears that the rich and powerful—the Bill Olivers and even the Brother Bens of the world—have avarice to thank for their stature. Their veneer of glamor and power serves as a false paragon to the millions of little men in the world. It has the same pernicious effect that the false ideal of movie stardom has upon the young and impressionable. The key in either case is immaturity. It takes maturity to recognize the fact that the ideal "big man"—as the little man wants to see him—does not really exist. In *Death of a Salesman*, except for the medium-successful Charley, the only such idol allowed on the stage is, significantly, an apparition.

In business, according to Willy's failure to charm his way to the top, the big man survives because he is the fittest, and his fitness is in his ruthless aggression. The little man is incapable of ruthlessness, because he is too sensitive. (Being "down" so long "sensitizes" him?) His bruised nature is what is needed to move the audience, and Willy's weakness has the same air about it as George Barnwell's whining impotence in *The London Merchant*, the latter having been so unmanly as to let a woman coax him into crime. Willy's Linda seems another vestige of the sentimental tragedy. She is like the long-suffering and incredibly patient women of the lachrymose eighteenth-century dramas who brought tears to

12. Quoted in *The Misfits*, review, *Saturday Review*, 4 February 1961, p. 26.

the audience's eyes with their ability to forgive in the face of their husbands' infidelity.

I think we still look in vain for the equation between Willy's common rank *or* stature and tragic heroism. Miller's big intent, of course, is that the society in the theatre will pay Willy some attention because society in the play has abandoned him. Because capitalism ran him into the ground? Or because he represents the universal misery of the Little Man? Linda's famous "attention" speech only reflects the new heroic values Miller would like to develop, or those of a society unable to conceive of a big and noble man. Since the playwright makes no suggestions about man aspiring to spiritual worths, Willy's worth will have to be equated with having his name in the paper and making a lot of money—the indexes which Linda uses. Not having achieved these things, he is less than great. But Linda does not define his worth. She says, "such a person." This phrase only refers back to "human being" and she does not add anything to show why he, more than any other human being, should receive the attention. Literally, this means that no matter what a human being does, he is worthy of the attention Miller hopes we give Willy.

Linda also concludes that "a small man can be just as exhausted as a great man." But the significant point is determining what exhausts him. In sentimental social drama, a "hero" may be exhausted by simply staying out of trouble or existing. Any human being can be exhausted on the greatest variety of quests from the ridiculous to the sublime. He may also make a quest that is for himself only. The tragic hero's goal is an affirmative one and affects far more people than himself. What he does is something not everyone works for every day. Willy's industry, on the other hand, is not tragic exhaustion because he works for his family, his company, and his creditors with certainly no greater results than thousands of breadwinners like him. His benefactors include a "philandering bum," an understandably ungrateful vagrant, and a wife who, however sweetly and patiently, only does the wash "as of old." The too-long held pessimistic attitude results in this notion of Miller's that heroic stature consists in simply managing to exist without becoming a criminal or complete savage.

The pessimist apparently doesn't believe in greatness in any measure. Miller's defense of the tragedy of the common man in no way proves that we don't still want to get involved with heroes of significant strength—

and stature. Concluding his criticisms of our writers' "insignificance neurosis," Colin Wilson ends on an even more urgent note: "The responsibility of literature in the twentieth century becomes appallingly clear: to illuminate man's freedom."[13]

13. *The Stature of Man*, p. 171.

6. EFFORT and ENERVATION

OVERVIEW

In the last century, one of the more important theories of the drama was Ferdinand Brunetiere's law of conflict—that drama must be a struggle of opposing wills. This has since been qualified by theories pointing out the acceptably dramatic character of plays that are not obvious displays of conflict but expressions of the internalized struggle of mental states. Any respected traditional tragedy, however, does not really refute Brunetiere; there is struggle in it, and the protagonist is expending vast effort to overcome an obstacle. Prometheus may be chained, but his efforts seem more physical and overt than those of many a modern running around in existential "freedom." In the modern pseudotragedy, effort is even seen as inappropriate and mindless and, in the few times it occurs, it can be regarded as the inability to see that it cannot get the character anywhere. Eventually, an atmosphere of enervation must take over. In the visions of the playwright as Sacrifical Priest, as the Accursed One, or as Icarus—and often enough elsewhere—living has drained man of energy, power, and will.

What does this do to the sustained and aware effort that is basic to tragedy? First, in such pessimistic tragedy, the actual or subconscious death-wish predominates, making dramatic struggle and our empathic identification with a fight very rare. (I will answer the question, why must there be struggle? in the course of the chapter.) Second, the pessimistic character, if he acts at all, is concerned with localized self-gratification (anaesthesia) as in recompensing himself for having to exist in the first place. That effort being private or illusory, it is difficult for us to share the process. Finally, much less a will-to-power, the pessimist has no power to will. Characters lack spirit, enthusiasm, or real passion. Their view or experience of the world, according to the playwright, has taught them the mood of accidie or ennui. Too often, the tragedies of our epoch seem more capable of spending energy in competing for further ways of saying "it's no use."

STRUGGLE AND SURRENDER

The death-wish is alarmingly popular in our tragedy, and not simply as a last resort after all other reactions to problems have been tested. It is only the end of Act One when Alan Squier supposes that the stars know "that carnage is imminent, and that I'm due to be among the fallen. . . . It's a fascinating thought." This is a particularly likely imperative for the tragedy of Martyrdom, Imprisonment, or Inheritance. Within other visions—where there may be some slight will to live—the intent is tied to narrow and rather private purposes, usually no more than a depressing plan for acceptance, and an endurance of suffering. From Zola to Dreiser to Miller and Williams, increasing analytical focus on man and the postulates of his condition have tended to picture struggle as a waste of time and effort.

The very nature of pessimism—positing hopelessness—asserts that struggle is pointless because life is a known downgrade, with no transportation available for going up. No other attitudinal position so rules out exceptional action. Skepticism means that things are bad enough to doubt, but that the doubt itself can improve conditions by evoking action, correction, and reform. The darkest of classical tragedy is skeptical in this way and much of it, ultimately, is optimistic.[1] The Chorus in *Antigone* can say to Creon:

1. See the later section in this chapter on "Un-Will and False Fate."

> Pray not again. No mortal can escape
> the doom prepared for him.

But at the end of the play the Chorus can also take a constructive view of the tragedy:

> Our happiness depends
> on wisdom all the way.
> The gods must have their due.
> Great words by men of pride
> bring greater blows upon them,
> So wisdom comes to the old.

It may be said such wisdom is cynical: keep your mouth shut to reduce the god-administered beating. That objection has more relevance to the question of free will which I reserve for a later section of this chapter, but let me say now that even scenes of despair are seen for what they are, as running counter to affirmation, struggle, and *life*. This is well understood in the Messenger's speech:

> Yes, when a man has lost all happiness,
> he's not alive. Call him a breathing corpse.
> Be very rich at home. Live as a king.
> But once your joy has gone, though these are left
> they are smoke's shadow to lost happiness.[2]

That is, happiness and an alive life are still conceivable images somewhere in that atmosphere.

True tragedy is dramatic in its picture of a desperate attempt to avoid catastrophe. Poetically, the unhappy end is of course assured, but the hero does not assume this at the start of the proceedings and instead fights until it is too late. The authentic tragic figure hates and fears suffering and death; this "fear" is not noxious to us, because it is fear of an extreme moment and not the undefined fear as a constant of life. Consequently, when the tragic destruction comes, we know it is the worst thing in the hero's life and thereby feel the sense of the *meaningful loss*. Contemporary vision, on the other hand, often expects and welcomes an

---

2. All quotations from *The Complete Greek Tragedies*, ed. David Grene and Richmond Lattimore (New York, 1954).

end to the troubles of existence; instead of tragic struggle, therefore, we see the act of waiting for the end. Plays such as *Key Largo, The Wingless Victory, Winterset, The Petrified Forest,* and *Long Day's Journey* completely substitute the death-wish for the tragic ideal. The typical rationale here would be that modern thinking man, as in existentialism, is horribly awake; that is why he sees meaninglessness and embraces surrender. Whitehead has the best challenge to this thinking: "Each tragedy is the disclosure of an ideal—what might have been and was not: what can be. The tragedy was not in vain. The survival power in motive force, by reason of appeal, to reserves of beauty, marks the difference between the tragic evil and the gross evil. The inner feeling belonging to this grasp of the service of tragedy is Peace—the purification of the emotions."[3]

The tragic motive to resist, then, must be broad rather than selfish, determined rather than abandoned. And the means of resistance must be heroic and admirable, for they are part of the ritual of excitement, too. The essential question here is whether death or destruction can be considered tragic when the victim, from the start, welcomes death as an escape from the total evil of life.

Even the pessimistic Schopenhauer, who believed resignation had a sanctifying effect and that one appropriate way to live was to cease willing (as in suicide), writes that tragedy can be an artistic relief to the assertion of the will in real life. Tragedy shows the will fighting itself: "[Tragedy] is the strife of will with itself, which here, completely unfolded at the highest grade of its objectivity, comes into fearful prominence. . . . It is one and the same will that lives and appears in [all men]."[4] Schopenhauer goes on to find the surrendering of life too important and even joyful, but even he acknowledges the fact that resignation in tragedy only follows significant struggle and assertion of will. His pessimism is in his seeing man dominated by will as his punishment—for the will, according to Schopenhauer, is irrational, aimless, and a constant threat to such peace as Whitehead has mentioned.

Nietzsche's tragic man has a will to live, while Schopenhauer's is tragic because he has a will; but in both cases there is still willful struggle. As Nietzsche said in *The Birth of Tragedy,* interpersonal conflict is either

3. Alfred North Whitehead, *Adventures of Ideas* (New York, 1933), p. xx.
4. Arthur Schopenhauer, *The World as Will and Idea,* trans. R. B. Haldane and J. Kemp (Garden City, N.Y., 1961), pp. 264–65.

Apollonian or Dionysian. In the Bacchic Dionysian form, the individual soul appears and is purified of the guilt of being an individual. The individual knows he asserts his will at the expense of someone else (as in Schopenhauer) and thus destroys the harmony of nature by being an individual. The Apollonian form is too carefully sculptured to permit the drunken will-assertion of the Dionysian and is therefore less tragic. In these two great classic illustrations, even the chief pessimistic and nihilist philosophers recognize the drama of struggle in tragedy, although the philosophical implications depart from the tragic ideal. The bulk of modern tragedy falls well short of this.

Street Scene's Sam Kaplan doesn't see any alternative to surrender. He is painfully conscious of his surroundings: "Oh, God, why do we go on living in this sewer?" His pessimism is total and he asks Rose why she does not join him in a suicide pact as the only means of escape. Earlier, Rose is only slightly touched by Sam's need for her—pathetic as it is— and, learning a lesson from her family's destruction, she considers the imprisoning factors of marriage:

> We'd be tied down then, for life, just like all the
> other people around here. They all start out loving
> each other and thinking that everything is going to be
> fine—and before you know it, they find out they haven't
> got anything and they wish they could do it all over
> again—only it's too late.

Sam's despair eats at every breast on that street. The pain of life there is symbolized from somewhere in the tenement by the cries of a woman in labor. Sam equates this with the cycle of life beginning and ending in certain pain, the time between being a living hell of suffering and meaninglessness.

Similarly, Anderson's Mio and Miriamne cannot be passionate about any passion. They must talk as if their love is doomed even before it has really begun. *Winterset* makes it clear that they probably couldn't enjoy love even if they knew how to express it, or were allowed to live long enough to let it grow. Mio says to Miriamne:

> There's too much black
> whirling inside me—for any girl to know.

> So go on in. You're somebody's angel child
> and they're waiting for you.

The obsession with blackness seems ill-suited to courtship, but that is Anderson's point: why bother? Later, Mio says:

> I've seen some lambs
> that Jesus missed. If they ever want the truth
> tell them that nothing's guaranteed in this climate
> except it gets cold in winter, nor on this earth
> except you die sometime.

Miriamne asks Mio what he believes in, and he replies: "Nothing." As to getting on with his main task, Mio's lack of aggressiveness weakens the attractions of the revenge theme on which the play is based. His actions are simply not much to watch. In one of his rare moments of initiative, he gets Trock's gun and has the frightened gangster in his power. But after another of his too-frequent discourses, he allows Trock to walk out the door; he does not want to remove his potential executioner from the scene. Life is not something to covet. After all, to Mio the earth is just "a ball of mud" and life "purely mechanical, like an electric appliance."

In Anderson's *The Wingless Victory*, Nathaniel—an adventurous sea-captain—returns home from the south seas, bringing with him a dark-skinned exotic wife, Oparre. In the provincial atmosphere of Salem, the interracial marriage stirs tensions, prejudices, and social fears. Against the background of Puritan pride fighting Christian humanity, the wife commits suicide. Nathaniel, after Oparre's own welcoming of death, says:

> I go
> to be with her while I can. What I've left of life
> I shall know what it is to love one dead,
> and seek her and not find. Let the sands of years
> sift quickly and wash long. I shall have no rest
> till my dust lies down with hers.

In *Key Largo*, King McCloud, guilty over deserting his comrades during the Spanish Civil War, goes on a self-abasing tour to see the survivors left by the dead soldiers. Visiting the last bereaved family, he finds the father and sister prisoners of a gangster. He sacrifices himself, taking the gangster with him, to make some retribution for his guilt. McCloud's belief toward the end is that

> the mind, the bright, quick-silver mind,
> has but one purpose, to defend the body
> and ward off death. Because it's the law of earth
> where life was built up from the very first
> on rape and murder—where the female takes what she gets
> and learns to love it, and must learn to love it,
> or the race would die! Show me one thing secure
> among these names of virtues—justice and honor
> and love and friendship—and I'll die for it gladly,
> but where's justice, and where's honor and where's friendship,
> and what's love, under the rose?

He goes on with his document about the fruitlessness of love and all the other "illusions" of meaning to life, but

> there comes a day when there's no sustenance,
> and you jump, and there's nothing you want to buy with money,
> and Christ hangs dead on the cross, as all men die,
> and Lenin legislates a fake paradise,
> and the girl holds out her arms, and she's made of sawdust,
> and there's sawdust in your mouth!

And these are not isolated sentiments. They are Anderson's, for he offers them up often enough in most of his other plays, in nearly the same spiritless "verse." Eventually Alegre does challenge McCloud:

> But if this were true,
> then why would one live—woman or man or beast,
> to grub in the dark?

King answers:

> To eat and sleep and breed
> and creep in the forest.

The rats inherit the earth again. The fact that Alegre goes on to speculate about the possibilities in accepting life's challenge are not supported by what Anderson does with the play. As King dies, he asks:

Is this dying, Alegre?
Then it's more enviable than the Everglades,
to fight where you can win, in a narrow room,
and to win, dying.

And he dies, and another character observes:

You can't be sorry
for a man that planned it, and it all worked out,
and he got what he wanted.

True enough, and this is the note we leave on.

In *Long Day's Journey*, surrender is basic to the "fog" people. The fog is the Tyrones' one blessed illusion, a means of suspended animation that is the closest thing to escape they can achieve. Edmund describes it:

The fog was where I wanted to be. . . .
Nothing was what it is. That's what I wanted—to be alone with myself in another world where truth is untrue and life can hide from itself. . . . It felt damned peaceful to be nothing more than a ghost within a ghost.

It is no accident that Edmund has morbid tastes and prefers philosophers and poets with a distinctly pessimistic bent. To his father, whom at best he can only wryly accept, Edmund says Baudelaire's poem about being always drunken is the best answer to life.

TYRONE: All we can do is try to be resigned—again.
EDMUND: Or be so drunk you can forget.

Tyrone, who favors Shakespeare as the man with the right thought for any occasion, finds all of Edmund's poetry, which Edmund reads or writes himself, to be "filth and despair and pessimism." Acting on his Irish Catholic principles, Tyrone tells Edmund: "When you deny God, you deny hope." But Tyrone's own life is a document in favor of pessimism, and Edmund is able to silence his father by pointing out the latter's poor record as a churchgoing Catholic. Most of all, the Tyrones find scapegoats to release them from having to work at life, not to mention any exceptionally taxing obstacle. And their protestations cannot even be original. Edmund himself admits that he is not equipped for any real struggle (even a verbal one) toward changing matters and fighting fate. He negates, with O'Neill, the whole idea of living *as a man* on the earth:

> And several other times in my life, when I was swimming far out, or lying alone on a beach, I have had the same experience.
> Became the sun, the hot sand, green seaweed anchored to a veil of things as they seem drawn back by an unknown hand. . . .
> It was a great mistake, my being born a man. I would have been much more successful as a sea gull or a fish.

Doris Falk concludes that, in *Long Day's Journey,*

> O'Neill returned to his tragic conception of life as an endless struggle between opposite images of the self. Now, however, the conflict is not only hopeless . . . but worthless. Man is not even endowed with dignity by virtue of his struggle; he is a bare, forked animal, unredeemed by heroism, who spends his life trying to live up to a lie, trying to perpetuate an illusory conception of himself. All values are equal; neither the self nor its conception has any real existence or importance, and all we can ask of each other is pity and forgiveness.[5]

In *Streetcar,* in a somewhat rare example, there *is* struggle and conflict —between Blanche's fragility and Stanley's bestiality. The moth must tempt disaster from the flame. Blanche confuses and upsets Stanley without his understanding why, and *because* he can't understand why. He is bothered by the affectation which is her protection; he feels she is pretending to be better than he is. But the drives which cause this much struggle are psychological ones of which the characters are insufficently conscious. Stanley is helplessly insensitive and Blanche is paranoid, and what little will they have reaches no farther than transitory personal gratification. Stanley is weak as a *tragic* antagonist because he does not know he is evil; he does not know why he is evil in being insensitive. Blanche is psychically too weak for a great tragic struggle. Being destroyed by a helpless animal adds to the pathetic, not the tragic quality, of the situation. The exercise of effort becomes a demonstration of hopelessness.

Martyrdom in Anderson, masochism in O'Neill or Albee's *Who's*

5. Doris V. Falk, *Eugene O'Neill and the Tragic Tension* (New Brunswick, N.J., 1958), p. 194.

Afraid of Virginia Woolf? or permanently certain destruction in Williams: it all synthesizes into *ex nihilo nihil fit*. Nothingness of effort makes for nothing. Of course defeats are a fact of real life, but the surrendering man in art hardly compensates for that reality even if we accept the dubious notion that defeat is universally inevitable. As Erik Erikson has noted, "Ego strength depends, above all, on the sense of having done one's active part in the chain of the inevitable."[6] Or, as Hinduism teaches, man's problems can be a blessing because he alone can aspire to a satisfying *karma*. Angels and other heavenlies cannot act because they are so well off as to be unchallenged. Animals below man know no moral choice and hence live only a sensuous bestial life. The game of life itself makes it worth *being* when one realizes the alternative is a void where there are no problems because there is no existence. How man can morally and spiritually respond to challenge constitutes the truly mature context of effort.

THE NEW AMBITION

The tragic goal and the ambition that drives toward it are essential for involving the spectator in the *form* of the attempt at an answer to life. The goal holds up before us the idea of the future; we do not know what will happen with it, but we are coinvolved in moving toward something. *We want*. As Mandel says, "all tragedy concerns ambition; more fundamentally, all tragedy concerns the will."[7]

What are the ambitions and goals in the modern attempts at tragedy or serious commentary? In *After the Fall*, it is to recognize and not to do. Quentin wants to know if he is cruel, and why he is cruel. In Albee's *Who's Afraid of Virginia Woolf?* and *Tiny Alice*, the characters' dramatic action is to protect themselves from emptiness. In *Long Day's Journey*, if anything, it is to clarify blame. Or Edmund Tyrone simply wants to dissolve into a bank of fog. In *Of Mice and Men*, ambition is to be left alone to enact the tiny dream of safety. *Beyond the Horizon's* Robert Mayo also wants to dream, to go to far-off lands to escape materialistic and unspiritual society. In the myriad "farm" tragedies, the goal of all effort is to find placating "love." In *Winterset*, Mio Romagna

6. Erik Erikson, *Insight and Responsibility* (London, 1964), p. 119.
7. Oscar Mandel, *A Definition of Tragedy*, (New York, 1961), p. 103.

says he wants to avenge his father and he does some detective work to that end, but simultaneously he undercuts the notion of purposive effort:

> But I have no dream. This earth
> came tumbling down from chaos, fire and rock,
> and bred up worms, blind worms that sting each other
> here in the dark. These blind worms of the earth
> took out my father—and killed him, and set a sign
> on me—the heir of the serpent—and he was a man
> such as men might be if the gods were men—
> but they killed him—
> as they'll kill all others like him.

Significantly, this godlike hero is already dead and Anderson cannot tell us anything specifically worthy about him. Yet the memory of the man keeps Mio from living and striving on his own.

Willy Loman struggles with lies and dreams, for his motive is to "belong." And Miller says of Willy's story that "the fateful wound from which the inevitable events spiral is the wound of indignity, and its dominant force is indignation."[8] Yet indignation is not national or societal indignation in Willy's case; it is personal, selfish, and ingrown. The question that arises from the lack of struggle over larger motives in such tragedy is whether man is the potential Titan or merely the subject of titanic meaninglessness.

Like Willy's, other contemporary goals may be no larger than our own purely mortal-physical ones. They may even be smaller. In *Orpheus Descending*, Lady's highest aspirations are for the opening of her confectionery. Val has no plans except to remain detached. When Val underscores Lady's own loneliness, she seeks detachment too. As Val warns her, corruption is widespread:

> I'm telling you, Lady, there's people bought and sold in this
> world like carcasses of hogs in butcher shops!

We would need more evidence than these characters' private visions for us to join behind their ambitions in their dream of escape into mystic transfiguration. Moving to other plays, Blanche in *Streetcar* wants kind-

8. Arthur Miller, *Collected Plays* (New York, 1957), p. 35.

ness and protection. She does not so much want to begin contributing something as to stop being hurt. We agree that there is inhumanity in the environment which has made this woman suffer, but her goal and effort, per se, are no bigger than that of any derelict or invalid or reformed criminal: to rehabilitate, to gain health and peace through love. Our own goals are at least as large. We may sympathize and even identify with ordinary goals, but the notion of human ambition leading to a farther ideal is not exactly stretched in the process. In contrast, the authentic tragic hero must believe he's going to be meaningfully alive for quite a while yet and that there are some bigger horizons left which might be reached.

Current protagonists' goals, then, are very often connected with personal medication or soothing distractions from harsh life rather than large and active issues affecting life, or affecting living conceived as *motion*. Their aspirations could be called unimportant. It may be asked, don't some of them nonetheless aim at ideals? Yes: Blanche, for example. But what ideals are involved are limited and inner-directed ego-ideals which have little or no relevance to us, our society, or men-at-large. They are salves, not quests. Another possible objection: does Othello, for instance, want much more than to settle down to a good happy life with Desdemona? Possibly not. But look how the play moves, even on the basis of that ambition. Eventually Shakespeare has got Othello struggling around that simple little goal in such a way that the play has to start commenting outside of its domestic relevance. Pentheus in Euripides' *The Bacchae*, for all his naïveté, wants to purify his kingdom and rid it of madness. That goal *matters*. In Miller's *The Crucible*, Proctor wants to uphold the truth—not in the manner of Quentin's passive self-analysis in *After the Fall*, but for the sake of all the Salems in the world. And Proctor (and Elizabeth) *acts* on that quest.

In short, ambition and desire needn't be relegated to Schopenhauer's sense that they necessitate someone else's pain. The tragic artist, selecting and crafting his protagonist's ambition, can order at least a temporary net rise for having gone beyond, aiming at a goal which accepts the possibility of pleasure and progress. We might extend the psychological insight of Erikson here that "purpose, then, is the courage to envisage and pursue valued goals uninhibited by the defeat of infantile fantasies, by guilt, and by the foiling fear of punishment."[9] In tragedy, we want to join behind someone who can overcome some of the barriers to goal-seeking which inhibit us—towards goals which represent uncommon experience.

UN-WILL AND FALSE FATE

Fatalism and the irrelevance of ordinary earthlings' will form the basis of much of the best Greek tragedy. Given this, how can I chastise modern pessimism for its mechanistic image of man doomed?

This argument is common and well-founded (up to a point), deflating a more Romanticist criticism which—like mine—seems to value the spectacle of man in his free will running head on into a tragic destiny which is made of the paradox of his character, as noble but sinning. (See chapter 8 for further remarks on this issue.) Mandel, for one, presents the case, noting the critical traps one falls into with generalizations about fate and will, and the differences in implied fatalism. Furthermore, while the modern tragic figure may seem a puppet, he may still exercise free will in being, as Mandel describes it, the puppet of "his own desire." He may feel free because he is not nearly as aware of a deterministic scheme of things as the Greek man. Mandel's conclusions are that "all forms of necessity, including fatalism, are compatible with tragedy"[10] and that "as long as we can mourn for others, whether they be free or not, we shall not find ourselves incapable of writing or understanding tragedy."[11]

Let us consider some examples of the inevitable fate position. Especially in Aeschylus, man is not free to choose: the gods have ruled, and man follows their rule without choice. This may be full predestination. Perhaps Oedipus, too, is a mere pawn of Fate. He doesn't make his play, the prophecy does. Euripides is more psychological and therefore less oriented to god-directed-Fate, but the passions which rule his people (Phaedra, for example) still move them choicelessly to their destiny. At least that is the belief of the theorist who permits fatalism in tragedy. Mandel also cites Othello as robbed of free will by Iago. But here, already, the case is not the same: Phaedra and then Othello are pushed

9. Erikson, *Insight and Responsibility*, p. 122.
10. Mandel, *A Definition of Tragedy*, p. 121.
11. Ibid., p. 137.

to destruction by their special character, and the *author* has exercised free will in conceiving these particular persons as most relevant to the tragedy to be revealed. In Aeschylus, at least, I can see the determinism, through the gods, touching all men on earth; and I will admit for the moment that Orestes, Clytemnaestra, and Oedipus never have a chance. The gods know the prophecies and the timetable and it is up to the tragic figures to follow their predestined routes. Clytemnaestra, we know, cannot escape *The Eumenides* even in the middle of the *Agamemnon*. Even if this is true of earlier Greek tragedy, however, one rarely feels the poet making a pessimistic refusal to grant his audience a tiny hope of a fate which might be colored by some shred of free will. In Shakespeare's case, life is not seen to be full of Iagos at every turn. And all the old characters have purpose and desire which at least poetically exercises the dynamic of some free will. Oedipus does not *know* all doors lead to the same destination.

Today this feeling goes unsalvaged. We are very chained to a fatalism that, with Hobbes and his like, became determinism. The will is thus never free. Facts are made entirely by laws, not by human hopes. So what do we miss? The truly free will is not bound by past conditions, but is open to free and alternative choices and the possibility of self-determination. This is how a tragic hero is able to *act* on our behalf. If we ourselves are burdened with endless tensions in our own willing, one gain of the proxy effort of the protagonist is our witnessing of his freedom, and his testing. The central condition in man which inevitably affects his search for an answer to the life question is his will to power. The effort to merely adjust, accept, or surrender is the denial of this most manlike drive. Tragedy certainly accepts that tension, and the tragic man accepts his terrible and partly existential freedom. The fact that he is born is the first challenge, not the cause of the first complaint of the pessimist: "I didn't ask to be born." In nonpessimistic tragedy, will coexists with the implications of the facticity of man. Modern tragedy, like pessimistic Christian dogma, says our existence is paying the penalty for sin, for falling. Man is freedom, say the Sartrians, but man starts as nothing because his existence precedes his essence. Less existential philosophers know that existence posits ideal. Perhaps the most beautiful concept is Plato's anamnesis, which tells of the primal ideal that existed before man —which man loses in the "shock of birth" but strives to recollect in the efforts of his imagination. The ideal is not realizable without will, because no one can realize it but man himself erring and succeeding and because freedom without wanting (or exercising freedom) becomes a meaningless concept.

All successful tragedy does not conform to the same mold. From Aeschylus to *The Crucible*, tragedies have obviously had variable secondary views, such as in their political themes. But they do hold to the same primary view. Either through poetic suggestion or specific philosophical vision they allow the idea that, while there may be no answer to the problem of life, there is some value or hope in struggling against the narrow part of life which we see toward imagining the whole and the future. The spirit which permits struggle is clearly the more optimistic one, and one which realizes that man exists at once in time (he is in the present, the present defined by where he is) but also in eternity (which is to say the essence of all man). The fact of death is the final root of tragedy for the protagonist, yes, and that is indeed an inevitable Fate. We are left to contend with the continuing problem of evil, and that becomes the root of tragedy for us. This, and the net gain—however tiny—means that effort must continue. The tragic scapegoat has functioned to increase our personal potential value. There is an inevitability about connotations of the future in real tragedy, but also an admission that the future includes possibility. Suffering becomes enjoyment for, as Kaufmann says of real tragedies: "Even the worst misfortunes are compatible with the greatest beauty. Far from being persuaded that life is not worth living and that we should leave the world, we are confirmed in our determination to hold out."[12] Whitehead talking about the relationship among God, value, and moving time seems to me to ease the mystery about an opening in our fate: "The purpose of God is the attainment of value in the temporal world. An active purpose is the adjustment of the present for the sake of adjustment of value in the future, immediately or remotely. Value is inherent in actuality itself. To be an actual entity is to have self-interest. This self-interest is a feeling of self-evaluation; it is an emotional tone. . . . This self-interest is the interest of what one's existence, as in that epochal occasion, comes to. It is the ultimate enjoyment of

12. *Tragedy and Philosophy*, p. 347.

being actual."[13] This also says something to the surrendering and enervated protagonists of modern tragedy. And the core answer to the pessimists on the question of making an effort toward the future is that no
one can *prove* that Fate is closed.

13. *Alfred North Whitehead: An Anthology*, selected by F. S. C. Northrop and
Mason W. Gross (Cambridge, England, 1953), p. 504.

7. *THE LANGUAGE of DEFEAT*

A spectator at a Wagnerian opera may be "inspired" by a particular passage, by how it sounds as sung, even when he understands no German. An ordinarily gifted orator may still have insights so exceptional, and worded so well, that they set off audience enthusiasms never before experienced.

When tragedy is true, its text manages the best effect of both such situations. There is an edifice of words which is not empty, but stimulates emotion and sensation in such a way that it offers the listener a new horizon of experience, perception, and imagination. Tragedy instructs in its fictional promise by above-average excitements—as in the display of will fighting—and this must be just as true of listening to the sound of its ideas and the connotations of its sounds.

Twentieth-century tragedy, however, has set a record for understimulating language. Its pessimism has led to four principal weaknesses in words and sound. First, the necessity for the message of despair results in a repetitious monotony of statements which, by definition, cannot test, examine, or speculate on new limits for man. Second, the predominance of despair necessarily emphasizes a standard and single kind of tone and compositional structure for speech: the tone of fading, downward inflection. The sensual pleasure required of tragic language is therefore harder to come by. Third, since pessimism requires a view of man as weak and unfulfilled, the characters' speech is drab and inarticulate much of the time, the speakers expecting little from the process of communication. Fourth, the lack of any poetic effect in the language used in the pessimistic tragedies greatly reduces the transcendent philosophical implications of their situations and statements, in some cases to the level of melodrama.

THE NEW SOUND OF TRAGEDY

The introverted speeches of most of our would-be tragedies, and the neotragedies of the sixties, muttered or growled by fatalistic protagonists in *Long Day's Journey into Night, Who's Afraid of Virginia Woolf?*[1] *Death of a Salesman, Winterset, After the Fall,* or *Street Scene* —for only a few examples—can sometimes be quite dramatic in the dejected context of the play, but they cannot produce the upward lift of traditional tragic language. Historically, we have expected much of the substance and emotion of a serious play to be carried by language, and content and sensory stimulation in language are vital to tragic pleasure. Yet the vast majority of characters in any representative moment of our century's tragic dramas feel—and therefore sound—like the character in *Winterset,* who says:

> [We] live here among the drains,
> where the water bugs break out like a scrofula
> on what we eat—and if there's lower to go
> we'll go there when you've told your story.

Listing some more specific weaknesses in today's "sound," we have: little enthusiastic speech, whether in anger or joy; low sensual reward in the pure sound of speech; unthrilling word choice and word structure; dialogue put into broken or listless rhythms; and deliberate nonmeaning,

---

1. We must grant, however, that there is an excitement of negativism, the scathing and perfect retort, and the *mal mot* in *Who's Afraid of Virginia Woolf?* It is a curious contribution, but this quality is rather original with Albee. It is even "entertaining" and blackly humorous—and it is language that does the job.

semantic runarounds, catch-as-catch-can symbolism, or simply weak meaning.

Of course one accomplice here is the unprecedentedly militant influence of the antilingual theatre, as in absurdism and certain other avant-garde movements, although it has been an influence only since the 1950s. The fountainhead, however, remains some species of pessimism denying the very premise of language and moving (which is to say dramatic) speech. It is no accident that we must hear droning explications of characters' failures (*After the Fall* and most of O'Neill, for example); their disgust with the curse of being born into life's treadmill of recirculated corruptions (*Orpheus Descending* and most other Williams, plus O'Neill's *Long Day's Journey*) and the cursing of their dirty fortunes (any number of personal greivance plays). The implication, the philosophy, of the following "sounds" remains generally typical of the whole period of attempted tragedy:

> It was a great mistake, my being born a man.
> I would have been much more successful as a sea
> gull or a fish. As it is, I will alway be a
> stranger who never feels at home . . . who must
> always be a little in love with death.

> Ah, it's a dog's life. I only wish during the
> war they'd a took me in the army. I coulda
> been dead by now.

> Funny, y' know? After all the highways, and the
> trains, and the appointments, and the years,
> you end up worth more dead than alive.

You will have noticed that these sentiments (from *Long Day's Journey* and *Death of a Salesman*), and perhaps even their tones, can also be found in *Hamlet, King Lear, Brand, Oedipus,* and other old models—but I think I can show that there is a difference in the dejection. Or one might think the tone depends on the actor—but that also is not a significant defense. The fact is that the modern speech of despair is deliberately or unquestionably self-limiting. There is *no* way to act, or to direct an actor in speaking, this dialogue inspiringly and gloriously—without obviously violating the playwright's intention and the context of the words.

"Inspiring," "glorious," "noble," etc.: the old bugaboos of essays on what tragedy should be—what *law* denies the tragic to the modern sound? I grant that illustrations are not proofs. Practically any modern play is rich in speeches which sound glum and indecipherable—which may only go to show it is a modern play. It is even possible to find unthrilling passages in Shakespeare or Sophocles, if I present the excerpts by themselves. The relevant point is what happens to the *tragic* purpose. The only way out of this is via the end of the limb: to say there is a definite aesthetic for tragic language—and then to validate it.

I propose to begin this with a more technical discussion than in the other chapters involving a closer examination of the attitudinal content of current texts and then of the general aural characteristics of their speeches. Lastly, the notion of an "aesthetic" becomes clearest in considering the "poetic effect" of tragic language.

WHAT IS SAID

There is a significantly new, even unique, difficulty with what is being said in the modern would-be tragedy. In this I include word choice, the simple denotative thought in the words, and the connotative idea stimulated by the words. But how important is such language content to tragic effect?

A preliminary illustration might come out of Hamlet's soliloquy, "O that this too too solid flesh would melt. . . ." Suppose I rewrite that to cover essentially the same "content," but do it in one of the modern idioms:

> Stuff it. I wish I had the guts to kill myself.
> What a drag it is—this living business. Stuff it.
> Garbage is the only thing that grows. Not even dead
> two months and my father's forgotten. She can't
> even wait two lousy months, before she hops in
> with this bum. But Dad was real: he was real to her.

If you know the jargon of a *Viet Rock, La Turista*, or a *MacBird*, or even of general modern slang, my speech states to you all the basic points of the Shakespearean original. Of course it is not aurally as pleasing, but the point for now is that—while the basic facts, ideas, and attitudes are unchanged—the composite content *is* changed somehow by the new word-choice and structure. "Thought" has been affected. Cast in that modern idiom, the attitude of the language connotes a narrower vision, with the speaker's bitterness ingrown to the point where we are sure he cannot differentiate between single incidents of hopelessness and a world-wide potential for at least as much good as bad. That kind of content and that one-sided view are typical of twentieth-century pessimistic tragedies.

Wherever we have gotten really good serious theatre in this century it has been as a result of talented manipulation of characteristics other than language. Exceptions are Miller's *The Crucible*, Albee's *A Delicate Balance*, and no more than two or three other plays. In *The Crucible*, a major reason for finding stimulating tragic content (the styling of the dialect is another matter) in language plus a workable tragic drama is that John Proctor knows himself and the implication of what is happening to him and thus can speak out about his fight against a relevant fate. Miller's other dramas are about his characters' failure to know themselves. Perhaps Quentin's most excited speech in *After the Fall* is the one where he narrates his being appalled when his friend's wife paraded herself half-nude before him; he is saddled, like many of his contemporary protagonists, with the job of narrative recall rather than speech which can grow "right now" through cumulative, felt, experience. *Death of a Salesman* is generally a magnificent achievement but, in speech "thought," Willy Loman is never able to give his audience an articulate speech of what he believes in, what he sees from coping with existence. Much more recently, *A Delicate Balance* is a rarity: a major triumph in the use of stimulating, literate, insightfully poetic speech. But, as I have shown in chapter 2, the play is not intended as a tragedy. Significantly, one of the reasons it has been mistrusted and underrated in several corners is because it does depend about 98 percent on language—against all trends for the *visual* in contemporary art and culture.

What about modern serious drama outside of America? In the few semitragic scripts from abroad—Osborne's *Luther*, Bolt's *A Man for All Seasons*, Whiting's *The Devils* (but not Shaffer's *Royal Hunt of the Sun*, by the way, despite its ritual genoicide with interesting Inca-talk and chanting)—it seems we can only justify a play conscious of rich words and word structure when we write about characters and worlds of long ago.

The historical character, we see, has somehow enough fiction about him for us to accept him as eloquent.

Now go back to the characters *created* in the premodern theatre. They may well be dejected and confused in relation to how things are going for them. For instance, in Aeschylus's *The Libation Bearers*:

> Numberless, the earth breeds
> dangers, and the sober thought of fear.
> The bending sea's arms swarm
> with bitter, savage beasts.[2]

Or, in *King Lear*, the King can say of faithless women:

> Down from the waist they are Centaurs,
> Though women all above.

This leads him to the dim view that

> When we are born, we cry that we are come
> to this great stage of fools

but, after experiencing the revelations that his and Cordelia's tragedies exhibit, he can say in anguish but also in tribute:

> Howl, howl, howl, howl! O, you are men of stones:
> Had I your tongues and eyes, I'd use them so
> That heaven's vault should crack. She's gone
>   for ever!
>
> . . . .
>
> Cordelia, Cordelia! stay a little. Ha!
> What is't thou say'st? Her voice was ever soft,
> Gentle, and low, an excellent thing in woman.

Lear's word choice, in the midst of an agony, betrays an awe, respect— even a love, still—for the challenge and game of trying to express life and the enormity of existence. *The tone is the content*: what a mighty thing is existence, he is saying; I still exist, and think, and *feel*—mightily. Lear and others, while down in the mouth, elsewhere and in other hemispheres of their vision are allowed to reflect some balance, the peripety of for-

2. Quotations from *The Complete Greek Tragedies*, ed. David Grene and ed. and trans. Richmond Lattimore (New York, 1942).

tunes, contrast in attitudes, and a variety of thought-images and colors. Not simply because their playwrights are more talented, but because they are prepessimist. Going further back, the darkest lines of Greek tragedy are virtually always relieved by contrast with some exalted positives, and the final impression is always an upbeat of thought. The last two stanzas of the earlier-quoted speech from *The Libation Bearers*, for example, proclaim agony in terms transcending personal pain and pity:

> The sword edges near the lungs.
> It stabs deep, bittersharp,
> and right drives it. For that which has no right
> lies not yet stamped into the ground, although
> one in sin transgressed Zeus' majesty.
>
> Right's anvil stands staunch on the ground
> and the smith, Destiny, hammers out the sword.
> Delayed in glory, pensive from
> the murk, Vengeance brings home at last
> a child, to wipe out the stain of blood
> shed long ago.

This vision, despite modern translation, has an indestructible essentiality which would always suggest that basic tenet of Greek thought: man can improve.[3] And, to take a final instance from Shakespeare at his least effective, even Timon's curses of his particular society are founded on images of contrast with great natural glories:

> O blessed breeding sun, draw from the earth
> Rotten humidity; below thy sister's orb
> Infect the air!
>
> . . . .
>
> Who dares, who dares,
> In purity of manhood stand upright,
> and say "This man's a flatterer?"

3. I think we must be beyond the point where there's any controversy about this. Some years ago it was widely asserted that the Greeks had not believed in the possibility of progress. The opposing case for positive attitude in the ancients' thinking is thoroughly supported in Ludwig Edelstein's *The Idea of Progress in Classical Antiquity* (Baltimore, Maryland, 1967).

Against this, the modern character is chained to the retaining wall of pessimistic bitterness. He is basically incapable of the vocabulary and style that are part of the reward of perceiving tragedy. And yet it is terrifically important that the sufferer on stage says and expresses something better than we could do it ourselves.

Even the most skeptical stream of invective in the classical character did not go over the line into total and permanent pessimism, to imply the rightness or the inevitability of negating the act of living for all mankind. The most harsh illustrations of the sins of men were written on the assumption that man could affirm something in himself or that his descendants, at least, could make a better adjustment to fate through gaining a clearer understanding of their relative impotence next to nature, the gods, and other eternal antagonists. Old discussions of the seeming senselessness of life, outside of the relieving factor of their verse, are tempered with moments and opportunities for verbalizing a discovery of meaning or just that one outside chance for achievement—because that was what going through the whole agony and ritual was about. In short, the character of old speaks because his creator believes talking will do some good and knows that some praises of life are still worth singing and can still be sought. The modern speaks only to vent despair, but he does not thereby stretch himself in vocabulary or insight and he experiences a cold and centripetal catharsis without the hope in enlightenment. His assumption, moreover, is that nobody much will listen to him anyway and what little is perceived by an equally (we are told) powerless audience will do man no good. Clearly this has to affect the amount of thought and verbal-minded might he needs to put into speaking. To support the "I told you so" irony of this assumption, the playwright in most standard serious drama of the era ends his play just short of the classical moment of *anagnorisis*—the speech of insight and enlightenment. The most we can do now is feel sorry.

Possibly the twentieth-century playwright has been intimidated by the old showman's dictum about long speeches (and poetry) being "death" at the box office. Revealing some lack of confidence in his characters' talk, the representative dramatist has been either painfully true to the naturalistic belief that ours is neither a very articulate race nor a stylistically very literate one or else has interspersed his text with visual tricks, nonverbal symbols, or flashbacks—as if hoping to keep things going by other means than allowing language a full free rein. Kaufmann describes this well as fear of writing "memorable phrases." He observes that our playwrights "are afraid of ridicule and seek security in large numbers of small words. More and more writers serve notice that no words can bear the burden of their offering. Security is sought in the obscurity of symbols, of absurdity, of incoherence. After the retreat from poetry comes the retreat from prose, and finally the retreat into darkness."[4]

In a way, the situation is only logical. The playwrights have chosen characters and situations of smallness which justify pessimism and thus ill equip characters to speak well. In many plays, the characters are not well educated and have seen little of the world. Biological and psychological realities enforce thought and attendant speech which have limited range. In some O'Neill plays and in *The Petrified Forest*, the hero *is* well educated but spends his intellectual and lingual energy on one line of thought, and his philosophy brings him back again and again to the same fixed idea that he must mouth hopelessly. A closed mind can't evoke stimulating dialogue. In general, however, it is a matter of "realism": the modern pessimistic playwright simply cannot envision a character of life's current drama producing speech which contains grandeur of thought and mood. The *base* for this is essentially no different than in the crude Darwinian hell which Dreiser's Isadore confronts in *The Hand of the Potter*:

> But look at me, anyhow! I ain't no good, much.
> I don't amount to nothin'. Here I am of a
> Saturday afternoon when everybody else is off
> sportin' around, and I ain't got no place to go,
> an' no work, an' no money. . . . I'm not right,
> I know that. I ought never 'a' been brought in
> the world. . . . I ought to kill myself, but
> I ain't got the nerve, that's what's the matter.

Fortunately, later playwrights could write a vastly better speech than that, but has there been much progress away from the problem of the single point of view unwilling to grow? Has there been much talk which really says something in response to the essential tragic question? Anderson may seem to have gotten away from the norm when he gave "poetic" and embellished speech to the gangsters and underprivileged people of *Win-*

4. *Tragedy and Philosophy*, p. 414.

terset. But in such a case he certainly exposed himself to the criticism of manipulating his characters beyond belief, the "verse" being hardly good enough to protect him. Tennessee Williams, on the other hand, is the best writer of dialogue in the modern American theatre. But his excellence (those limpidly beautiful, pining, speeches) is devoted to the dark poetry of his atmosphere of despair in this "hell on earth which we have created for ourselves." Albee's *Tiny Alice*, thought by a few to be true tragedy, employs grand-sounding speech (partly in the sense that it is polysyllabic), but there is strong suspicion that Albee himself did not know what his meanings were; the talk is full of Strindbergian clevernesses and gratuitous imponderables.

Am I missing the point amid this campaign for optimism? Is it naïve to expect a playwright who is necessarily writing about the blood, guts, nuclear terror, and psychoses of today to woo, lilt, placate, and narcotize with pleasing words and grand statements? My simplistic dodge here could be: "No, it's not; He *can* do it. Shakespeare and the Greeks managed uplifting language, and they wrote about some pretty horrifying themes too." But I still haven't defined this business of "uplift." I think I can do a better job with that after we have considered the technical aspect of language sound and the issue of dramatic poetry. For now, let us say it is a question of writing *recording* or writing *expression* as against conveying the artist's *knowledge* of the felt experience. It is something above actuality because tragedy is a weighing or testing—something above a stasis of thought. Pessimism is the repetition of pessimism; skepticism or optimism operate more "at war" as active considerations of alternatives toward a coveted goal.

HOW IT IS SAID

Since I've already insisted that tone can be content, I now need to discuss the pure sound, the sensual power, of the modern tragedy's speech. First I'll work up a kind of checklist of technical acoustic factors. Contrasting the overall practice of today with the sound signals implied in premodern dramatic language, only the factor of silence is in first place in our century. This is how I think they would rate today:

Pitch: a lesser variety is possible or implied. *Duration*: long speeches and long sounds are suspect. The argument is that they defy the verisimilitude of the times, in our clipped and staccato age. *Silence*: more than simply having the caesura within meter, there is more silence today than before. This might be like the layout-man's "white space," but, because it is the silence of deliberate incommunication, it is not dramatic in contrast with nonsilent moments. Pauses are less pregnant. (Pinter and Beckett represent exceptions, but outside tragedy.) *Rhythm*: broken and deliberately unexciting. *Meter*: difficult for the actor to capitalize on. While there's nothing inherently wrong with speech which is unmetrical, there is something wrong when dramatic speech does not tend to "build." Certain use of rhythm and meter can accumulate power and impressions of emotion and thus mount. The normal approach today is away from cumulative meter. *Intensity*: scarce. This is directly shown by the disappearing will-to-live that should be literally and metaphorically basic to drama. Characters caring less and being less gifted fighters today, there is far less chance of intense speech stimuli than in theatre which is known to have satisfied man's listening before. *Tone*: essentially flat. Overtones and harmonics are rarely motivated by modern word choice, arrangement, and thought. All-important inflection clearly tends to downward turns at the ends of units of speech thought. Enervated characters or absurdist mannequins naturally preclude tone choices rich in nuance and color. Inflections must usually be centripetal: they "throw off" few further or larger suggestions.

In short, it is uniquely difficult to find much contemporary dramatic language which physically or symbolically moves onwards or upwards. Tragic language *should* convey an onward and upward movement.

Pessimism almost automatically insists that our sense receptors are not stimulated. (It is only a half-humorous suggestion that one check a feature of this by noting the decline in the use of exclamation points in today's texts, let alone the quality of the word-symbols preceding them.) Part of this is due to the popular preference, first significant in the last century, for realistic or naturalistic prose over poetic language or real verse. The largest fault, however, is the playwright's complaint that "nothing is any use" these days. Speeches assigned to carry that attendant, suspenseless bewilderment are automatically destined to dead or dying patterns and sallow color tones. Characters tend to speak as robots because they or their authors are acutely aware of the "pessimistic facts of life." For rationale and result, Edmund has the keynote speech, in *Long Day's Journey*:

> I just stammered. That's the best I'll ever do. I mean, if I
> live. Well, it will be faithful realism, at least. Stammering is
> the native eloquence of us fog people.

Verbosity doesn't lessen the robot motif. O'Neill's last play, *More Stately Mansions*, runs on just as much "mouthpiece" dialogue as his earliest work. Now the O'Neill figure is Simon, who concludes:

> ... Our whole cowardly moral code about murder is but
> another example of the stupid insane impulsion of man's
> petty vanity to believe human lives are valuable, and
> related to some God-inspired meaning. But the obvious
> fact is that their lives are without any meaning what-
> ever—that human life is a silly disappointment, a liar's
> promise, a perpetual in-bankruptcy for debts we never
> contracted, a daily appointment with peace and happiness
> in which we wait day after day, hoping against hope, and
> when finally the bride or the bridegroom cometh, we
> discover we are kissing Death. . . . And at last we die
> and the starving scavenger hogs of life devour our carrion![5]

The language is both unlikely and uneconomical.

In the preceding section I experimented with the "thought" of one of Hamlet's soliloquies. Now, I'd like to consider "tone" in what might superficially be regarded as one of Shakespeare's most pessimistic passages —in *Macbeth*.

> To-morrow, and to-morrow, and to-morrow,
> Creeps in this petty pace from day to day
> To the last syllable of recorded time.
> And all our yesterdays have lighted fools
> The way to dusty death. Out, out, brief candle!
> Life's but a walking shadow, a poor player

---

5. It is true that *More Stately Mansions* is somewhat incomplete. But considering the body of O'Neill's work, there is little reason to believe he would have greatly revised such a speech had he lived to see the manuscript through the polishing stage.

That struts and frets his hour upon the stage
And then is heard no more: it is a tale
Told by an idiot, full of sound and fury,
Signifying nothing.

Now I'll rewrite this to say the same thing, but reducing it to something like the modern tone:

Time drags on, and the past is just whatever's
been used up of the time we happen to have.
Might as well throw in the sponge. A life isn't
a very noticeable thing. Sometimes it takes
a lot of doing—but it's empty in the end.

In the "pessimistic" Shakespeare, is the tone limited to descent and dying, and is it sensually unexciting? Just possibly, some might say. And of course the modern author can come up with a better modern "translation" than mine. But the main point is this: the Shakespearean version *can* be read to sound dull and dumpy, while my condensed version *has* to be read that way. (Also, Macbeth's pessimism is *not* Shakespeare talking: the rest of the play shows no sign that this is the author's personal outlook. Macbeth despairs because he is so caught in a moral trap, while Malcolm sounds his note of joy at the end because he has discovered purpose.)[6]

Once again we wonder if an exceptional actor couldn't ignite some of the peculiarly modern idioms, to speak to us in our own way using the experiments of progressive new kinds of "poets." Does an expectation of such things as spirited pitch inflection have to be based on the standards of yesterday? Here my answer is that the words themselves should be complete enough signals to imply a range of pitch inflection and tone, especially as the arrangement of several words produces *context*—and I like to believe that good playwriting chooses words (and context) fairly precisely. True, there are "fifty-two different ways" to say "yes,"

6. See F. R. Leavis, "Tragedy and the 'Medium:' A Note on Mr. Santayana's 'Tragic Philosophy,'" in *Tragedy: Modern Essays in Criticism*, ed. L. Michel and R. B. Sewall, pp. 312 ff. Leavis catches Santayana in the assumption that pessimism in Shakespeare is necessarily Shakespeare's own. The argument is over the sentiments of Macbeth.

but that "yes" in a playscript will appear within an overall context which will make the pitch signal, with its inflection and tone, more specific. Otherwise the playwright takes no credit for his notation of intent. He should signal a range of appropriateness because tone *is* interpretation.

Moving on to other sound problems, I would also say that the monotone is unusually common in the modern tragic speech—because it is required by a pessimistic world view. (Nothing's going to get better, good people and good intentions aren't going to change the system, etc.) Yet a monotone is by nature undramatic, "drama" suggesting some kind of a dynamic, some sense of motion along a continuum. Monotones are cured by contrast values, but contrast is philosophically alien to pessimistic premises.

To illustrate, even the most chaotic dramatic moment need not be shapeless to represent chaos; the drama in chaos is known by its contrast with relief moments and lesser chaos. Our sensual participation is aided by perception of "major" moments and "minor" moments—i.e., variety—in which some components are more important and stimulating than others. Thus the basic advisability of the pleasurably unpredictable pattern of sound and tone which therefore invites greater intellectual and emotional participation through speculation.

If there is an aesthetic for tragic language, it could become confused with the conception of the "beautiful" in language, and whether beauty was relevant to tragic statement. A test was once given to poll which words people thought were ugly and which beautiful. In English, the beautifuls were such words as "golden," "azure," "lullaby, and "April," while the uglies were "mange," "scram," "cacophony," etc. The results indicated that a beautiful word was simply a word which had beautiful associations, and an ugly word one with ugly associations. I think that conclusion might have been too generalized. There is the possibility of equating "the beautiful" with some kind of exceptional higher experience, including the sensual, in a "beautiful" idea or "beautiful" insight. Reasonable (associational) or not, something might just strike us as better than what we have known before. If there is an acoustic reason for disliking "mange," could we then like "gnädiges" if we didn't have the translation?

Mario Pei, in *The Story of Language*, said that "the application of an esthetic criterion to language, which has objective reality and a practical function, is bound to be not merely unscientific, but unsatisfactory."[7] But he also admitted that acoustic beauty *would* involve a limit, for instance, on consonant clusters. "This is because vowel sounds carry musical pitch far better than consonants."[8] Hence language (not just national language, but a kind of artistic language) is more likely to convey a richer range of stimuli when it is rich in vowel sounds; and therefore it has a better chance of being "beautiful." If we can get that far, we can admit other things (partly instinctual, I acknowledge) in building towards an aesthetic.

The poet Wallace Stevens, in his book of essays, *The Necessary Angel*,[9] had some of the same misgivings about the sound of word usage today that I do, and he believed the cause was the failure in the coexistence of reality and imagination. This failure came from, he said, the "pressure of reality." (Meaning both that life is more "real" today—and more capable of pressure.) Stevens said imagination and reality needed to interdepend as equals. He used the word "nobility" in defending imagination, which sounds dangerously like the old reactionary criticism that we've got to regain our stories of kings, queens, and princes. Yet we *would* regard "nobility" as false, dead, even (politically) ugly. In this way Stevens saw us surrendering to reality and accepting limits. On the other hand, with what can we associate a depressed and depressing tone?

The converse would be an aesthetic containing several hints of make-believe—and I wouldn't hesitate to accept that as part of the aesthetic for tragic sound. Some could call this wish for something better a kind of sonic escapism. Although I don't want to go back to the flowers of elocution and tragic bombast, I would acknowledge the charge—because there is a human and timeless motive for taking pleasure in transcending and stretching the possibilities of expression. Tragedy deals with this, and all of its component stimuli should work to the same end. Through pitch, tone, intensity, and the like it is a question of what they enlarge for us—better than we ourselves can say, or do—as the "poet" speaks for the best and most ambitious in us. The sensual reward of the poetic effect becomes an intriguing statement in itself.

7. Reported by Mario Pei, *The Story of Language* (New York, 1960). See pt. two, chap. 10, "The Esthetics of Language."
8. Ibid., p. 157.
9. Wallace Stevens, *The Necessary Angel* (New York, 1951).

THE QUESTION OF VERSE

The fact that nearly all great tragedies of history were written *as* poetry is impressive evidence for the contention that tragedy must be cast in verse. There is no totally logical reason, however, for denying the possibility of a prose tragedy. Under a somewhat relaxed definition of the genre, we can pick out several successful prose tragedies—some plays by Ibsen and Strindberg, and perhaps a few from our own era.

Probably it is better to say that, while the mere presence of poetry in a serious play cannot elevate it to tragedy, the absence of some sort of poetic tinge—whether in prosaic or poetic form—handicaps even that play which has all the other necessities for tragedy. George Steiner noted that high verse tragedy was last seen in the French neoclassical period and that its absence since then has finally pronounced the "death" of tragedy. I don't believe tragedy is gone forever but, at any rate, Steiner is convinced that:

> So far . . . as tragic drama is an exaltation of action above the flux of disorder and compromise prevalent in habitual life, it requires the shape of verse. The stylization and simplification which that shape imposes on the outward aspects of conduct makes possible the moral, intellectual, and emotional complications of high drama. Poetic conventions clear the ground for the free play of moral forces.[10]

The "shape of verse" may be asking too much. I can't think of any way to support a theorem for out-and-out metrical poetry. Nor could I prove that full-blown poetry was mandatory for a more satisfying "sound" or tragic sense—although the premodern writers used verse almost as a matter of course and thus must have regularly enjoyed the use as naturally advantageous. Today there are various technical reasons why the playwrights don't attempt poetry (the taste of the audience being one mighty influence) but a really basic reason is that the pessimistic vision cannot stomach the fancy required for the use of verse in its actual metrical form, or in the mood it subsumes. I think a case can be made, however, for language that is *poetically conceived,* and for why it is effective and essential in tragedy.

10. George Steiner, *The Death of Tragedy* (New York, 1961), p. 246.

Poetic language by its very nature voices an expression of limits reachable (but seldom reached) which challenge finite man. It fights the "pressure of reality" cited by Stevens if only because it is contrived; good "poetry" is then self-evidently a *rare thing*. The various realistic speech expressions—although workable for conveying information or actual emotion—only remind man of finitude.

Whereas "poetry" can economize time spent on description and exposition, the pessimistic tragedy dwells on the repetition of dejected grumbling to waste time in the interest of showing, not avoiding, monotony and descent. It is not sufficient for expository and rhetorical communication to sustain matters, as heard in the raw power of O'Neill dialogue which is nonetheless consistently awkward and clumsy at catching any evocative essences and therefore rarely illuminating. We have to probe life emotionally as well, and the graceful generalizations of the poetic can take the place of prosaic statements which—in the pessimistic tragedy—are necessarily degraded to the situation and the mood.

Verse or poetic language actually frees both playwright and spectator, making it easier to believe and participate in the vital fictions of tragedy. In other words it answers philosophical-artistic needs. As Martin Halpern[11] points out, the discipline of formally patterned language makes it especially sensitive to contrasts—and contrasts are the essential tension of tragedy. Not that we must have the formal metre, but language conceived poetically (I think of Williams and Albee in their best moments) carries some of the same benefits. We ought, and want, to react to the boredoms and frustrations of real and stage-life by insisting on the freeing effect of this larger conception of speech.

For tragedy, perhaps the clearest advantage is that suffering can be seen better through poetic description—for the obvious reason that it allows for a more desirable aesthetic distance between the display of pain and the meaning of pain. The writhing of the central characters in *The Hand of the Potter, Beyond the Horizon, All My Sons, Summer and Smoke, After the Fall, Desire Under the Elms, Anna Christie,* and so many more semitragedies of the modern American theatre is display far more than meaning. In traditional tragedy, the meaning and the poetic effect are synthesized with the act of the suffering.

11. Martin Halpern, "Verse in the Theatre: The Language of Tragedy," *Massachusetts Review* 8 (Winter 1967): 137–48.

There's also something about the connotation of "melody" or rhythmic structure. In music, we have a kind of sonic judgment problem illustrated in the conflict between harmonic-melodious music and dissonant music. Brahms, say, is easier on the ear and perhaps on the pleasure centers connected to the ear than Alban Berg, or Arnold Schönberg, or Bartok in the Violin Sonata, or Karlheinz Stockhausen in his concrete music. Of course this is not a meaningful way to distinguish what is intended as *artistic* satisfaction; it does not allow for the artist who wishes to murder your ear, confound your pleasure centers, or figuratively get you off your complacent rump. It is like the earlier discussion of the "beautiful," and one cannot be dogmatic about melody or consonance, either. For one thing, what is dissonant to us may be the consonant norm in another culture, and expectation of "nice" sound is (as the traditional fear goes) for people who go to theatres or concert halls just to be pleased, to be entertained. Even so, I wouldn't discount the factor of entertainment in tragedy.

We get a little closer to the answer in the consideration of poetic structure: poetically conceived language is more likely to have a beginning, middle, and end working toward the cumulative building of impressions. This old "law" still complements the chain of command of sensory to emotional apparatus. In music—and in sound generally, I think—we like to hear that "coda" of sonic thought. We like to get the perspective on things afforded by the arrival of the tonic chord: we have gotten somewhere through a complex route. The sonata form, for example, is no arbitrary whim—it is structure which helps the composer and listener get together. To find a parallel in an aesthetician's approach, one theory of artistic patterning is that—because our own physiology is gravitational—there are lower limits on the satisfaction we can get through antigravitational stimuli, such as wild jaggedness, dissonance, and excessive downward movement in the artist's medium. That is, beyond or beneath these limits the artist won't be getting through to us with his intent because our senses respond in relatively definite sets. There is no consensus on the theory,[12] but it suggests a likely problem in the action of plodding pessimism: it operates beneath a good, workable level of attention and enthusiasm.

What all this comes to is that poetically conceived language can impart a "moral sense" to the proceedings of tragedy. "Free play of moral

12. The theory comes from philosopher-aesthetician John Hospers.

forces" was Steiner's term, and in *The Poet in the Theatre* Ronald Peacock similarly notes that the chief and special contribution of poetry is always "moral." Of course the term should be thought of very connotatively, as in poetry being moral to the extent it can be hand in hand with life and yet free from it. All the specific advantages of the poetic sense in speech, that is, help it to suggest man and man's thought *as we might wish them to become*. Dealing with the inevitable question of fate and existence-meaning, it expresses what we cannot say for ourselves. The ordinary (nontragic) man's limited speech says only what is for who speaks it. The poetic sense substitutes vision for observation through simplifying, taking specifics away, getting to the abstract essence which lets it speak for "Man" rather than "a man." Thus it is moral. The function of speech is not moral in an atmosphere of utter defeat compared to one which searches better truths as an active mission. Poetic speech implies control and coordination of sense and meaning. To Eliot poetry was "wise excitement," and poetic effect must be a kind of legal minimum for tragic language.

WHAT REMAINS

My central conclusion on this point is that tragedy is inescapably a very special, even entertaining, means of achieving a view. If its language is relevant to the main task of tragedy, it will and must automatically go "up" in sensual, denotative, and connotative eloquence and impact. Surely we need not be limited to a serious theatre which says we are either permanent victims or burlesque mannequins and nothing more. Tragedy exposes evils at the same time it asks the artist for his positive insight into experience, namely, that which can foresee the progress that language was originally created to seek. In a sense, we may have a very honest theatre in hearing the facts without embroidery or rhetorical deodorizers, but artistic language—tragic language—is built on a principle of symbolic expression of what is seen as the essence of facts as they relate to the questions: "Does life make sense?" and "What can we do to improve our fates?" In the "false" hope of improvement lies the interesting concept of its "entertainment."

Finally, I don't subscribe to the Artaudian thesis that our language has outlived its usefulness. No alternative has been presented for creating a method of expression whose meanings and suggestions are obtainable to anything like a universal audience. None of the attempts have shown themselves as validly potent or as accurate as the old words, imperfect as the words may be. Moreover, theatre was born so that words could take on life—tragedy being the form of that birth—and words alive enough to justify existence on a stage then lived in mutually enriching interdependence with the other modes of expression inherent in theatre.

Despite the doomsday neurosis, and even because of it, words and writing can still become a sort of encouraging temptation, can love the potential idea of man while damning his error, and can fight rather than withdraw.

$8.$ MORAL STATEMENT

Pessimism gives modern tragedy a moral vision very unlike that of traditional tragedy. Its implicit moral statement is nearly always weak or equivocal. This contrasts with the classical notion of tragic suffering, as in Krutch's description: "For the great ages tragedy is not an expression of despair but the means by which they saved themselves from it. It is a profession of faith, and a sort of religion; a way of looking at life by virtue of which it is robbed of its pain. The sturdy soul of the tragic author seizes upon suffering and uses it only as a means by which joy may be wrung out of existence."[1]

I can see we might not want to accept some of these images too quickly: robbing existence of its pain, for instance, as against some learning *amid* pain. Or the "sturdy soul" of the author may just sound a bit too Edwardian. Nonetheless it is clear enough that today's general situation is completely at odds with the Krutch ideal. Today's view pictures suffering, evil, and sin as the standard elements of existence and in effect welcomes

1. "The Tragic Fallacy," in *European Theories of the Drama*, ed. Barrett Clark, p. 521.

pain and the sight of injustice as further proof of the pessimistic conclusion that we live under an indifferent God—or no God at all.

Pessimism hurts moral statement in several specific ways. First, man is seen as not really responsible for what he does or what happens to him. He cannot really sin, because his behavior or fate may be only arbitrary whims of Nature. Therefore he makes no moral choice leading to a conflict which imparts meaning to the choice. Furthermore, agnosticism or atheism figure in nearly all modern playwrights' world-views— resulting in plays which do not allow for the possibility of a fundamental moral standard, let alone a Higher Judge. Instead of morality, the code is amorality: nothing is certain, and all is anchored to phenomenalism. With no "God," the plays can tell us little about immortality-questing or existence-meaning. The conclusion or "warning" comes from science or the newspapers; basically, it is something we already know. Or, man's moral values (e.g., situation ethics) grow as wild weeds in the jungle evolving as his material society. Finally, the sin and suffering which occurs is simply a constant—happening universally and at random. This is an ambiguous moral view or no view at all.

ERROR, SIN, OR ACCIDENT?

Like Theodore Dreiser, many modern dramatists have found Nature, or Evolution, or a terrible inevitability, to be a more likely supreme power than God. For example, Alan Squier, in *The Petrified Forest*, is cynical about a determinist law but his pessimism still accepts it when he asks to be shot: "You see, Duke, in killing me—you'd only be executing the sentence of the law—I mean natural law—survival of the fittest. . . ." True, the dramatists could be right about all this; what Albert Schweitzer called "the pessimistic facts of life" may even bear out their conclusions. Tragedy, however, is fact plus hope based on some idea of the worth of conduct, and the playwrights' pessimistic view of causality affects the conception of "sinful" conduct in the structure of the modern tragic drama. Man is not seen as liable for his sins, or the ambitions leading him into "sinfulness." This is formulated on three possibilities: there is no sin; sin is everywhere and hence accepted "custom and usage"; or, sin can never be defined and judged.

The chief cause of this outlook is knowledge, largely scientific-logical. "Man does not make himself," etc., etc., and thus we have the "irresponsibility" rationale linked to such things as the theory that the violent murderer may influenced by X-Y chromosomal abnormality. Back in 1920, this was the whole basis of Dreiser's conception of a tragedy—in *The Hand of the Potter*. As a character in that play, an Irish newspaper reporter, says [*sic*]:

> If ye waant to come out exactly right in this world, which nobody ever does, ye waant to be pairfectly balanced, or nearly that—an' few are that. It's more luck than anythin' else.

Because of "hormones" and the evidence in Krafft-Ebing and Havelock Ellis (as per Dreiser's dialogue) the Isadores of the world cannot be blamed if they "don't come out all right." A crude but reasonable case for seeing the sexual psychopath not as criminal but as someone needing understanding and treatment: fair enough; but present enough of this and there is a total reversal of the traditional tragic code of willful individuality leading to destruction, and destruction leading to high knowledge for the society left behind.

Whether it is a helpless horror or simply a man who can't triumph any more than he can stop being vile, pessimistic exploitation of Darwinian and scientistic doctrines of natural weakness are at the forefront of the problem. The derivation of Auguste Comte's scientism and positivism is enlightening in the extension of such "sophisticated" beliefs. Comte advanced the idea that man's highest stage of belief came when he progressed through the fiction of theology and the abstraction of metaphysics to the positive belief in science which, in part, he termed a "religion of humanity." In effect, zealous Comtians see positive values only in things which can be "scientized" or made into science-obsessed doctrine. The playwrights who see conduct as accident more than error and disregard the possibility of clear sin indirectly erect this same kind of shrine to natural science. It also means they do not ask the big tragic question, let alone attempt an answer.

This ignores the truth that, as T. R. Henn concludes in *The Harvest of Tragedy*: "the central problem of tragedy, from Aeschylus onwards, has always been the moral or religious problem of the place of evil and suffering in the world."[2] Not that modern tragedy ignores suffering, but an obsession with suffering precludes perspective on its misery. Where is *real* sin? In a good, solid, well-defined antagonist, in an illuminatingly sinful Iago, Claudius, or Clytemnaestra? It is not for us today: the antagonist is most likely to be part of the central character's own general confusion, or the collective "they," in the rest of the world. Man's life is accidental, and his destruction has the same tinge. In *Golden Boy*, the improbably sensitive hero Joe Bonaparte and his girl friend Lorna get into a car and drive because "somewhere there must be happy boys and girls who can teach us the way of life!" Joe says, "We'll drive through the night. When you mow down the night with headlights, nobody gets you! You're on top of the world then—nobody laughs! That's it—speed! We're off the earth—unconnected! We don't have to think! That's what speed's for, an easy way to live!" And it is an easy way to die, as we hear in the final scene. Then there are the O'Neill heroes destroyed by tuberculosis which obviously has no connection with character or thought, and even before that someone like Robert Mayo can say "I'm a failure, and Ruth's another—but we can both justly lay some of the blame for our stumbling on God." The only blame O'Neill could mean is the "accident" that put Robert on the farm instead of the deck of a tramp steamer as premature deus ex machina.

Our plays imply that the world is purposeless and chaotic to the point that evil exists outside any question of individual control. Tennessee Williams's basic position is this: "I don't believe in 'original sin.' I don't believe in 'guilt.' I don't believe in villains or heroes—only in right and wrong ways that individuals have taken, not by choice but by necessity or by certain still-uncomprehended influences in themselves, their circumstances and their antecedents."[3] But this aspect of the playwrights' personal pessimism, while excusing man as morally irresponsible child, also robs man's error of tragic (sinful) dimension. Reinhold Niebuhr says: "The temptation to sin lies . . . in the human situation itself. This situation is that man as spirit transcends the natural and temporal process in which he is involved and also transcends himself. Thus his freedom is the basis of his creativity but it is also his temptation."[4]

2. *The Harvest of Tragedy*, p. 65.
3. "The World I Live In," quoted in Goodman, *Drama on Stage*, p. 295.
4. Quoted in *The Harvest of Tragedy*, p. 74.

If the possibility of an ethics or a morality has been increasingly colored by psychoanalytical insight to result in this elevation of accident over sinful error, is science wrong for tragedy? Must knowledge be held back? That is a broad question for the whole scope of tragic vision, which I will get to in chapter 10 in the idea of form-tempo. As far as sin and evil are concerned, science has challenged tragic statement only when insistent pessimism has overreacted to those findings which are convenient for the preconception. It comes back to formal or informal philosophy. All the modern serious visions, including the nontragic absurdist genre, tend far more to blame existence than to blame man. Existentialism teaches that theories of good and evil are not relevant to the business of living. Man's ability to identify himself through a great sin—which I must define in a moment—is considered a remote or impossible thing, and thus characters are secondary to philosophy aimed at the statement of uselessness. The audience for tragedy, however, must define existence in terms of men. "We" are not an audience of "existences"; we have instead an almost prurient interest in seeing one of our number sin in the process of testing an exceptional ideal.

To try to make this point more specific, consider the functional weakness of the accidental amoral protagonist of today. (Blanche can't help "putting on"; Quentin doesn't know why he is always "hurting" people; The Young Woman is a classic case of frigidity; Lennie can't refrain from petting soft and furry things, thus hurting them; Mr. Zero is driven to homicidal madness.) Why *must* he be more heroic, i.e., moral? And is the deranged nonheroic protagonist anything new?

A hero-villain such as Shakespeare's Richard III or Euripides' Dionysus in *The Bacchae* is immoral, and in that sense he is not traditionally "heroic." But dramatically, at least, he is attractive and forceful. He has courage and conviction within his evil, something which can be admired in the subjectivity of the theatre. Consider also Richard's straightforward murders, and even the rending-to-pieces of Dionysus's victims—here are quite definite, "moral" acts. They are moral in the sense that a clear choice has been made in favor of what is immoral judged against the norm but moral in the sense it is a necessary contribution to an ambition the character believes is right for his world. No audience really wants Richard or Dionysus to fail—*at those points in their dramatic lives*. On the other hand, some modern like Dreiser's rape-slayer Isadore is disgustingly helpless and choiceless. He is not distanced from us, and the *act* he commits is all. In the premoderns, the act is a component of a larger presence and purpose and implies moral commentary on an ambition. "Amorality" is of no interest to us. Science and psychology excuse Lennie in *Of Mice and Men* when he kills the flirt, *Streetcar's* Blanche in the newsboy scene, or drug-addict Mary of *Long Day's Journey*. Their acts, however, do not eventually and ironically combine with their greatnesses in a moment of conscious, moral knowledge. Moral neutrality, determinism, and claims of irresponsibility can pin no tragic significance to an act since it is diluted in its moral meaning to the character and to his society. Richard's society, for example, is not so scientifically altruistic that it cannot be horrified by the willful individuality and creativity of his "evil" deeds and accordingly experience and evoke a dramatic awe. The Romans denied the existence of evil and the modern pessimist sees nothing but. The Greeks, however, saw evil as discoverable, and their tragedies are the dramatization of such discovery—though "evil" was codified as disobeying the gods. The classic hero-villain's playwright is not chastising his audience into giving quarter to some arbitrary unfortunate. Finally, if the tragic race is won or lost on accident or luck, the tragedy is vaporized because there is no motive for admiring a winner (temporary and partial winner though he always proves to be) or sympathizing with a loser. Mere sympathy for amorality is a one-way street. Tragedy requires a sudden and mighty awareness of definite error. Error is beyond location in the pessimistic tragedy; pessimism regards that as a mere constant also. And, as for morality in moral statement, we may define this as common law, not necessarily as theological law.

These general pronouncements are perhaps too easy. For one thing, there remains the apparent contradiction in sin and heroism: how do real heroes sin? Nietzsche said of Sophocles' thinking in *Oedipus* that the conclusion would be interpreted this way: "The noble man does not sin; this is what the thoughtful poet wishes to tell us: all laws, all natural order, yea, the moral world itself, may be destroyed through his action, but through this very action a higher magic circle of influences is brought into play, which establishes a new world on the ruins of the old that has been overthrown."[5] This is not the action of pessimism; the main idea

5. *The Birth of Tragedy.*

is the constructive influence of the protagonist's scapegoat role. But it is superficially obvious that noble men *do* sin: Oedipus, Orestes, Macbeth, and Othello have no lack of company here. Later in our experience with these men we come up with the usual qualification: they sin in a way that is a result of their nobility. Hence we emotionally put Othello very nearly 180 degrees away from Iago on the morality scale. The *fact* of sin, though, still remains; reading Nietzsche's comment again, we see his noble man *is* sinning against the status quo. For the man on the street, there's little ambiguity about given breaches of the common-law morality, i.e., regicide, cold-blooded strangling, and so on. Then there's the higher implication. For all heroes, part of their stature is that they "sin" by exceeding limits in an unlawful way—that taste and ability for excess being also their greatness. The law in question here is the law as constructed by limited man to define his limitation. The errant hero then is punished on our behalf, in the manner of Christ, for what was *at that time* illegal. Metaphorically, the hero therefore helps to rewrite the law, but not before he falls victim to it. The Christ myth—he "died for our sins"—mythically and tragically means he died for doing what we should have been doing, or should have wanted to do, ourselves. We cannot, however, and no non-mythic sinner can change this status quo. In tragedy, the sin becomes noble because it will suggest what it means to the very temporal notion (typical of tragedy) regarding where man *was* and where he *can be* later on. The hero's particular hubris means sinning against "natural" morality in favor of helping to write the new morality of maximizing ourselves. "The recognition of sin is the beginning of salvation," said Martin Luther; his context was very Christian, but the basic truth is still very correct for tragedy. Which brings us to a very popular problem.

GOD AND TRAGEDY

Somewhere audiences for tragedy confront the idea of morality equated with a presence of something like God. I have made a start at supporting this, speaking of the concept of sin in the mostly aesthetic sense of taking some definite, somehow "attractive," plunge for which the character is responsible. The premises of modern would-be tragedies ignore a clear and balanced view of evil, but they also contain the larger failure of being rarely moral in a true, wide philosophical sense. The dynamic of what happens in the play doesn't "say" much morally. Now, where does the fundamental rightness of a morality come from, and where is its relevance to tragedy?

One older concept which has often been accepted, perhaps surviving only as dogma, is that man starts life and starts tragedy with a definite moral burden. To the Hindu, this stems from a past incarnation. For the Christian, the likely reference is original sin—and George Steiner seems willing to insist on it for tragedy. He speaks of it as the real object of the art form, of and beyond peripety:

> But the rise and fall of him that stood in high degree was the incarnation of the tragic sense for a much deeper reason: it made explicit the universal drama of the fall of man. . . . By virtue of original sin, each man was destined to suffer in his own experience, however private or obscure, some part of the tragedy of death. . . . the prologue to the tragic condition of man is set in Heaven and in the Garden of Eden.[6]

This I cannot believe: if nothing else, the instinct for tragic make-believe predates the story of the Garden of Eden. Where does this "universal drama of the fall of man" come from, and how can it be used for the contrived tragic pleasure? Where, for instance, is the Egyptian peasant's emotional knowledge of "the Fall" amid his identifying with Osiris-Horus in the myth of 4000 years ago? (We need only turn to the Ramesseum Dramatic Papyrus to see tragic myth which propagandized for obedience to faith in god-ness without reference to guilt—and which undoubtedly worked.)[7] Cold logic proceeding from the original sin concept leads near the scientistic position: sin is automatic. Yet should not man be able *to sin again*, as I have said earlier, because he is a special man —wherein he chooses a "sin" neither vague nor predestined? He must; otherwise all the power of the God-presence is somewhere "back there" on the temporal scale. Where would be the contemporary challenge of God throwing tests at us as we come along the scale? I think tragedy must put some concept of God or Moral Law into its own time period. But

---

6. *The Death of Tragedy*, pp. 12–13.

7. A reconstruction of the text of this ancient coronation play can be found in Theodor H. Gaster, *Thespis: Ritual, Myth, and Drama in the Ancient Near East* (New York, 1950).

most of all, the "Fall" is "Fortunate," in the words of Lovejoy and Weisinger, and "is felt to be simultaneously harrowing and ecstatic, for at the very moment when man is thrown into the deepest despair, at that moment, and at that moment alone, he is made aware of the possibility of realizing the greatest good, and in this way, and only in this way, does good come out of evil."[8] Thus the famous paradox. He has learned something about *not* "falling" which must depend on a scenting of something outside himself—a fictitious god at the least—which gives a mythology to the dynamics of reversing fortunes.

Contemporary pessimistic tragedy, of course, rejects the idea of any higher control and order which a thought of God posits. Man, we can see, is only a burlesque of what he should be, so there can hardly be some supreme presence structuring his existence and development. Kaufmann says of Shakespearean tragedy that it does not "revolve around moral conflicts,"[9] and I think that is to put it in the same boat with the contemporary view. Optimistic tragedy *does* assume a kind of morality inevitably related to God or god. E. E. Stoll puts this in practical terms of making the tragic statement comprehensible. He says that both Greek and Shakespearean tragedy contain "an absolute, unquestionable moral element"[10] which conforms closely to the moral judgment of the audience, thus encouraging an immediate and united response. For Herbert Muller, "the tragic sense is the deepest sense of our humanity, and therefore spiritual enough. But all men may profit from it, whatever their faith." (So much for the Old Testament's context of "Fall.") Muller adds that tragedy "sizes up the very reasons for religious faith, the awful realities that men must face up to if their faith is to be firm, mature, and responsible."[11] Note that he says the *"reasons"* for it, not the religious faith itself. And Shakespearean analyst A. C. Bradley says of the result of the tragic destruction: "[In the central force of the tragedy] the ultimate power or order is "moral" [in that] it does not show itself indifferent to good and evil, or equally favorable to both, but shows itself akin to good and alien from evil."[12]

8. Herbert Weisinger, "The Psychology of the Paradox of the Fortunate Fall," in *Tragedy: Modern Essays in Criticism*, p. 107.

9. *Tragedy and Philosophy*, p. 366.

10. *Shakespeare and Other Masters*, p. 27.

11. *The Spirit of Tragedy*, pp. 332–33.

12. *Shakespearean Tragedy*, p. 36.

But why the equations, tragedy = morality; morality = God? The combination is automatic, and it is best expressed in Whitehead's very major insight that all order "is aesthetic order, and the moral order is merely certain aspects of aesthetic order. The actual world is the outcome of the aesthetic order, and the aesthetic order is derived from the immanence of God."[13] I can't hope to prove this (I could only refer you back to Whitehead), but the last idea might be eased a bit more: for our purposes, "God" should be defined as the focus of a system of values and virtues, not necessarily as a full and Christian Father. For instance, Meister Eckhart's image of God as the mystery that is nonetheless "there" carries the consciousness I take to inhabit tragedy. He says: "It is God's nature to be without a nature. To think of his goodness, or wisdom, or power is to hide the essence of him, to obscure it with thought about him."[14]

Pessimism accepts God as dead. O'Neill's Edmund reads Nietzsche a great deal, and believed with the philosopher that (as he quotes him): "God is dead: of his pity for man hath God died." Evidence from the Death-of-God theologians *or* philosophers is immaterial, however, for tragedy is a fiction which must believe in extramortal ranges if not in extraterrestrial rewards and ever-afters. The experience of religion as institution is very relevant. Freud spoke for much of the sense of the century when he several times referred to religion as a "delusional remolding of reality," and one of the harmful "mass delusions." It survives, he said, only because "no one who shares a delusion ever recognizes it as such."[15] To Freud, religion restricts because it depresses the value of life and distorts the picture of the real world in a delusional manner, intimidating the intelligence with its "psychical infantilism." I think it is clear in their plays and their many public statements that twentieth-century tragedians embrace this kind of exposé. Dreiser's disenchantment is typical: "The very best that religion can show is no better than that which Life, or Nature herself, could and did do long before any religion appeared, namely, a rough equation, a balance struck; so that if a

---

13. *Alfred North Whitehead: An Anthology*, p. 506. Plato, of course, could be mentioned as having a somewhat similar insight in equating art, the ideal, and "the divine," but Whitehead commits himself to a more specific meaning.

14. In Crane Brinton, ed., *The Fate of Man* (New York, 1961), p. 192.

15. *Civilization and Its Discontents* (London, 1963), p. 18.

man had done a consciously wrong thing in one place he was chemically or emotionally moved to do a right thing in another."[16] The last statement is of course nonsense, but the basic posture is shared by the playwrights who then sit down to write their tragedies. The religion-and-God problem thus seen causes, or supports, pessimism. On the other hand, Freud is objectively quite right, and I know few people who wouldn't be perfectly convinced by his type of attack on religion. But Freud nowhere shows that there is no "god." *Of course* religion is a fiction, but that, also, is not in turn a proof that there is no supreme being or inherent necessity for believing one exists. It was man who invented religion, not God.

Now we must come to the problems of seeing tragedy as Western-Christian and of making contemporary tragedy as atheist. Both are wrong positions, I think, and it is clarifying to discuss them together. (But only with reference to the pessimism issue.)

If you accept the atheist tragic vision of our time, then man is put in the precarious position of thanking chance and nonethical bases of selection for his survival in the universe. Nature, however, has no capacity to care which of her gifts is used, or how, and by whom, for good or for evil; Nature cannot be considered a god-substitute or a substitute for man's natural theology, such as in the Golden Rule. The branch of a tree can be made into a club. It is man—as a whole or as the best within his number—who does care and makes a statement about it. The tree can then be used as a shelter—or as a shrine. Man improving implies something like god-ness in man. In this way his survival may be Christian, or what have you: it doesn't matter. At least it uses a code of virtue which sets him a little outside sheer utility and himself alone.

Does pessimistic atheism, in which man is not improving, kill the tragic vision because it is non-Christian? For one thing, as everyone knows, it depends on how death is viewed. One pro-Christian theory is that: "Tragedy has as its concern the experience of mortal man undergoing the trials which a mysterious providence appoints. This concern is Christianity's too. Death ends tragedy as it does life, but neither church nor theatre treats death as the ending end."[17] Others say tragedy's picture

16. *Hey Rub-a-Dub-Dub*, p. 172.
17. A. M. Eastman, "Mimes and Morals," *Christian Century*, 26 December 1956, p. 1508.

of death must be final: "There has been no specifically Christian mode of tragic drama even in the noontime of the faith. Christianity is an anti-tragic vision of the world. . . . Real tragedy can occur only when the tormented soul believes that there is no time left for God's forgiveness."[18] Eastern culture has no tragedy because death is not the end and life is only an indeterminate stage between incarnations. Then perhaps tragedy could be defined as opposite to this? Or is God a reward—or a judgment? Sylvan Barnet[19] says that the Christian view insists "that the good are rewarded and the bad are punished." I doubt seriously that this is necessarily always true, and for that reason reject it as a proof against Christian tragedy.

Let's take Alan Squier in *The Petrified Forest* as an illustration. Once Alan had wanted to live, but, as the play says and shows, he was "blinded" at that time. Now, through what he sees in the course of the play, *"he can see."* And what he sees is welcome death. Gabby and Sherwood insist on concluding that Alan died happy. The question for us is, is Alan going to a "new life"? The line of comedy is said to go from death to life, while tragedy seems to run from life to death. The Christian regenerative form, however, is from life to death—to life again. This is apparently in keeping with Alan and other pessimistic martyrs: they are "redeemed."

But this approach, theorizing over the life-to-death or death-to-life line of the hero, overlooks one essential complexity of tragedy. Alan Squier's Paradise is not necessarily ours. Even more so, Hamlet's absolute and final death without hint of "Christian" redemption is not necessarily intended to reflect our own progression. Of vast importance is the tension and the irony between the hero's pattern and ours as we witness life-to-death. They are not parallel tracks. It is true that we would not want the character to be so Christian that he looks ahead to a second chance; *his* catastrophe must be unqualified. But there must be some vision of "time left" *for the audience.* We must know about the finality past the character's finality.

Now look at the apparent finality of *King Lear.* Clifford Leech, with a number of others, notes that *Lear's* conclusion finds evil just as strong as ever. This is matched with the opinion that "the theme of renewal is

18. Steiner, *The Death of Tragedy,* pp. 331–32.
19. "Some Limitations of a Christian Approach to Shakespeare," *ELH* 22 (1955): 92.

absent from most of Sophocles and Euripides."[20] *Lear* seems a good case because its whole basis is a non-Christian chronicle. But isn't there still a code, a system of virtues, some moral order? What is the metaphoric impression of the supposed finality of *Lear* and the other dark-ending traditional tragedies?

Fundamentally, tragedy decreases as the vision of death becomes less final or less of a contrast (and this is where pessimism clouds the whole issue), and conversely as it becomes more final in the view of the spectators. There is a dramatic irony,[21] an opposing set of tensions, between the stage world and the real world which is vital to this feature and once more it is a matter of perspective. Does Faust's Catholic-like redemption at the close of Goethe's play remove from it the aura of tragedy? Is this similar in effect to Anderson's misty view of sacrifice in *Winterset* and *Anne of the Thousand Days* and *Key Largo,* or Albee's infinite ambiguity for the end of *Tiny Alice*? I have said before that the tragic ending cannot be gilded with the halo of martyrdom.

Pessimism in tragedy, ironically, sometimes agrees with Christian-Catholic hope in that it will prefer whatever death consists of to the meaningless thing called life for the *protagonist: not* us. Still, exact religious attitude is not the key to the tragic as long as it can exceed the Christian and find a universal conception whereby endings and strivings square with a notion of "God" as "that factor in the universe whereby there is importance, value, and ideal beyond the actual."[22] It is more a matter of a clear ethical attitude. Much has been argued, for example, about Shakespearean tragedy being Christian or non-Christian, with the weight against the idea that Shakespeare emphasized God and Christian thought in his conception of what was tragic—as in the matter of *Lear* mentioned earlier.[23] Even if Shakespeare is not considered Christian, however, his tragic heroes have some idea of punishment and reward after death. Othello has a superstitious and primitive view of paying for his

20. See Clifford Leech, "The Implications of Tragedy," in *Tragedy: Modern Essays in Criticism,* ed. L. Michel and R. B. Sewell, p. 172.

21. That is, the spectator has privileged knowledge in accumulating impressions of the whole denied the protagonist in his experience of only his own particular. See J. L. Styan's potent discussion of this "dramatic irony" in *The Elements of Drama* (Cambridge, England, 1963), chaps. 3 and 4.

22. Whitehead.

23. See Barnet, "Some Limitations of a Christian Approach to Shakespeare."

sins, while Hamlet has a more intellectualized attitude. But they do at some time have a consciousness of ethical values. The point is in how the tragic characters view moral responsibility and its attendant struggles on earth, while they live. It is perfectly true that Elizabethan morality was different from the Periclean, the Periclean unlike our own, and ours different from those of still other ages. But only up to a point. Men as a whole are still aware of an essentiality of moral values in a civilized society. The world at large, for example, has always been able to define murder.

Agreed, the hero must not have any hope of salvation, nor must "heaven" make it all worthwhile. But what is never mentioned in all these arguments about Christian or non-Christian tragedy, or final or transitory endings, is the difference between the fact of the hero's destruction and our knowledge of his intent and his fate. Following up now on this earlier observation, the hero must be destroyed, *but we are still physically alive and have the benefit of the entire tragic experience from all viewpoints*. For the hero, "the rest is silence" indeed. Yes, Othello is damned. No enlightened cherubim sing around the corpses in *Hamlet*'s last act. But who can claim Elsinore is no better, and that we the spectators have no more insight into morality, despite what is a final finality for Hamlet?

Artistic illusion means we are capable, like the hero, of simultaneous experience with the explicit and the implicit. When I suggest there is a kind of redemption for *us* in true tragedy, in its moral and ethical revelation, I do not refer to a sentimental *Jane Shore* type of conclusion. The heroes and heroines in real tragedy are not forgiven. So tragedy goes from life to death for the hero. Our aesthetic partnership with the experience parallels this, *but then shifts*. We imagine the life-to-death in tragic art. Then, as in Christian regeneration, we see life reappear in the continuum —but only for us, not the hero. We touch immortality from the hero's mortality. He has shown us a relationship between a code of virtues and an overlarge ambition.

Thus a fear of some moral arbiter, whether God or not, is present in great tragedy. Consequently, an atheism or agnosticism about the existence of such a power seems antitragic. Such fear can be the beginning of wisdom, and it certainly gives meaning to sin—whereas the pessimistic heroes and heroines exceed this fear (as respect, a balanced fear) and know only dread. This morality-consuming dread places them in the Void which Kierkegaard criticizes: "When death is the greatest danger, one hopes for life; but when one becomes acquainted with an even more dreadful danger, one hopes for death. So when the danger is so great that death has become one's hope, despair is the disconsolateness of not being able to die."[24] Because this sickness is "*self*-consuming"[25] there is no moral awareness of tragic circumstances: where one was, how one arrived here, where this leads—always that temporal-moral continuum.

Is man really immortal, through *soul?* Is this a rational belief? It doesn't matter: tragedy exists, in part, to ritualize our belief, and our need to believe, in whatever we might call a higher potential—the only constant goal or value as we move uncertainly along in time. A kindred situation: beauty has no use, other than to "intoxicate" in Freud's context, but still civilization cannot do without it. It is a continual bait which is not intrinsically linked with harmful immoral goals and which aids our momentum. Judgment from a perspective outside ourselves—and even a consensus of the most ethical thinkers on earth will do as a substitute for standards we think derive from God—is necessary. As Whitehead puts it, "God is that non-temporal actuality which has to be taken account of in every creative phase."[26]

To conclude the commentary on moral statement, we need some more specifics in the form of some amplification on values versus virtues.

VICTIMS AND VALUES

Most characters created under a pessimistic tragic vision have lost contact with a system of workable values, such as the common-law moral order I have already suggested. Albee's George and Martha are cast loose to play the games they can without benefit of the strong father authority they both would welcome. Blanche has values ("don't hang back with the brutes" and "there are *some* finer things in life than mere animal gratification," etc.) but her better ideas along these lines are not as directly involved in her story as her peculiarities and psychological confusion. The Tyrones express only a cynical code of life as suffering

24. Kierkegaard, *The Sickness Unto Death*, p. 151.
25. Ibid.
26. Whitehead, p. 502.

because they have given up on it long ago. And Willy Loman's idea of values is not even a case of good situation- or contextual-ethics. The questions of conscience and code rarely seem relevant to modern tragic characters. They have few values because they are first of all victims; they are not able to understand what's going on. They learn pessimistic "values" (codes for survival, really) rather than discover values as virtues which pay off in progress.

Values come into the picture because the modern tragedy could be effective in stating a value position where it might have justifiable difficulty with more explicit statement on morality, good, evil, and sin such as discussed in the previous sections of this chapter. The statement of "values" only as schemes for surviving or "beating the system" is contrary to tragedy because it exhibits "wrong" moral codes. I do not mean that tragedy must moralize and preach, "giving the moral" quite in the Aesopian sense. For one thing, tragedy's dependence on values is part of a questing suggestion, something poetized and never absolute. (Which is part of the reason we can interpret it and share it through our own impressions.) The playwright, however, does not lead the enactment of values into an ambiguous or equivocal position.

Rights and wrongs are never clear with modern victims. They do not represent consistent codes: existence and action are guilts in themselves, or their severely limited happiness may justify an ethical modification. The code will influence the victim's *ethos*. It follows that a non-victim has been better able to think about his values and, while we certainly do not require a guiltless Christian tragic figure, he will have more to say to and for us if he is consciously virtuous enough to make him a worthy opponent for a clear and deliberate evil. He cannot just be a victim of a system which has not especially singled him out, which has only caught him in its net along with other prey. Pessimism is prone to this situation because in maintaining that nothing is any use, it denies an ordered system. No reaction to life requies codifying, and sincere laws, morals, and ethics tend to be precluded. It sees false tragedy because it rejects an interplay of right and wrong values. In authentic tragedy values are assaulted but never fully unhooked so that, as Stoll upholds the effect,

> the verities are in the end unshaken, the moral values and even the social sanctions are unbroken. On the one hand, there is

not the transcendental consolation of evil as but negative, barren, and self-destructive, nor, on the other, the desolation of good and evil merged and confused. There is no skepticism or cynicism, no enveloping irony, as in Ibsen and O'Neill; no bitter despair or mockery on the lips of the survivors or (except the villains) of the dying. There is no hollow echo at the close.[27]

I will illustrate the problem through *Death of a Salesman*. Miller has responded to the charge that Willy has no values:

The trouble with Willy Loman is that he has tremendously powerful ideals. We're not accustomed to speaking of ideals in his terms; but, if Willy Loman, for instance, had not had a very profound sense that his life as lived had left him hollow, he would have died contentedly polishing his car on some Sunday afternoon at a ripe old age. The fact is he has values. The fact that they cannot be realized is what is driving him mad—just as, unfortunately, it's driving a lot of other people mad. The truly valueless man, a man without ideals, is always perfectly at home somewhere.[28]

Yes, there will be a tension in him, but does Willy's tension show that he has "ideals"? For ideals, I refer back to my comments in chapter 6: they are wishes, not ideals in the sense that universal literature and philosophy must define Ideal. And later in the above statement, Miller says his aim in *Death of a Salesman* was to "set forth what happens when a man does not have a grip on the forces of life and has no sense of values which will lead him to that kind of a grip."[29] So Willy dreamed because he failed on both levels. The dream is *not* a value, and certainly not an ideal.

Willy Loman is an excessively material creature. His externals-minded set of values is in league with the Loman theory of the excusable immorality. Stealing is all right for Biff because he's going to charm people and go places. Cultivating an athletic personality is better than studying, because "appearances" are what count. Willy's love for his boys stresses their exterior attractions: their builds, looks, physical ability. It dislocates

---

27. *Shakespeare and Other Masters*, p. 80.
28. Transcript of radio Broadcast, in *Tulane Drama Review* 2 (May 1958): 66.
29. Ibid.

them because it is a denial of natural order. Instead one must *act* one's way into being noticed, through sham. Biff is characterized as "carrying a football which he keeps squeezing as though to locate himself in the world." Biff and Happy know you build a future by getting ahead of the next guy—but without understanding the process or the necessity. Happy's name is an irony, for he does not know pleasure even in his repeated sexual conquests. Without clear good, evil pales as well.

Part of the atmosphere of perennial defeat in this household comes from the impersonality of the automated, mechanized society that has substituted mass mediocrity for slowly cultured quality. The Lomans know intimately the seemingly petty defeats of broken-down refrigerators, carburetor trouble, and the like. At the same time, they respond, with all "common" men ("common" by the advertising industry's definition of mass attraction) to the mass-production values. Willy himself, as a salesman, must represent those values to the consumer. Willy and Linda can leak out their earnings for a mountain of minor repairs, and then justify their decision to purchase a particular brand by saying: "They had the biggest ads of any of them!" Miller's comment in another interview points to another aspect of such adopted values; "Willy is a victim; he didn't originate this thing. He believes that selling is the greatest thing anybody can do."[30]

Miller says he was careful not to inject a personal statement of his philosophy into the play. Yet Willy is so obviously wrong in all he does, all the while "meaning well" and loving his family, that a statement of values seems especially needed. We only see a world which is mutually infected by Willy's helplessly perverted dreams and codes. If the characters are deliberately and pessimistically drawn as limited intelligences, there can be little perspective on values from within the play. Could Linda be a source? She seems most sensible and most objective, but she has a policy of single-minded support of Willy. Her love is then impressive but her values routine.

Willy's self-building only develops the ground for his later paranoia, when he decides the world has treated him badly in the light of his greatness *as he imagined it*:

30. Quoted in Philip Gelb, "Morality and the Modern Drama," *Educational Theatre Journal* 10 (October 1958): 192.

> And they know me, boys, they know me up and down New England. The finest people. And when I bring you fellas up, there'll be open sesame for all of us, 'cause one thing, boys: I have friends. I can park my car in any street in New England, and the cops protect it like their own.

Thus the Loman men feed on each other's empty values, resulting in their eventual cynicism about modern life in the city: eat, sleep, work, and then more of the same. Lack of values means lack of ethic plus lack of knowledge. The result: pessimism and cynicism. Eventually Biff vaguely wants to marry "somebody with character, with resistance:" that is, both Happy and Biff agree they must seek someone to challenge them as Linda and Willy have not.

The object of Willy's code is understandable. He's got a poignant dream and we can sympathize with it. We all desire recognition, and we want him to have it, wrong and false though he may be. He will share it with his family, too. But his means to this object remain at least amoral if not immoral. While Miller naturally criticizes Willy, it is nonetheless clear that Willy is Miller's (and our) pathos-object. It is sad what was expedient to the Lomans, but this is not a moral statement, even though Miller is normally one of our more moral playwrights.

Willy's dangerous thinking, forced on him by society, is also somewhat inherited, and Willy in turn will pass this on to Biff, and Biff would pass it on to his children. Willy's brother Ben says to Biff what is probably the same thing Willy heard from his father years ago: "Never fight fair with a stranger, boy. You'll never get out of the jungle that way." There are two interesting suppositions here: that they *are in* a jungle, and that one must force one's way out. They are keystones of the Loman pessimism, and ironically Willy is not aware enough to be a fighter. These only explain and do not justify Willy's perennial defensiveness. The main conclusion is that those who get out of the jungle are the treacherous battlers and connivers and thus the earth is inherited by some cross between rats and apes. Accordingly, Ben's repeated boast that he was rich at seventeen is Willy's favorite piece of literature: "That's just the spirit I want to imbue them with! To walk into a jungle. I was right! I was right! I was right!"

So Willy is destroyed by his values, and they are not moral or ethical values, but situational and material codes. They alienate Biff even as Biff learns of no alternative to this type of value. That is Willy's greatest loss and the final impetus for suicide. Simply put, Willy is a professional failure. His values wouldn't matter to the company if only he could maintain his quota and not act so strangely.

Death of a Salesman, for all its excellence as a drama, then shares the typical weaknesses of the other pessimistic plays when it comes to moral statement. Nothing has been said distinctly or strongly in any of the areas that might pass for such statement—not on sin, or error, or moral belief, or mere common-sense values. But even this is not the ultimate problem with the pessimistic would-be tragedy. It is finally a matter of enlightenment, and I will finish the point in the next chapter.

9. ANAGNORISIS

Anagnorisis, or, as Lucas translates it, "the recognition of the truth," is the by-product of tragedy which probably most determines that the expression *is* tragic. If the victim goes to his death bewildered by himself and blind to the real source of his destruction, that destruction is meaningless as philosophy-in-action. There must be insight and enlightenment in tragedy.

In fact, *anagnorisis* helps make the destructive crisis happen. In traditional tragedy, the hero's insight into himself is often in direct relation to his suffering, and his insight into error spills out into the audience in the form of enlightenment about the universal implications of that error. When Oedipus and Othello finally recognize themselves and their actions in this severe light, they destroy themselves. After the tragic upheaval, the surviving enlightenment sets values upright again.

Is there enlightenment in the modern pessimistic tragedy? At the least, we could expect the play to say something about the problem of existence —how much and in what way life does not make sense. But even admitting debatable judgments on what is concluded, it can be frustrating to look for the mere incidence of such statement. Here, the majority of modern serious plays contain either no speeches making such an attempt, no action of character implying it, or else make the position even clearer by proclaiming categorically that there is no hope of understanding the meaning or "value" of tragic downfall in the world of the play. The catastrophe simply occurs, and the playwrights nearly always jump straight to pity and fear, bypassing *anagnorisis* or recognition. Another fault is that pessimism emphasizes characterization of the psychological disorder supposedly inevitable in a despairng, chaotic world, precluding characters' ability to have an insight into themselves and their dilemmas. But doesn't psychotherapy give one insight, we might ask? It does, but what there is is retained by the playwright and then force-fed to us. The character is left out of the picture, remaining caught as clinical focus: while interacting with his fictional problems, he does not gain wisdom. Finally, because the very basis of many modern pessimistic tragedies is the constant bewilderment of the characters, there is no tragic sense of developing enlightenment for the audience, but rather static confusion. We see defeat—to no purpose of meaning.

PSYCHOLOGIC SIGHT

Today's characteristic psychologic level of perception is specifically psychological but also figuratively subpoetic and subphilosophical. In the first instance, it is easy to note cases of a Dreiser or an O'Neill clearly acknowledging his debt to Freud's classic analyses. Anderson's *Night Over Taos* is straight out of *Totem and Taboo*. Lynn Riggs said of his *Cream in the Well* what applies to the vision of almost any of the modern "sex" tragedies: "Freud is part of our heritage. Everyone ought to know his work—and most people do. Like an artist—for he is that too— he illuminates, stimulates, reminds."[1] That last verb is the significant one. Then there is the use of expressionism, as in scenes from *Streetcar*, or *Salesman*, or *The Great God Brown*. The style is chosen to get inside the brain of the interestingly abnormal character. We see things through his eyes, distorted. Like the Apollonian protagonist, we are seeing rather often "as in a dream."

Poetically and artistically, if tragedy is hoped for, I suggest this can be comment below the level of wisdom, perhaps even of true knowledge.

1. Quoted in W. David Sievers, *Freud on Broadway* (New York, 1955), p. 308.

Popular reaction might say this is only to be expected, what with the twentieth-century characters being so much more "sick" and "confused" than those of old. In the epoch of modern tragedy, however, these are as nothing compared to the willfully psychosexually sick perverts of the latest radical theatre, and old tragedy portrays its share of sick minds too. Still, the modern victims of major spiritual and mental disease experience few healthy moments in which to base a statement of the recognition of truth. Robert Mayo, Edmund Tyrone, The Young Woman, Alma, Brick, Laura, Mr. Zero, Blanche, et al.: these are people often sick in both mind and body, or with the minimum symptom of the chronically broken view of living. Remember Williams's familiar focus, directed at the weak and unusual people for whom he feels. "Williams' special compassion is for 'the people who are not meant to win,' the lost, the odd, the strange, the difficult people—fragile spirits, who lack talons for the jungle."[2] Elsewhere, people like Happy and Biff are not "sick" but they are just as confused. Their society allows men to succeed who can hardly box, run, or weight-lift at all: their knowledge of values as gained from Willy Loman. Isadore Berchansky in *The Hand of the Potter* is both sick *and* confused by any measure, and Dreiser chose significantly weak people to be the only "friends" Isadore has. His parents are the victims of their poverty and misassimilation in a new social order. His sympathetic sister Masha is herself crippled and powerless: nature at work again. True, this is by no stretch of imagination a major play, and the expression of Dreiser's sympathies is extremely crude, but the bias is essentially the same as in Williams and considerable amounts of O'Neill.

No doubt the neuroticism of our "sick" characters is more annoyingly evident because the playwrights of this century are naturally more armed to talk about anxiety problems in more informed clinical detail, or are simply aware that dilemmas usually produce psychological problems in the end which are key difficulties—more than alternatives of action or dependence on dogmas of religious or other faiths. Yet the openly depicted neurotic does not necessarily command our aesthetic admiration merely because he is helpless. John Gassner points out: "The neurotic is cured only when he is brought out of the nightmare world of his inner conflicts by his recognition and understanding of their nature and source.

2. "The Angel of the Odd," *Time*, 9 March 1962, p. 53.

. . . When a dramatic character lacks the stature to understand reality
. . . to understand after he has had experiences that compel understanding,
we are deprived of the possibility of achieving identification on a sufficiently high level of enlightenment."[3] Identification again? Partly, but
directed now toward an insight. It is a simple matter: we ask at least as
much strength and vision from the tragic protagonist as *we* have—*somewhere* in the play. If he shows less, the theory is absolute: we are in danger
of comedy or pathos.

Let's check this out at some length, with a modern character who in
most other respects is quite wonderful. Blanche expresses *feelings*, often
beautiful and sensitive and right, but almost no knowledge.

Sick people, like Blanche, represent the "good," with whom we must
sympathize according to the emphasis of Williams's play. Blanche's own
comments affirm the premium placed on weakness:

BLANCHE: Sick people have such deep, sincere attachments.
MITCH: That's right, they certainly do.
BLANCHE: Sorrow makes for sincerity, I think.
MITCH: It sure brings it out in people.
BLANCHE: The little there is belongs to the people who have
experienced some sorrow.

Later she is forced to conclude:

I never was hard or self-sufficient enough. When people are soft
—soft people have got to shimmer and glow—they've got to put
on soft colors, the colors of butterfly wings, and put a—paper
lantern over the light. It isn't enough to be soft.

Blanche knows bitterly that softness is not allowed in the survival pattern,
but Williams prefers and defends softness. The weak are thus destined to
become weaker and the strong stronger. Stanley's stock increases by
natural selection. Ergo: to be weak is to be right, to be human? This is
obviously a very simplistic conclusion, but isn't it *emotionally* what
Williams is saying?

Notice how important the trauma over the perversion and death of
Allan Gray is to Blanche's character. It is essential that it be viewed as
somehow sufficient to bring her to her promiscuity:

3. John Gassner, *Theatre in Our Times* (New York, 1954), p. 65.

> After the death of Allan—intimacies with strangers was all I
> seemed able to fill my empty heart with. . . . I think it was panic,
> just panic, that drove me from one to another, hunting for some
> protection—here and there, in the most—unlikely places—even,
> at last, in a seventeen year old boy but—somebody wrote the
> superintendent about it—"This woman is morally unfit for her
> position."

This and kindred tendencies are to be her main weaknesses, but they say
nothing about Blanche's tragedy beyond the physical and psychological
level. Her sensitivity, which ought to be her tragic greatness, is largely a
function of traumatic derangement. As a case history more than a tragic
heroine, her derangement is actually rather ordinary. The pessimistic
facts of life tell us that insanity is all too common today. What should
be Blanche's exceptionality is not far enough removed, by Williams's
perspective, from the "sensitivity" existing in numerous types of patients
in mental hospitals. Blanche wants to live, and she understands a kind
of ethic in this better than do the other characters in the play. But her
heavy psychological bases make it inappropriate for her to project meaning into the world from what she understands about her downfall. Perspective is further weakened by the necessity of showing everyone existing
on a sensual plane. Although not necessarily neurotic, the other characters learn almost nothing from the lives they live; their senses are too
busy with animal satiation. Even the DuBois sisters, when their sexual
senses drive them, act blindly. This being one of the deliberate images
of *Streetcar*, no one is left to strike a tragic contrast between the real and
the ideal.

Williams knows life as a terrifying trial, but he claims that his artistic
outlook does not end in such futility:

> Q. Do you have any positive message, in your opinion?
> A. Indeed, I do think that I do.
> Q. Such as what?
> A. The crying, almost screaming, need of a great worldwide
>   human effort to know ourselves and each other a great deal
>   better, well enough to concede that no man has a monopoly
>   on right or virtue any more than any man has a corner on
>   duplicity and evil and so forth. If people, and races and na-

tions, would start with that self-manifest truth, then I think that the world could sidestep the sort of corruption which I have involuntarily chosen as the basic, allegorical theme of my plays as a whole.[4]

This "positive message" does not enter into Williams's plays enough to make him less pessimistic. The message comes to us indirectly, spurred by witnessing the horror on the stage. Williams certainly has the compassion of which he speaks, but only for the sensitive and abnormal persons his personality prefers—and Williams's pessimism proves over and over again that these people cannot live to reassert their sensitive values. Thus, it is rather a negative message, and it presupposes an objectivity and willingness in the audience to deduce the need for better human understanding because of the implicit warning in a violent display of corruption. This is a great deal to ask of a modern audience, so highly propagandized itself about psychoanalysis, political chaos, and the imminence of doomsday. Also, it is absurd to think that Williams would "involuntarily" choose corruption "as the basic, allegorical theme" of his plays so consistently were he not stressing darkness far more than light. Although he can show us how *not* to live, his pessimism does not equip him for displaying or suggesting a program for the ideal, for positive life, which is a product of tragic enlightenment.

Williams approves of more of us being friends and lending a helping hand, such as the doctor's hand offered at the close of *Streetcar* (as he states his central value: "When you ignore other people completely, that is hell."), but the process of evolution is only increasing the number of enemies. We cannot believe that Blanche, the only "human" person in the play, is strong enough to regenerate her kind, or is not too far degenerated herself to be considered a healthy "breeder" in the allegorical sense in which she is cast. In the trap of the world, her brand of sensitivity hopelessly exposes her to further abuses. As Williams defines it, sensitivity's own attributes are self-weakening because the sensitive person is too easily shocked by constant injustice, evil, and brutality. The insensitive can absorb life without serious trauma. They copulate and survive. As Stella says to Stanley:

4. Tennessee Williams, "The World I Live In," reprinted in Goodman, *Drama On Stage*, p. 294.

> You didn't know Blanche as a girl. Nobody, nobody, was tender
> and trusting as she was. But people like you abused her, and
> forced her to change.

And we see her only in this "changed" state. With Mitch's faith in her
destroyed, Blanche is completely alone. The Kowalskis return to what
they were doing before Blanche came, and the cycle of evil and meaninglessness, made gratifying only by sexual communication, continues. Stanley clutches Stella like a child seeking attention to distract its mother
from the act of mischief. Stella receives his obeisance, signifying the fact
that the world on the stage is unmoved and unchanged. Seeing the
world's corruption, Williams's rather fearful and pessimistic reaction is
to show, not what might have been, but what *is* happening to the weak
and unusual people for whom he is able to have feeling. With such
people, Williams is able to create great drama. But their stories are not
the matter for tragedy: the tragic loser must have the potential which
pessimism is unable to grant him and he must have been, at some time, a
supreme winner.

It is true that Williams does succeed in making such poetic use of his
symbols of sensuality and corruption that his work has broader implications than mere melodrama. The poetic expression of the dark side of
this life force is still Williams's prime meaning and contribution—and it
is a valid one even if it does not become "tragic" unless the spectator's
personal, subjective, and perhaps neurotic involvement interprets it as
such. But neurotic involvement would be perception without perspective
on the real, the poetic, and the ideal. Blanche's story, by implication only,
is a tear shed for modern, antisocial man. It might be tragic if we were
willing to recognize tragedy in man's becoming so antisocial that he communicates only in animal terms. But Williams's tragedy of sensitivity is
not so demonstrably universal, and I think we know there are more types
of men and possibility than in Williams's two simplistically warring allegorical factions. Moreover, symbols, like the statistics of war dead,
cannot have as much irrevocably tragic meaning as the loss of a single
great heroic figure, whom we know directly and fully, and who enacts a
meaning of life. It is no secret that Williams is unable to find real meaning in existence on which he might base *anagnorisis*.

Inevitable and consistent psychological damage thus ruling out some shred of positive discovery, a question of eugenics arises. Tragedy, most unrealistically as far as history and science certify thus far, posits a race of higher and stronger people capable of a moment of supralogical sight. Tragedy finds the representative of the troubled society in the person of someone with at least a hint of the superman in him, and allows its audience to assume that others might be around in the future. In a way, the tragic figure is even expected to procreate through his spirit: the activity of one Hamlet or Oedipus makes it likelier that there will be two, or four, or eight Hamlets or Oedipuses the next time man tries to answer the big question. The Greek and Elizabethan tragic characters become confused or "sick" largely after the obstacle appears, and their fatal conflict with it restores them to perceptiveness and a knowledge which is of use to us.

NEW TRAGIC MEANINGS

What is offered instead? The tragedies of the epoch have come up with certain substitutes for enlightenment.

When Willy talks to Bernard about the change in Biff after Biff had gone to Boston, Willy's conscience troubles him. He knows Biff's discovery of his philandering crushed his son's faith in him. Willy has to ask the young man he had once ridiculed as a bookworm why Biff gave up after that. Bernard tells him, and then gives Willy some more advice:

BERNARD: Good-by, Willy, and don't worry about it. You know, "If at first you don't succeed. . . ."
WILLY: Yes, I believe in that.
BERNARD: But sometimes, Willy, it's better for a man just to walk away.
WILLY: Walk away?
BERNARD: That's right.
WILLY: But if you can't walk away?
BERNARD: I guess that's when it's tough.

Not being able to "walk away" is Miller's idea of tragedy: "I take it . . . that the less capable a man is of walking away from the central conflict of the play, the closer he approaches a tragic existence."[5] Well, *what* man? And *what* conflict? This may only point out the obvious inevita-

5. Miller, *Collected Plays*, p. 7.

bility of any tragedy, and there remains the question of the significance of the contest. Willy does not walk away from suicide because he sees it as an escape and a way to give his family money. Thus he is partly a martyr. During his career, however, he walked away from many things many times—one of these being the truth.

Willy is the unenlightened man who is correspondingly inarticulate. The Lomans cannot talk to one another. When the final blow comes, and the last plan for having Biff realize himself for the sake of the family is defeated, Willy can make only a pathetic attempt to communicate with the earth to ease his disorientation:

> Oh, I'd better hurry. I've got to get some seeds. I've got to get some seeds, right away. Nothing's planted. I don't have a thing in the ground.

He *feels* emotional loss, but *knows* little about it. Compounding this, Willy never stops lying to himself: "Ben, that funeral will be massive!" But the suicide produces nothing, and hope is not in the least increased. Worst of all for Willy, almost no one comes to the funeral. Nobody even pays him the attention of blaming him:

> LINDA: But where are all the people he knew? Maybe they blame him.
> CHARLEY: Naa. It's a rough world, Linda. They wouldn't blame him.

So the pitiful and sentimental, not the tragic, mood persists to the end. Linda can only say in eulogy what is meaningful to her small existence, thus increasing pity:

> I can't understand it. At this time especially. First time in thirty-five years we were just about free and clear. He only needed a little salary. He was even finished with the dentist.

The scene is almost unbearably sad, and even quite beautiful, but the pathetic effect then is precisely that Willy Loman did die in vain. What happens to him is the pessimistic illustration of existence in our monster society. The author evaluates the meaning of the conclusion this way:

How can we respect a man who goes to such extremities over something he could in no way help or prevent? The answer, I think, is not that we respect the man, but that we respect the Law he has so completely broken, wittingly or not, for it is that Law which, we believe, defines us as men. The confusion of some critics viewing *Death of a Salesman* in this regard is that they do not see that Willy Loman has broken a law without whose protection life is insupportable if not incomprehensible to him and to many others; it is the law which says that a failure in society and in business has no right to live. Unlike the law against incest, the law of success is not administered by statute or church, but it is very nearly as powerful in its grip on men. The confusion increases because, while it is a law, it is by no means a wholly agreeable one even as it is slavishly obeyed, for to fail is no longer to belong to society, in his estimate.[6]

Thus for Willy this is a law of pessimism. It is pessimistic to believe, in the first place, that such a law exists. The defensive attitude which it manufactures in the protagonist further negates the possibility that life includes happiness and mutual assistance among human beings. Willy sees it as a law of society because his perception of society is ordinary and limited—like that of the ordinary spectator.

Miller believes that tragedy springs from "the underlying fear of being displaced, the disaster inherent in being torn away from our chosen image of what and who we are in this world."[7] Any related *anagnorisis* would thus concentrate on the *effect* of loss. This means the tearful and dim view of the little human being who was justified in dreaming anything he wished about himself. (He is quite an autistic thinker; he has undisciplined imagination in his wishful thinking.) He can do this because, pathetically and in his pessimistic knowledge, he was destined never to make the grade. "Both Miller's theory of tragedy and its application to the play are subject to debate. Is 'our chosen image of what and who we are' always acceptable, and is it, in Willy's case, worthy of the respect that alone can give us tragic exaltation? Since Miller refused to accept

6. Ibid., pp. 35–36.
7. John Gassner, *A Treasury of the Theatre* (New York, 1950), p. 1061.

the validity of the hero's fictitious view of himself, did the author waste compassion and respect on him?"[8]

If Miller denies the possibility of insight, Maxwell Anderson makes a self-conscious try for it in several of his pseudotragedies. Take that mock-Elizabethan speech of enlightenment at the end of *Winterset* provided by Esdras. He proclaims: ". . . this is the glory of earth-born men and women, not to cringe, never to yield, but standing, . . . [to] die unsubmitting. . . . I find no clue . . . no certain answer, yet is my mind my own. . . ." This surface hope bears no relation to the play just ending. Mio has found and learned nothing save the slimy evil he expected from the very beginning. We remember, for instance, that Mio even doubts the justification of revenge:

> It was bad enough that he
> should have died innocent, but if he were guilty—
> then what's my life—what have I left to do—?
> The son of a felon—and what they spat on me
> was earned—and I'm drenched with the stuff.

Anderson's real belief is that spirited striving is senseless, and Eleanor Flexner's comment on the speech of insight is also an apt summary of the effect of final meaning competing with attitude:

> With his useless wisdom, his purposelessness, his hopelessness, Esdras is the incarnation of futility, of a philosophical idealism completely dissociated from reality. Yet Anderson so constructs his play as to make Esdras the survivor who pronounces over the bodies of Mio and Miriamne . . . a valedictory which is unequalled for its empty idealism, whose phrases are devoid of any significance in terms of actuality. Now either the architecture of the play fails utterly to convey the dramatist's real meaning— which in the case of a craftsman such as Anderson is hardly likely—or it expresses his intention justly and we are driven to analyze it. The message of *Winterset*, as conveyed in this denouement, is that effort and strength are of no avail. A vague emotional concept is the be-all and end-all of existence. Best of all is to die young.[9]

8. Ibid.
9. Flexner, *American Playwrights, 1918–1938*, p. 111.

Elmer Rice tries, rather suddenly, to do the same sort of thing with *Street Scene*. He shows how Rose Maurrant's experiences with her surroundings, culminating in the horror of her parents' violent end, lead her to develop a hard-bitten philosophy of isolation as the safest way of life. This is part of Rice's pessimistic message in the play, and he treats it as a denouement of insight. Rose decides she must live through, and depend only on, herself:

> I don't think people ought to belong to anybody but themselves.
> I was thinking that if my mother had really belonged to herself,
> and that if my father had really belonged to himself, it never
> would have happened. It was only because they were always
> depending on somebody else for what they ought to have had
> inside themselves. . . . That's why I don't want to belong to
> anybody, and why I don't want anybody to belong to me.

Rose does go away from her terrible environment, but the closing words of the play (from a neighbor) show that she is still trapped. She will not escape the stamp of her surroundings:

> Well, you never can tell with them quiet ones. It wouldn't surprise me a bit, if she turned out the same way as her mother.
> She's got a gentleman friend, that I guess ain't hangin' around
> for nothin'. I seen him late last night, and this afternoon. . . .

This is essentially Rice's attitude toward the existence which has been pictured. Every development in the play, in faithful naturalistic reflections of the life that Rice apparently sees as empty, supports the belief that things will be no better wherever Rose is going.

According to one reviewer, however, the play caught hold of a great truth "that no matter what may be the pressure of one's environment, the only true power to meet the life of today must come from within the individual."[10] That would be fine, but terming such a selfish philosophy as Rose adopts as "truth" misses the sardonic and pessimistic point of the play's conclusion. Obviously, Rose's new belief is dangerous and false. Her parents lived alone, although jammed amid a teeming sea of people, without communicating with each other. Sam Kaplan lives alone in his sense of persecution and his intellectual overawareness of the futility of

10. R. Dana Skinner, review, *Commonweal*, 9 (January 23, 1929): 348.

life. The marriages pictured in the tenement society feature wrangling and infidelity rather than real love or happiness, and the husbands and wives are living for themselves. Rose's philosophical solution lacks the same element that had led to her mother's destruction: love. Inability to love will be the source of Rose's destruction. Her environment has taught her that mutual human dependence is destructive, but she has not seen a representative sample of mankind and his worldwide environment. Her environment has also retarded her in keeping her from having the spiritual equipment to be independent. Finally, that no man is an island is a far greater truth than the supposed message of her new convictions.

Instead, Rose's insight is cold-blooded defensiveness. It has destroyed Sam, the other "sympathetic" character in *Street Scene,* and it will defeat Rose as well. The lack of true enlightenment on the stage precludes our heightened understanding of misfortunes presented with about the same kind of helpless inevitability and ordinariness as an automobile accident. Stark Young concludes:

> Is it possible that anyone who could understand the values of the first act of "Anna Christie," for example, or a play of Chekhov's, could fail to see that the last act in "Street Scene" . . . is empty and made-up? The girl has found her mother shot, seen blood, at the hospital she has seen her mother die without speaking, she has seen her father caught and torn and bleeding, the Jewish boy, who loves her so much, offers to leave everything and go away with her, and she stands there making a little speech about dependence on one's self. . . . If this Anna Maurrant's life and death really bit into us, cost us something, instead of providing a mere thrill and the comfort of pseudo-thought afterward, would we not wreck the stage for rage when we see how little this matter has stung the dramatist?[11]

If Rose's epilogue is enlightenment, it does not even develop in the same key or line of reasoning as the body of the play. The preceding scenes are merely displays, with very little sign of commentary or symbol, and their reasoning is the arbitrary pattern of life in an environment of helplessness. Suddenly, however, an attempt is made to shift the action into a lesson

11. Stark Young, review, *New Republic,* 57 (January 30, 1929): 297.

and a credo aimed at combating the environment which only ends in midair. The only conclusion is that the credo is no match for a pessimistic view of the power of the environment. It is transient observation unrelated to the big sweep of the continuum of human spirit.

A final illustration of the new conception of enlightenment is the way in which O'Neill ends "The Haunted," the last play of the *Mourning Becomes Electra* trilogy. In the final moment, Lavinia says to the world:

> ... I'm the last Mannon. I've got to punish myself! Living
> alone here with the dead is a worse act of justice than death or
> prison! I'll never go out or see anyone! I'll have the shutters
> nailed closed so no sunlight can ever get in. I'll live alone with
> the dead, and keep their secrets, and let them hound me, until
> the curse is paid out and the last Mannon is let die! (With a
> strange cruel smile of gloating over the years of self-torture.)
> I know they will see to it I live for a long time! It takes the
> Mannons to punish themselves for being born!

And as the very last image of the play, "Lavinia pivots sharply on her heel and marches woodenly into the house, closing the door behind her." O'Neill has made his version of what is "learned" very clear. Enlightenment is out of the question. The new *anagnorisis* is reveling in the inheritance of despair.

ENLIGHTENMENT LOST

I believe the final impression of the authentic tragedy is a hint of the future, and the future's possibility, colored by the enlightenment gained through the extraordinary interaction of tragic extremes. While there has been (on the surface) more evil than good in the plot, the final thrust is one of optimism. Understanding has been left behind for the world of the play, and for us. Understanding means placing things in a system, and this system, for tragedy, derives data on where we go from here. The catharsis is meaningful pain, the process from *Poiema*, to *Pathema*, to *Mathema*.[12] The *Mathema* belongs to an apt etymology for "perception."

12. As used by Kenneth Burke via Francis Fergusson.

But the fall is paradoxical, as we have seen earlier and as others have analyzed far more thoroughly. And how do we know the enlightenment is worth something, since we cannot test it against the future? Why can't it simply end in exclamation: weep for this man, this was unjust, see what we do to one another? Myers, for one, says the climax of the tragedy is retrospective, *not* prophetic.[13] The pessimist playwright wishes us to *recognize* our evils and guilts, or respond intelligently and frankly to the world as it really is. Fine: recognition is a worthy end-product. But this is no kin to the "recognition" implied in the older sense of *anagnorsis* as enlightenment. Mirroring, or "facing up to it," is not necessarily under-standing. Recognition as understanding means measuring degrees on a scale so we know more about how and where evil was evil, *along with* confronting it as a fact. Not that matters are totally explained. Again, they are linked to the future, to an unknown possibility. But the whole notion of linear progress involves a mixture of improved understanding at the same time it affirms mystery in self-discovery. It is very like Karl Barth's opinion of God as wholly *other* than man: we must trust his system even though we don't understand it or know it. Why? Because otherwise man is doomed. Recognition as acceptance of the already known parallels such doom. In chapter 1 I noted Morse Peckham's strange opinion of tragedy as tranquilizer. Now consider the whole state-ment: "It has been said that tragedy reconciles us to life. Perfectly true. . . . And therefore tragedy says to us, 'If even an Oedipus can fail, if even a Lear can fail, you can forgive yourselves if you fail. Relax! . . .' In short, tragedy reconciles us to life by persuading us to submit to it. Tragedy encourages what Nietzsche calls the slave-morality of the Philistines."[14] That way, being swept along toward a future or more of the present has nothing to do with what you are. But it is just the reverse that is satisfying about *The Crucible* or *J. B.*, despite certain imperfections or moments of averageness elsewhere in the scripts. At the close of their play, J. B. and Sarah, through love as enlightenment, have acted in such a way as to be able to say, ". . . we'll know, we'll know. Blow on the coal of the heart." In *The Crucible*, Proctor will not let his name be used to further the propaganda of his confession, and the whole point of the final scene is his and Elizabeth's resistance through knowledge—and a gained attitude

13. Henry A. Myers, *Tragedy: A View of Life* (Ithaca, N.Y., 1956), p. 6.
14. In *Beyond the Tragic Vision*, p. 369.

on what they have done—so they can do what they must do to be human beings. "Show them no tear," Proctor warns, and he will not submit because: "I have three children—how may I teach them to walk like men in the world and I sold my friends?" Elizabeth maintains, "He have his goodness now. God forbid I take it from him." Are there tears as the execution drum rolls? Some perhaps. But there is something else—otherwise why the whole form of the play, building toward what is revealed in the action of the Proctors? It is enlightenment. As Kant defined *Aufklärung*: "Enlightenment is the liberation of man from his self-caused state of minority, which is the incapacity of using one's understanding without the direction of another." The rest of Salem was unable to do that, but we are able to take Proctor's cue.

Part Three:

TRAGEDY in AID of LIFE

10. LIVING and WRITING

In these two final chapters, I wish to examine the central difficulties of the pessimism-tragedy relationship and then suggest some alternatives to that condition. In this chapter, the focus is on the problem of living—and writing—in our time. As for the final chapter, perhaps a reaffirmation of the nature of *optimistic* tragedy can enrich a new look at the question of our future.

THE TRAGEDIAN'S ENVIRONMENT

How many protagonists, or playwrights, really accept having been born in this century? Are they psychologically so unique that they would be equally pessimistic in the nineteenth, seventeenth, or twenty-first centuries? And just how much useful work can a philosopher do when he rejects living with his present? Perhaps the dramatist of today must live in a uniquely anti-Utopian environment. What can he do with it? My argument against pessimism thus may be with this environment and not the man for, in a kind of Watsonian sense, it is what creates the pessimism and molds the playwright.

It is a truism that environment, broadly meant as physical and spiritual surroundings, must be especially right for the artist attempting tragedy.

The delicacy of the aesthetic-spiritual operation involved is suggested in Goethe's confession: "I am terrified at the idea of undertaking to write a tragedy, and I am almost convinced that I might destroy myself by that very effort."[1] Critics and historians have long theorized about the conditions which would define "favorable surroundings." They give us the insularity theory, the solidarity of national-ethnic *esprit*, or the presence of a strong mythic theology. Another theory is that great theatre—which usually involves a strong tragedy—is always preceded by a kind of renaissance syndrome, featuring an atmosphere lusting after thought and discovery which serves as a buffer between the present artistic aspiration and the relatively dark age preceding it. A reasonable notion—except that it doesn't explain the Greek tragedians, who overachieved straight out of nowhere.

Possibly statements of minimum requirements are more defensible. For tragedy, let us say, we need a cultural environment reflecting basic love of ideas, of wisdom following upon knowledge, where free investigation of creeds and credos is possible—perhaps with a society that is attracted to humanistically uplifting sensation, a society which has experienced its world and come back to know itself. (Even a primitive society, often the author of tragic ritual, almost meets the definition through the arranged knowledge of its magic.) It would seem that history tells us this much is demanded. The society of this environment should be aware of the sense of a future more than busy itself with the present alone. Another possible flaw, then: the Golden Ages of tragedy were much built on man's more usual desire to base himself on the past, and our own age is the one seeming more concerned with being attuned to the future. The problem is that this newer concern is only technologically and materially oriented. Nevertheless, our current environment could probably meet most such minimum requirements—*except where attitude derives from that environment*. Paradoxically, with our freedom of ideas, movement, and so forth—greater by far than in the Golden Ages—the attitude we conclude from it seems more restricted. Emotionally we feel commanded by the predominant attitude: conclude what you will, opine what you like—as long as it does not cling to a happy ending.

Yet just as self-consciously as in most of the other ages which were not

1. Quoted in T. R. Henn, *The Harvest of Tragedy*, p. 36.

golden, we wonder about and look for our *pietás, pathetiques,* and *appassionatas.* Our intention for environment still agrees with something like Shelley's conclusion that ". . . it is indisputable that the highest perfection of human society has ever corresponded with the highest dramatic excellence [that is, tragedy]: and that the corruption or extinction of drama in a nation where it has once flourished, is a mark of corruption of manners, and an extinction of the energies which sustain the soul of social life."[2] America never had an Elizabethan drama thus referred to, but we still believe in the goal. (Thus concerned, Shelley sat down and wrote *The Cenci:* far worse than the poorest of our contemporary pseudo-tragedies largely because the poet had no sense of the dramatic. Shelley's better intention did not narrow the near-perennial gap, whereas today we have the talent without the necessary attitudinal intent.) If only subconsciously, we hunger no less for tragedy; this is common to our environment and that of centuries ago. Leslie Fiedler sees America as the greatest remaining market for the vision, where the conflict of its polarities can still be recognized in perspective. "Of all peoples of the world, we hunger most deeply for tragedy; and perhaps in America alone the emergence of a tragic literature is still possible."[3] On the other hand, we know some significant new things about control of environment. Karl Jaspers defines "Seinvergewisserung" as reality-testing, verifying one's inner condition and relationship with one's environment. An objective kind of *Seinvergewisserung* seems indicated.

Even if social science hasn't proved it (though I think it has), one can see in modern serious plays that the twentieth-century playwright has an apparent new burden: a world in which man does not make his history, in which environment *is* without being the sum of socially united motives and drives. It is Society the Automatic Mechanism. Loren Eiseley, writing on "Science and the Unexpected Universe," thinks Nature contains that which does not concern us and that she has no intention of taking us into her confidence. He also says the unexpected will always confront us: "We are more dangerous than we seem and more potent in our ability

2. H. F. B. Brett-Smith, ed., *Shelley's Defence of Poetry* (Boston, 1921), pp. 38–39.

3. Leslie Fiedler, "Our Country and Our Culture," *Partisan Review,* 19 (May–June 1952): 294.

to materialize an unexpected which is drawn from our own minds."[4]
What about an unexpected *good*? The testimony of the plays shows that
the contemporary playwright would empathize with Albert Schweitzer's
summary picture of man in this world:

> The man of today pursues his dark journey in a time of darkness,
> as one who has no freedom, no mental collectedness, no all-
> around development, as one who loses himself in an atmosphere
> of inhumanity, who surrenders his spiritual independence and
> his moral judgment to the organized society in which he lives,
> and who finds himself in every direction up against hindrances
> to the temper of true civilization. Of the dangerous position in
> which he is placed philosophy has no understanding, and there-
> fore makes no attempt to help him. She does not even urge him
> to reflection on what is happening to himself.[5]

"To help him," he says. He must mean something more than philosophy
as the study of man thinking and living: in fact a positive philosophy of
where to go, as in tragedy. As for the climate in which there is no reflection: what kind of reflection? Several playwrights do reflect on what
we are like or what is happening to us; in this context Miller, Williams,
and Albee are deeply humane. But reflection is not necessarily philosophy, as when today's plays carry that unmistakable air of mere demonstration, and something special must happen to reflection in its artistic
container to allow tragic art. What we can say is that virtually no modern
tragedian likes his environment, and the scattershot condemnation that
sometimes follows *is* thinking—but it is sloppy thinking. Many such reflections can be challenged with the question: what is the difference
between *environment* and *existence*? Basic life environment I take to
mean nature, other people, current physical conditions for the organism,
and the like. Is *this* what is rejected, or what happens *in* it? Existence, the
fact of being, is timeless and essential; we have no data for saying it is
different in some Periclean high as contrasted with a Nuclear Age low.
Environment, however horrible, is redefinable every moment—a temporary historical condition. The pessimist's reasoning is flawed in tending

---

4. Loren Eiseley, "Science and the Unexpected Universe, "*American Scholar* 35
(Summer 1966).

5. *The Philosophy of Civilization*, p. 20.

not to distinguish the two. For example, in Euripides' *The Trojan Women*, there is no doubt at all that the environment posits utter sorrow. Troy has perished. Hecuba, the complete sufferer, concludes that "our fortune's course of action is the reeling way a madman takes" but she is conscious of the suffering being also "a theme for music, and the songs of men to come." Existence continues, is still worth informing; Troy is dead, but its death may mean knowledge for some man of the future.

If environmental psychology has relevance to this discussion, it *is* apparent that the artist's environment has changed for the worse. We have moved from some "tragedy" in the 1920s to none in the 1960s and early 1970s. He must now create in the age of the visual (how do you express ethical and philosophical statements without words?) and the transitory sensation, a time of sociopolitical shocks and psychic instability, an era of amoral antiabsolutism, the collectivized anti-individual, nonwill, determinist economics—and unprecedented permissiveness. Happiness is purchasing power, which I suppose is as good a reason as any for abstract antihumanism in art. A generalization about the atmosphere of the 1920s will hardly do for today, but the changes which have occurred are those which do not refute pessimism. That very movement contains the problem. Our "ages," as we popularly labeled them, used to be ten years long; before that, a score or more. Now we have an "age" every three years or so; perhaps next it will be two, and so on, until time as container and anchor loses all value and meaning. The epoch's tragedian or serious dramatist finds this unsettling, of course, because a moral view by, for, and of the society is never at the head of any of the movements which define these mini-ages. There is no settled frame of reference to convince him he can offer men a look at where they are or ought to be going. This is where Schweitzer's view of a surrendering philosophy seems most justified.

Thus there is no blanket modifier for our time. Atomic? Space Age? Concerned? Psychedelic? Pornographic? No one is enough, and no one can be sufficiently elastic of description. The change and dynamism suggested in this little semantic dilemma should be implicitly exciting, except that the names we would try to apply would usually refer to something we are trying to control rather than to any agreement as to what we are and what we believe in. That's not a very positive situation to be in. The appropriate names for the Age of Discovery, the Age of Reason, and the Age of The Enlightenment justly suggest a rather different sort of society. Political disunity, for one thing, did not have to mean widespread cultural and ethical disunity. Granting the material accomplishments of our age, it has so far held no universal purpose and no style for modern man in general. The ordinary man of the day accepts the style made for him by the secondary forces of industry, technology, advertising, and other nonphilosophical systems of thought. The world is frenetic, true; a handy excuse. Yet he himself does not believe in positive change amid the energy. Typically, he and we meet conditions of the moment but the next moment can demand an amendment to our ethics, morals, or credos. Principle not being a primary force, we can rationalize anything. Tragedy reflects such contemporary beliefs. Where does it posit order: in sex, success, God, love? From *Machinal* to *The Adding Machine* to *Death of a Salesman* to the latest experiment in confrontation we see reflected the belief in little if anything; small wonder a hope for united conviction is unreasonable.

The relatively mysterious nature and universe of Sophocles and Shakespeare have become, through the labors of science, far more knowable, and they no longer require our rituals of homage and explanation. Environment cooperates or harms according to its own laws, and there is little we can do to change it. Our materialism tries to mollify us in this knowledge, only to show the modern image of man as dwarfed beside the edifice of automation, institutionalized satiation, and increased consciousness of man's psychobiological smallness in relation to nature and history. So instead of making tragedy, it may be understandable to express what little real drama can be found in our rootlessness:

> It is no wonder, then, that the greatest artists of the theatre feel isolated. They have looked farther and deeper into the private and public chaos of the century, and their shudder is not easily exorcised by a full larder, by a temporary rise in employment and income, and by a few more factory-made conveniences. They turn to existentialism, to communism, or to the sheer nihilistic despair of O'Neill's "The Iceman Cometh." . . . The most creative artists become the most disoriented. They favor hybrid forms that are rootless and therefore are incapable of ripening into fruit.[6]

6. Gassner, *Theatre in Our Times*, p. 12.

This estimate by John Gassner, true of theatre some years back, is still true of living and writing today. The forms are even more hybrid, and purposes less aesthetic—for example, the new expression geared to "blowing the mind." This is the "atrophy of sensibility" that Herbert Read speaks of in connection with his urgent conclusion that alienation is "inimical to art."

Is the "rootedness" of conformity and nonquestioning a cure? In contrast to our mini-ages, it may have been too uniform a situation to have almost nothing (comparatively speaking, relative to today's situation) but Mozartian music in the Age of The Enlightenment, or hardly anything but Romantic art in the mid-nineteenth century. But is the opposite extreme a net gain? History, at least, supports something like the idea that one cannot stand for everything and anything and expect to produce genres of art which require a universal moral statement and vision of the problem of life. There are limits to the principles and styles by which men live and aim their ambitions. "Principle" by nature includes "limit."

Not that we have any monopoly on alienation. As Erik Erikson points out, earlier man felt a lack of link with his environment, estranged by the agricultural, industrial, and mercantile labors that helped mark him human. The mobility of modern man means further psychological loss of roots. So man's identity is artificial and acquired while the animal's is instinctive: what, then, is a good relation to one's environment? Is "rootedness" always the goal? Progress, ironically, means fewer roots because today progress must add complexities to the conventions of living. We would probably have to pay for our rootedness through regressive policies regarding mobility, social change, and the like. Thus we experience fear, as Erikson says, because we know our identity is technically augmented. However, he concludes that "there is no reason to insist that a technological world, as such, need weaken inner resources of adaptation which may, in fact, be replenished by the good will and ingenuity of a communicating species."[7] But what attitude is prerequisite to such helpful communication, and who is to stimulate and organize it? Once we counted on our humanist artists. Now, how do our tragedians' visions contribute?

In our fragmented world, there are as many disparate attempts to cap-

7. Erikson, *Insight and Responsibility*, pp. 103–4.

ture man's "modern malaise" (and thus communicate) as there are play-wrights who have attempted tragedy or the play of serious commentary. The range runs from Anderson's martyr to Williams's erotic psychotic; from O'Neill's pathetic dreamer to Miller's pathetic liar. The more they aim for tragedy, the more pessimistic they are. The playwright is just as susceptible to the environment—if not more so—as those with whom he communicates. Thus he finds himself in disagreement with the identity-giving practices of the past. Today's critic and spectator then ask him to do things which he is both unable and unwilling to do, so the playwright (when he turns critic or expresses his theory of tragedy) often plays a defensive role which sounds a note of something less than "good will." Arthur Miller defends the tragedy of the common man—more endearing politically than artistically. Maxwell Anderson, in "The Essence of Tragedy," endorses tragedy as a "religious affirmation" without achieving any kind of affirmation on stage. And, although he produces a one-sided and pessimistic view on the subject of tragedy's most central function, Eugene O'Neill supports a didactic social-problem role for the tragic genre.[8]

They, and we, apparently know the environment and its facts too well. According to some, the darkest conclusions of the knowledge are all to the good. As the philosopher Gurdjieff puts it, "so long as man is not horrified in himself, he knows nothing about himself."[9] I suspect Krutch would have said to that that we know too much. As he viewed pessimistic and jaded knowledge:

> A too sophisticated society . . . one which, like ours, has out-grown not merely the simple optimism of the child but also that vigorous, one might almost say adolescent, faith in the nobility of man which marks a Sophocles or a Shakespeare, has neither fairy tales to assure it that all is always right in the end nor tragedies to make it believe that it rises superior in soul to the outward calamities which befall it.
>
> Distrusting its thought, despising its passions, realizing its

8. O'Neill proclaimed: "The playwright of today must dig at the roots of the sickness of today as he feels it—the death of the old God and the failure of science and materialism to give any satisfying new one. . . ." Quoted in M. J. Moses, ed., *American Theatre* (New York, 1934), pp. 267–68.

9. P. D. Ouspensky, *In Search of the Miraculous* (London, 1950), p. 218.

impotent unimportance in the universe, it can tell itself no stories except those which make it still more actuely aware of its trivial miseries.[10]

Will the environment get worse? Without a doubt, the facts of the sixties and seventies can motivate more terror than those of the twenties. As to the years beyond, this is a question I wish to build toward on the way to a discussion of the concept of the future in my final chapter. In the meantime, it is clear enough that the environment has not been good to the tragedians of the epoch—so long as they operated under pessimistic attitude. But if attitude cannot relate to existence for all its interdependence with environment, why blame the playwright? First, change the environment.

That priority is impractical, if not philosophically cowardly. At this point, a revision of attitude would have to precede significant reform of the surroundings. In any event, furthermore, the issue of blame for the nature of the playwrights' vision is unimportant. The obvious fact is that we need different playwrights—who will either be selective about reaction to environment, or transcend its admitted limitations with stories of a different shape and substance. What would happen if we experimented with *hope*?

HOPE AND PERCEPTION

The hypothesis would be: add hope to the perception of environment, and to the conception of life therein in expressing a philosophy for the life. Here we move above recognition and reality into an area of myth and purposive imagination. What does hope *do*?

The archetypal tragedy is ritual baited with hope. In my conclusions on modern tragic dramaturgy I have already suggested that the shape of tragedy is very much a special manipulation of time; it becomes *mythic time*. Myth in tragic experience is an adventure in a sacred or superhuman history, and the oldest myths at least show how a concept of existence or a human condition was born through the actions of whatever supreme forces started Time going—by making an existence, where before there

10. "The Tragic Fallacy," in *European Theories of the Drama*, ed. Barrett Clark, p. 521.

was nothing. Myth concerns, Mircea Eliade notes, "what the gods did in the beginning."[11] As a major factor in the creative process, this principle was out of date as early as the late Hellenic tragedy, but the study of connotations in myth-time concepts can still lead us to a truer understanding of the action of tragedy's attitude. It's still a factor in figuring out the material for an effective tragedy.

Myth is mentioned constantly in essays on tragedy, and has received far more profound and scholarly treatment in some of the essays than I can or will give it here. For now, my only subject is the coexistence of myth and hope. This is how hope becomes a kind of dimension for moving above the environment. In it, a special perspective comes into play as we react to authentic tragedy's "suggestions." Time as dimension helps us measure either our looking ahead or looking back, to be able to place ourselves amid those perspectives. Hope and time interact in tragic myth as the artist recounts essential beginnings, mixing these with a contemporary fiction so that the spectator may imagine some positive possibilities in looking ahead. I will try an illustration.

Go back to the example of the real-life shocking event. Dwelling on it, in order to live with it or to understand it, what has to happen next? Where is the mind led? Keep at it and eventually one gets into guesswork, or religious credos, or philosophy generally. Earthbound reasoning leads to dead ends (such as: why war and aggression? why must that good youth die when an old invalid lives on?), and the art versus nature theory involved here is familiar and obvious. But the theory is more than that if we want to move on. There is no way out save by a certain leap of faith, where we make up "what might have been" and then transfer it to ourselves. We move into hope, and it is not unreasonable to say it is a selfish act. The archaic forms of tragedy illustrate this, though without such objective self-consciousness, in their strength-providing images of potential. (Fake? Only the future could ever tell.) Why did societies in the days of archetypal tragedies keep on going in the face of a dark present? Because primitive religion enforced certain tragic teachings: the stories, the myths, were rallying points of entertaining propaganda—to the effect that time would bring rewards. Later on, with a less impressionable

11. In *Myth and Reality,* which is an excellent summary of the whole question of relevance to myth.

proletariat, tragic myth was still an essential statement of the spirit with which the contemporary society *wanted* to agree.

The "passion" of the Egyptian man-god Osiris showed the common Egyptian man that his sufferings were part of his eventual ascension to a state of near-godliness, and that even a lowly man could identify with a god—becoming vicariously greater than he could ever hope to be in his real life, before he perceived the tragedy. (Five thousand years ago royal barges probably traveled up and down the Nile, fitted and manned strictly for the performance of the Osiris myth and its relevance to the coronation of new mortal kings, so that the hopeful propaganda was kept sufficiently before the peoples of the kingdom.) This fundamental function of tragedy was the same as that of most primitive religion: it made man closer to a mysterious supreme being or force, or to a vague state of "betterness," and helped him to believe he was better than he saw himself to be in his day to day surroundings—since his representative mortal hero could (by man's own invention) become heroic and godlike on behalf of ordinary man. Osiris suffered and was torn to pieces by a symbolic enemy of man, Setekh. (Characterized as a brother, i.e., the other side of self, the pessimistic fact of man's sometime aggressiveness?) His reincarnation as a god was the start of a great period of prosperity of the imagination through myth. As in most tragedy, man had simply decreed for himself a bit of immortality. Even the unhappy ending, the dismemberment, was "happy" and good for man; the deliberately scattered pieces of the body were symbolically seen as so many fertile "seeds" of nourishment for the land.

In ancient Mexico, there was Tezcatlipoca. He was a great war hero of noble lineage, physically and spiritually beautiful, and his passion was called "The Sacrifice of the Beautiful Youth." This Adonis's perfection and destiny were literally manufactured by the Mexican priests. Adored as the living likeness of the primordial, undismembered "soul of the world," he wandered about Mexico for a specified time for all to see and identify with him before his ascension (really a proxy "test-flight" quest of the most daring "plane" his people could build) on the part of his fellow men. The culmination of his spiritual growth on earth was a sacrificial ceremony in which he was dismembered, much like Osiris.

In old Tibet, an early form of the present Dalai Lama served as the people's heroic representative. Again, like Osiris and Tezcatlipoca, he was an ambassador to greater and more godlike (albeit imaginary) states. This great Bodhisattva, or messenger of joyous tidings, called Srimekundan, was the living dramatization of man's fate as the Tibetans wished to picture it—through the destiny they had fashioned for him to enact. The illustrated question was the same, only rephrased in Buddhist terms: "What is man, and what determines his *karma*?" And the classic Buddhist answer is that his destiny grows out of his former incarnations. The nature of the hope is certainly different from the more Western myths, but hope as the transcending dimension of the experience is still there.

Srimekundan, or "Immanuel, the Blameless One," was also reared with great care—as the tragedian must likewise do with his fictional character of today. Like the modern Dalai Lama, he was selected from among the newly born by a complex ritualistic determination, becoming the "Chosen One." In the manner of his counterparts across the world, Srimekundan was forced to suffer on his way to reincarnation—which, for him, was becoming a Buddha or "perfect vessel of divine redemption" —and the form of this suffering was that he could never refuse a request made of him by any living creature.[12] By contriving the requests, the inventors of his myth forced him into exile, took his eyes and children and left him to wander Tibet, blind, with only his wife to comfort him. But when his selflessness was exhibited (his self-sacrifice being the equivalent of Osiris's or Tezcatlipoca's death at the hands of others), he was reincarnated and given back his possessions. His Nirvana was in abandoning earth, but through him man left behind had a way for deriving hope even from the seemingly hopeless situation.

Hope, then, exists and insists on a complete jump across the gap which separates the fact and the ideal. It establishes a distancing effect which directly admits the promising generalization about destiny. Three dimensions and five senses are not enough to justify the generalization. Hope is not concrete; even the etymology of the word refers to "springing." It is the beginning of the useful fiction, and the New Testament motto is fitting: "Hope maketh not ashamed" (Romans, 5:5). Nonetheless, it is not a complete denial of responsibile reasoning and practical life. There is no real contradiction between the two, writes Norman Cousins, because "the capacity to hope is not the natural enemy of an-

12. This, of course, would delight the Schopenhauer faction, all pain being desire via will.

alytical intelligence. It is a source of energy for creating new options. It helps to create new uses for logic. It sets people in motion and thus gives rise to new swirls, new contexts, new combinations. It gives reality a new face."[13]

LIFE-TEMPO AND FORM-TEMPO

My own hope at the moment is the merely editorial one that more substance will come to the surface of this essay if I move next to considering hope and time in art versus time in life. The optimistic tragic vision which I urge includes a special attitude toward time. There is a depth to time which it is the special business of tragic drama to convey. It occurs, though we can hardly grasp it, somewhere between knowledge of time and wisdom about time—or about the item within time. George Kubler's description, I think, sets off the right imaginative effort for conceiving this depth: "It is the interchronic pause when nothing is happening. It is the void between events. Yet the instant of actuality is all we can ever know directly. . . . The perception of a signal happens 'now,' but its impulse and its transmission happened 'then.' "[14] That is, there is an unbridged space involved which is not only chronological. Kubler's illustration is that men cannot fully sense any event until after it has happened, until it is history; it is like light just reaching us now from a star dead long ago.

Apply this image to the implications of the tempo of our reality or contemporary history, as against those of art form—not just the artist's creation of form as container, but form as comment on the problem of life. At first, this only sounds like the old argument on the art-life separation, the tragic in art *vs.* the tragic in daily life. Later we should see what it means to contemplate form as open, closed, widening, narrowing, strict, and the like. Although I said earlier that tragedy is very temporally oriented, it still can transcend life—and time—because, while there is linear or cyclic time in life, and linear time in the *form* of tragedy, what is ultimately suggested is dimensional time. It is a spatio-temporal relation that is, like time itself, not fully knowable.

13. Editorial, "Is It Possible to Be an Optimist?" *Saturday Review*, 5 November 1966, p. 26. See also Sidney Hook, *The Hero in History*, especially as referred to in chap. 11.

14. George Kubler, *The Shape of Time* (New Haven, Conn., 1962), p. 17.

For example: modern dramatists put themselves in the paradoxical situation of trying to keep pace with current chaos while trying to speak to contemporary fear at its own level. With all its veneer of symbolism, or naturalistic detail, or deterministic pessimism, much modern tragedy does little to combat the cult of mediocrity and the evil of the commonplace which are the antithesis of tragedy. It settles, in other words, for *life-tempo*. But it has always been the role of tragedy to maintain a balance between the moral order as a constant and material existence as a turbulent variable, and then suggest the new momentum of an ideal. That is *form-tempo*.

O'Neill's *The Great God Brown* illustrates this—and it should be anything but an easy defense for my case. O'Neill can't be faulted for lack of desire to make metaphysical leaps in tragedy, as in his "big theme" plays: *The Great God Brown, Strange Interlude, Lazarus Laughed,* and *Mourning Becomes Electra.* Sizing him up against the usual paragons, he may even look better than Aeschylus in this respect (who, we should acknowledge, had thematic visions on a large scale but fleshed them out less with intellect than with poetic repetition and reinforcement). In *The Great God Brown,* in any case, we have a play by America's premier tragedian which attempts a transfigured and poetical metaphor for capturing the essential tragedy of the personality at war with itself and the norms of its culture. The famous—or notorious—masks enacting the personality shifts and conflicts are only the most obvious marks of O'Neill's grand scheme. O'Neill intended to make Dion Anthony and William Brown more than portraits of the artist *vs.* the effective conformist; not topically, not literally, he wished to universalize their story towards an essence of people and themes connected with striving and falling short. The spectator can even feel a reach beyond our normal sense of dimensions into the mysterious regions of the metaphysical for the O'Neillian God or Ideal.

But the pseudopoetic transfiguration of the contemporary-life "problem" is built on next to nothing: an unsupported and one-dimensional assumption about modern existence. The artifice is extraordinarily empty; we haven't left the earth at all. Dion is presented as doomed before we even know him, and the play once again acts out the old predestination of O'Neill's sensitive artist, leaving us with a monotonous, gimmicky chronicle of Dion's mocking endurance of his life sentence and then the gratuitous shift to Brown's handy doom which follows from Brown's coveting of Dion's personality. The poetizing is awkward, and it isn't long before the spectator is again faced with pedestrian life-tempo in the guise of metaphor. O'Neill does not practice insight into essential virtues and values but instead window-dresses his take-it-on-faith vision of the destruction of the creative man. What does the destruction matter?

Under his mask, Dion Anthony is as unpoetic as unpoetized life: man in a moment of toenail-cutting, for instance. Worse, Dion is a staggering bore. O'Neill would have us believe he is an admirable painter but over the long stretch of his wait for death (eventually, the whole play spans eighteen years) he never paints anything to give the slightest evidence of the artistry and creativity that today's world is destroying. Moreover, he never says anything beyond the level of broken-record posturing, self-pity, and cynical grousing about the contrast between his dissolution and the life that goes on. Should we assume an *ethos* for him? How, when we know so little about him? In tough-minded terms, an hour after opening his mouth, Dion would be dismissed as a vacuous fraud by any circle of working artists—or art patrons. Rather than say anything real, Dion hides behind his acting, his pose, his mask, his mocking. (Time after time, O'Neill uses the stage direction "mocking, mockingly," for Dion's speeches.) He was "born without a skin," but this supersensitivity says nothing *about* life. "Why am I afraid to live. . . . Or rather, Old Gray-beard, why the devil was I ever born at all?" Dion cries. Even at the height of his passion, he wants to "dissolve into dew"—but why? Who hurt him? By Act One (seven years after the Prologue), O'Neill says Dion's face has "grown more strained and tortured. . . ." From what? He turns alcoholic. Why? Because O'Neill precasts him as frustrated with life? But from attempting what? Dion hasn't enough dramatic flesh, blood, will, and command of self to make human contact. His death-wish is thus unaffecting, humdrum, anything but poetical. Dion speaks of his "next incarnation" and tells the prostitute Cybel that "you've given me the strength to die. . . . Come soon, soon . . ." so that "tomorrow I'll have moved on to the next hell!" Even so, Dion claims shortly thereafter that: "I've loved, lusted, won and lost, sang and wept! I've been life's lover!" But that's not the Dion we see at all. This is mere statement rooted in the O'Neillian preconception of life's movement.

Dion hides behind his Pan mask, in mocking cynicism about roles and identity, but the world cares neither for the man below nor the man above

—or so the logic of O'Neill's stress would have us believe, though he spends no time on the substantive worth of either identity. Again an *ethos* is presumed, not proven. The one specific source of Dion's malaise that is mentioned is the mundane trauma of the four-year-old Dion bullied by Billy Brown. (Specifically, Billy destroyed a picture Dion was making and hit Dion with a stick.) We are expected to conclude from this that Dion had enough of a wound so that he decided to become "silent" and design "a mask of the Bad Boy Pan in which to live and rebel against the other boy's God and protect [himself] from His cruelty." To Dion, God can't be loved or trusted as long as there are Billy Browns walking around destroying Art.

After Dion dies, Brown himself is made to decide that the "best good is never to be born" because, via the Dion mask he now wears, Brown begins to know what life is like for the supersensitive. Again this comes down to a reading of life hopelessly stuck at the level of life. The reading can't rise because O'Neill himself has no stretch of vision left; he is chained to his preconception of life referents. (These include his mother, father, and particularly himself.) The characters are drawn simplistically, the parents and their sons being sheer American stereotypes based on the playwright's apparently instant bias about the tragedy of the creative man. Simple execution is a problem too, as in the awkward exposition that has to set up the cycle of nonfulfillment. As mentioned in so many cases already, the language pushes and themes are overstated. The poetic sense is precluded by life-bias tones, as in such disasters as Dion's remark to Cybel: "Your hand is a cool mud poultice on the sting of thought!" The people are subordinated to an unexamined notion of an American twentieth-century life-problem: no wonder they speak in prolix mottoes, never really breathing in life and exhaling sense, whether fearful *or* hopeful. The experience of *The Great God Brown* leads us back only to the assumed beginning. Cybel's final speech about life's cycles is said "with profound pain": "Always spring comes again bearing life. . . . but always, always love and conception and birth and pain again. . . ." I think this is presentation, not revelation.

What I'm calling life-tempo is the taking of time and what it "documents" as is, jerking along its continuum until it reaches the blank wall of finality, which in turn only refers back to the start of things that wound up that way. No new energies are generated. In *The Great God Brown*

Dion dies and Brown dies and even the form of the play (note the way the Epilogue repeats the setting of the Prologue) reminds us of mere cyclical existence and implication: a closed cycle at that, episodes along the path to the end. In an aesthetically better conception of the tragedy of existence, what is enacted is the opening of the cycle or a constantly redefined linearity which touches new sections of other cycles and lines. It refers ahead in imagination, then back—even as far as the primordial—for a cross- and future-referral which is unique: a new chapter of the always changing story of an implied ideal and how things are coming with that ideal. Now Aeschylus moves ahead of O'Neill after all. *Prometheus Bound* is a metaphor for a huge attempt at daring new dimensions, new "time," new truths. Prometheus ends his play buried in that mountain cave and in time, but with clear hints of emergence as himself and as the spirit he needs to affirm. A form is created to reveal and examine this ambition.

Roughly speaking, we might just say the modern would-be tragedy is too often too close to its age. Even Eugene Ionesco, defending a theatre of far different shape and spirit, writes of the value of rephased serious theatre:

> Some people reproach the theatre today with not belonging to its time. In my opinion, it belongs to it far too much. That is the weakness and cause of its impermanence. I mean the theatre belongs to its time at the same time that it does not belong to it enough. Each epoch requires the introduction of a certain incommunicable "out of time" within time, within the communicable. Everything is a moment circumscribed within history, of course. But in each moment there is all of history: every story is valid when it is trans-historical; in the individual one can read the universal.[15]

In part, he means *perspective*. It should be obvious that any future tragedians would have to part company with the vision of the merely actual. The form of the greatest tragedies at first connotes a move back in time, in search of what the philosophers call primordial time, the time wherein Ideals stood, to give shape to the setting-in-motion of historical time.

15. Eugene Ionesco, "Discovering the Theatre," *Tulane Drama Review* 4 (September 1959): 7.

Thus it is capable of exceptional perspective on man existing in all time. The initial act of reference is conservative (early in the play we have some clear prechaos idea of old values, the simple and definite balance between the good and the evil), and Freud's phrase about "the conservative character of instinctual life" is relevant and important here. Why would the instinctual side of man be "conservative"? "Conservatism," for now, would have the value of holding tragic art slightly back from the pace of physical flux, chaotic politics, and so forth. Today there is a great tension between the philosophical polarities in the question whether order precedes progress, or progress, order. Could the latter risk an order without understanding? Note how this involves the myth-time dichotomy: apply it in art, then in life, then apply the art to the life. As Stanislavski noted the effect of keeping up with alien governmental-social stabs into the future: "What is this path of the progress of art? It is the path of natural evolution. One must travel over it without hurrying. But the Revolution and its generation are impatient. New life does not want to wait; it demands quick results, another and a quickened tempo of life. Without waiting for natural creative evolution, it violates art, stuffing it with sharpness of form and content."[16] The environment of the Russian revolution which evoked that sentiment was roughly similar to today's, and the warning still holds; but, more than patiently not "hurrying," the necessary stance for the tragedian raises the question of a whole new aesthetics and metaphysics of time. It means doing this: first we chasten the motives of the actual world, taking that step behind life-tempo. Something like this perspective was also suggested by T. S. Eliot in his observation that every major work of art forces upon us a reassessment of all previous works. Tragedy, then, takes a broader view of the continuum of spirit than history. But in terms of our actual future daily life and its most insistent issues, tragedy's perspective later looks well forward just as it always eventually looks well upward, building optimism and progress out of fearful doubt and evil. Unlike the work of the would-be tragedians of this century, true tragedy can never come close enough to real events and real time to specifically criticize and reform dated history. Even if (as some scholars maintain) Aeschylus is denouncing an

16. Constantin Stanislavski, *My Life in Art* (New York, 1956), p. 566.

actual tyrant of his day in *Prometheus Bound,* anyone can agree that the fine thing about the play is Aeschylus's creation of the poetic and metaphoric posture of heroic rebellion against tyranny. Notice that today we do not really criticize *death,* which is a fundamental "tragedy" of existence, but rather the specifics of our environment, the finite things of life-tempo. This is acceptable—but only as long as we aim no higher than the problem-play.

The tempo of life I am speaking about occurs on the surface of life: events, fashion, passing fads of thought and conduct. It is interesting how these shift. They *must* shift because we do not expect to *get anywhere* with them. What is the ultimate goal of a fashion? Style and the like, or "problems," or "issues," change because their marketability or relevance is derived from being "in step" versus "out of step." The change is all too easily arbitrary, or else a product of simple causation. The tempo is not made to happen through the exercise of essential thought.[17]

What I am really doing now is moving toward a suggestion of tragic perspective. (I won't say it's definable.) Plato's *anamnesis* is still valid for the effort: this perspective is a practical part of the tragic ideal, giving rise to a form which can produce a metaphysical stretch aiming at that primal Ideal "way back there." Freud hints at the same abstraction as our present ego feeling which is a "shrunken residue" of a much more comprehensive bond between ego and the world, a kind of missing link in the relation of our ego to its historic essentiality. Freud tentatively compared this "past" of the mind to the past traditions and image of a city. Mythological illustration will talk about going backward through time, retracing the meaning of lives, with such seeking of *anamnesis* meant to project man out of his historical moment. This is a key discussion in Eliade's *Myth and Reality.* For man as spirit, Eliade says, "the essential precedes existence." Sartre says the same thing in a different argument, but the image of this artistic-spiritual march to the beat of a very different drummer comes out of the need to know both what can have taken place "back then" and what may take place in the future. "The need to find one's way into 'foreign' universes and to follow the

17. Technology usually takes it on the chin as analogy, e.g., the SST is created just because "it's possible" whereas its total human and humane use hasn't been comparably thought out.

complications of a 'story' seems to be cosubstantial with the human condition and hence irreducible."[18] It is perception on an entirely new dimension, ordinary human perception being slow enough as it is when it seeks meaning for the shifts in life-tempo. In tragedy, this distancing involved in form-tempo and perspective is a measurement of duration toward the Ideal ahead as against the original implied in the original fact of man, in primordial time.

But in more practical terms, what is this perspective required in writing authentic tragedy? For one thing, it is a vision which relates to reality as experienced by its audience, which is true of life in its components of characters and actions, with which real people can identify—and yet which, taken as a whole and therefore needing to be seen as a whole, is *not* merely real. The vision's story sets out to become myth and mystery, reaching optimistically into a dimension that is not available to us in our real experience or by any other means, tempting us to recognize truths about the gap between our actual selves and the never-achieved potential that we think lies dormant somewhere inside us. (Which is why, as far as we know in the present of its performance, it is a "mystery.") To accomplish this, the artist must stand back from his work to accept its arrangement of seemingly real incidents into a totality which is necessarily suprareal. For example, there is the credibility of spirit next to an incredibility of form in *Oedipus the King* or *The Bacchae*. Oedipus's saga is about as pleasurably improbable as a James Bond escapade; Sophocles needs the saga to allow the exceptional experiences which generate the revelations that keep Oedipus's search for truth moving. *The Bacchae* is similarly free to act out the excesses of its theme. The play says that it is mankind's own tragedy that he is awed into the beautiful, hypnotic terrors of spiritual fantasy and cannot instead produce a balance between his desires to explain the universe in rationalist terms and his primal drive to escape from it in orgiastic, ecstatic leaps. In such plays we see that the form is unreal, therefore capable of the Ideal, and therefore capable of applying some new-found perspective to the man watching the tragedy.

The perspective requires a very formal pattern, though form is not all.

18. Eliade, *Myth and Reality*, p. 191. For entire basis of this point, see his chap. 5, "Time Can Be Overcome."

Revelations are not merely logical, because the tragic perspective does not intend to lead us back into what we already know of life but instead almost literally beyond it. (Thus its linear extremity, to run "off the edge of the world.") Therefore we come to the seemingly preposterous mystery which demands perspective even to approach: that is, the event of personal reality is so different from the contrived event of art in magnitude and spirit that it could be said that anything that can happen in such reality, used as being complete in itself, can never satisfy the needs of tragic art because it will automatically be too familiar or too close to our own individual finitude. We cannot idealize about that which we know. We cannot attribute meaning to the random event which is what we *see*. Pessimism, in its cyclical reference, slams us once again into a present we have not left, while tragedy creates problems of perspective similar to seeing oneself in multiple mirrors via the reflection of an infinite reflection. It operates in a sort of fourth dimension and exists in the seclusion suggested by the old joke, "you can't get there from here." One knows the tragic event only vicariously and, to paraphrase Bharata, it tastes infinitely better that way. To illustrate: it would be completely improper to require the tragedian to actually set out to make his story significantly incredible or the world of his play remote or even exotic, and yet I suspect such qualities are incidentally important to the effect of the "good" classics of tragedy. In this sense, the modern plays are more rational. *Long Day's Journey into Night, Death of a Salesman, A Streetcar Named Desire,* and all their lesser kin tell of essentially "credible," "real," "relevant," "authentic," or "identifiable" contemporary human conditions. Next to these, the tales in *Oedipus, Hippolytus, The Eumenides, Faust, Andromacque, The Cid,* or *Polyeucte* are hokum; they defy direct connections, direct meaningful parallels, or quick understanding. Of course the main reason the general audience likes those "old costume plays" is the wrong reason (having to do with the pleasures of curiosity and fantasy) but, as for tragedy in other worlds and times, there is a substantive reason hidden beneath.

Mimesis regarding *anamnesis* is not enough. Tragedy's perspective is the imitation *of* the "imitation of an action." The first level of such indirection is the hero-myth itself, imitated out of the imagination; the next is the illusion involved in dramatizing the fiction. There is a clearer hint of this in Krutch's rejection of the recording of natural tragic action:

> . . . to say that tragedy is the *imitation* of a *noble* action is to be guilty of assuming, first, that art and photography are the same, and, second, that there may be something inherently noble in an act as distinguished from the motives which prompted it or from the point of view from which it is regarded . . . [instead] it is certainly a representation of actions *considered* as noble, and herein lies its essential nature, since no man can conceive it unless he is capable of believing in the greatness and importance of man.[19]

It takes an optimist to *arrange* the irreparable tragic event, to be less concerned with the "facts," so that he may conceive a really extreme event as a test never before passed.

In this dimension, actual experience thus far is pressed by the mysterious and primeval longings of the always underfulfilled spirit. Hence tragedy is written to excite this unendable drive. Critic Richard Rosenheim writes that this "transmutation" occurs only in the play achieving that perspective, where

> the polarities of passive receiving [as in nature] and active sending [as in creative action, in "form-tempo"] coincide mysteriously. In one flashing instant of mutual permeation they become one. . . . We are confronted with that precious miracle of transmutation by transmutation—as illustrated . . . in the "Play within the Play" set by Hamlet as the "mouse-trap" for the treacherous king. [The spectator] *gives sense* to what he visualizes as the living representation of a higher truth. [Namely, something beyond Nature, beyond despair.] Behind the transparent veil of illusion he perceives the Archetype of Man in Metamorphosis. . . . He is transmuted by beholding transmutation.[20]

This is the miraculous perspective of tragedy which eludes us today, the vision which is able to see and show the side of man to which man's natural eyes are blinded. It is enormously creative, in a *different* space

19. Krutch, "The Tragic Fallacy," in *European Theories of the Drama*, ed. Barrett Clark, pp. 519–20.
20. Richard Rosenheim, *The Eternal Drama* (New York, 1952), pp. 6–8.

and time. It stands back from personal real life and provides the unique and carefully conceived catalyst which fuses natural perception with an ideal moral one—something never manifest in reality. But it enforces an attitude that unseats us by suggesting that possibilities change, that we cannot *prove* idealized action ought to be abandoned: "The great poet is the enemy of our everyday reality: he makes that which we have seen with our own eyes appear as a mere shadow of that reality which we encounter in *Oedipus, Lear,* or *The Brothers Karamazov.* He shows us that we live blindly on the surface and says in Rilke's words: 'You must change your life.'"[21]

21. Walter Kaufmann, *From Shakespeare to Existentialism* (Garden City, N.Y., 1960), p. 258.

11. TRAGEDY and a FUTURE

I have ranged from the practical problems of pessimistic tragedy to some implied philosophical stances in genuine tragedy. Perhaps tying these together now in conclusion constitutes some sort of practical philosophy—which is not a bad way to understand tragedy.

PESSIMISM VS. OPTIMISM

Is pessimism better than optimism as a guide to the future, or a means of relating to it? The question concerns tragedy, because tragedy is a way of coping with both a personal and a universal future—a device we need today probably more than man has ever needed it, something which could help us do what physicist Dennis Gabor calls "inventing our future."[1] Gabor, incidentally, is an able defender of the sciences against the usual charge that they cannot advance our humanity, and he believes science and its productivity is a better source for optimistic forecasts than the humanists and writers who have only thrown away the old visions.

I think pessimism has helped bring us to an unphilosophical tragic theatre, with the specific deficiencies of introversion, predestined plotting, degraded insight, and the like. These characteristics of the attitude

1. See his article in Brinton's *The Fate of Man.*

cannot raise thought up to a consideration of the future. More to the point, there is no faith in the future. Modern American pessimism is insistent, a blanket which covers all aspects of present existing. Pirandello's pessimism, for a contrasting instance, is revealingly more successful as philosophy (and perhaps might be as tragedy had Pirandello more consciously attempted the genre) because he does not insist on it for all men and all issues.

For a change, I'll turn to the argument against optimism—to get a perspective on the alternatives before going on to final conclusions.

Probably most of the social commentators assessing today's condition, particularly the American, would applaud the theme of Robert L. Heilbroner's respected book, *The Future as History*—more now than in 1960, when it first appeared. One of Heilbroner's main points is that America's "optimism" has led it to a false and unfruitful view of progress and the future, and his arguments about the failure of optimism as personal credo and professional stance for any social observer still form a very stimulating challenge to the notion I suggest of tragedy as future-oriented faith. My position, for instance, like the stereotype of the American facing the "promise" of the future with firm stance and uptilted chin and eyes, *can* be likened to, say, the unproven fantasy of optimism basic to the eighteenth-century philosophe, the Marquis de Condorcet.[2] (Thus optimism's bad name.) It is true that Americans developed and sustained a perhaps unreasonable optimism in the eighteenth, nineteenth, and early twentieth centuries, noting how fast and well the country seemed to move with its technology and fresh young democracy. Heilbroner's criticism of this, of course, is that the attitude came from "a unique and sheltered historic experience"[3] which should not have meant much when one looked at the whole sweep of history. For him, optimism's central shortcoming is that it equates the motion of history with the idea of progress, whereas "contrary to our generally accepted beliefs, change is not the rule but the exception in life."[4] Also, optimism does not give us a sense of what to expect from the possibilities of history and the realities of human ambition and ability. What Heilbroner concludes at the end of

2. His key work in this vein is *Outlines of an Historical View of the Progress of the Human Mind* (New York, 1955).

3. Robert L. Heilbroner, *The Future as History* (New York, 1960), p. 179.

4. Ibid., p. 195.

his critique of progress-thinking and optimism, rather too simply, is that we have got to be realistic about the record on progress, to know our attitudinal place (perhaps like the Europeans who long ago abandoned optimism as untenable) and see that it will be a long time before things improve even a little—as against continued violence, injustice, and the like, which clearly show that *lack* of progress in the quality of life is the rule. Instead of being optimists, he says, we should face up to our limitations; but Heilbroner also decides that we mustn't be uselessly pessimistic either. The West will need, he writes, "fortitude and understanding" in enduring a period of healing in which progress should not be expected: "The ugly, obvious, and terrible wounds of mankind must be dressed and allowed to heal before we can begin to know the capacities, much less enlarge the vision, of the human race as a whole."[5] Though most of his book states that we cannot expect to progress, he finally says that the "false despair" of pessimism is no better than misleading optimism. The thesis dissolves, in the very last pages, into a request for "compassionate" patience.

The necessity for arguing the implications of these points, at this moment in our history, cannot be overestimated. The attitude of *The Future as History*, I think, shares the failure of the modern tragedy: we are denied action and lectured on recognition. What is the purpose of mere "waiting?" Events have no doubt worsened since 1960, but, on the other hand, some new light has been shed on attitudes which beget accomplishment. (Responsible activism is an example.) Also, today, I question whether we are still a nation of optimists, and I doubt that we maintain any big popular belief in the possibility of change. Rather it is widespread belief in stasis and worst outcomes that constitute the problem for progressing and surviving. Moreover, the realistic waiting implied in Heilbroner's argument and in the similar prevailing pessimism of the numerous indignant social observers of the day tends to the same kind of passivity and inability to alter decline which Heilbroner attributes to "traditional American optimism." This misunderstanding of the potential of optimism does to conduct of national life what it has done to the life of the imagination in our tragic art.

The view of the social scientist (and the playwright enacting a similar role) who refuses to be consoled in his reaction to contemporary trends

5. Ibid., p. 205.

and events ends up in a very reasonable realism: a justified, rational, accurate recognition of the present and past history—which also happens to be an empty and unspecific introduction to our relation with a future, to running our personal lives, or hoping to influence national life. Do we really need more of these? *Additional* realisms will prove no more productive than simplistic optimisms. In short, pessimism is distinctly more passive than balanced optimism—while "balanced pessimism" is an inherent contradiction. Antioptimism is not necessarily the wisdom we seem to make it. Norman Cousins has a good reply in saying that "It is unhistorical to rule out the conversion of imponderables into positive forces under pressure from powerful ideas." He adds:

> It *is* possible to be an optimist in today's world—without having to strain or synthesize. It is necessary only to attach oneself confidently to a plan for accomplishing an essential purpose—and then to help bring that plan to life with advocacy and work. The only thing more dangerous than nuclear force in today's world is failure to perceive the lines of connection between the individual and the ideas and forces that shape his world.[6]

Note how this applies to the phenomenon of the contemporary activist; at his most sincere, and at work on a meaningful project, he inherently leans to optimism. Indeed, the signs of an antipassivity in some of today's demonstrations and other expressions of public concern can suggest a more useful program than guilt assessment and toleration of historical limits.

Certainly optimism has had its mindless and naïve moments. The nineteenth century, led by such titillating pronouncements as Ernest Haeckel's forecast on the attainment of all-knowledge,[7] saw perfection just around the chronological corner. American political rhetoric has often been another item on the critics' list of grievances against optimism, or a source for the generalization that Americans are improperly optimistic. But, other than the politicians, how many of those who speak for the society (thus affecting it) are such optimists? The politician's at-

6. Norman Cousins, editorial, "Is It Possible to Be an Optimist?" *Saturday Review*, 5 November 1966, p. 26.

7. His most notorious pronouncement being that science would have discovered everything by the early twentieth century.

titude is an obligatory paean to his own golden intentions. For years, where have been the optimistic writers and thinkers who have the public ear? I can think of exactly one playwright in the American serious theatre who is a consistent and demonstrated optimist. That would be Archibald MacLeish, and his major occupation has always been poetry rather than drama. Are all the others defying their constituency, not speaking for the prevailing attitude?

Again I would say that the recent trend is more of a reverse of the stereotype, at least in terms of aired opinions. One manifestation of our significant distrust of optimism is the habitual American guilt—over wealth, resources, and perhaps over the old nineteenth-century progress. Arthur Miller's worry in *After the Fall* is very representative. Quentin continually equates his success (monetary and material) with guilt and an inevitable cruelty to others. When universalized (and Miller wouldn't object to seeing his Quentin as Everyman), this is a mad argument. The play doesn't prove the general axiom. *Why* is success vile? Are success and progress always ego-serving? Can modern man never again praise ambition? Granted that Quentin's successful lawyerhood is no great goal, but there are kinds of success, and there are kinds of men. The concomitant to success depends on the man involved. Similarly, my preference for optimism stands: it is more capable of *degrees* than pessimism. Again the Cousins essay, with the conclusion: "The main characteristic of pessimism is that it tends to set the stage for its own omens. It is self-fulfilling. It shuns prospects in the act of denying them. It narrows the field of vision, obscuring the relationship between the necessary and the probable. The prime fallacy of pessimism is that no one really knows enough to be a pessimist."[8]

We live. Therefore we are asked the central question of tragedy. Therefore we are forced to relate to the future that will belong to all of us. And, of course, we have no way of knowing it; but optimism tolerates more areas in which we may think of an answer.

THE IDEAL TRAGIC VISION

So "where will the world go from here?" becomes a question of ideal tragic vision. Our first comfort should be that we cannot prove the

8. Cousins, "Is It Possible to Be an Optimist? p. 26.

world will not be a happier place for the poet sometime in the ages to come. I mean "happier" in the sense that it will allow him to depict an expanding fate for man rather than react to the present through mere submental, subspiritual, and subphilosophical sensation. It is even possible that soon the world of art will have no choice but to rediscover this, as its tragic vision—unless the people really do record their votes so as to give the mandate to doom.

Still the vision itself is a mystery. In a way, one cannot adopt or conceive of a political platform, a professional ethic, or a spiritual salve in this age of apparent failure and decline by rational means. It is Plato (or Plotinus or Hegel or others) again: aesthetics plus reason is needed to deal with those huge intangibles, the Ideals. And ideals are based on faith. So is tragedy: "This supreme preoccupation with the first beginning and the ultimate end of all things," wrote de Unamuno in *The Tragic Sense of Life*, "cannot be purely rational, it must involve the heart."[9] This is no light maxim, for very curious metaphysics lurk in the true tragic vision. Just a start comes with Herbert Muller's statement: "The tragic spirit is not cynical. If man is merely a base, selfish creature, and his idealism a mere pretense, there is no real problem in his fate and no reason to pity him."[10] Then very to the point is this: *Credo ut intelligam*, taught Augustine—believe to understand.

For an idea of this ideal, I now wish to draw together what I have said about hope, myth, the tempo of form, and the tragic perspective. This can follow a summary understanding of the irrelevance of pessimism to tragedy.

The ideal tragic vision can never be pessimistic. Pessimism negates life because it does not sufficiently fight death and mortality—a contest basic to tragedy. The skepticism that will occur on the way to the end is a subthought of optimism, not pessimism: doubt is an exercise in the hope of growth. As Krutch says, "Tragic despair is not nihilistic despair."[11] The weakness of the pessimistic vision as tragic theatre is contained in a deceptively simple fact: there is nothing tragic about the loss of some-

9. Miguel de Unamuno, *The Tragic Sense of Life in Men and Peoples* (London, 1921), p. 16.
10. Muller, *The Spirit of Tragedy*, p. 19.
11. Joseph Wood Krutch, "Why the O'Neill Star Is Rising," *New York Times Magazine*, 19 March 1961, p. 108.

thing (life) or someone (the protagonist) already self-proclaimed as being worth nothing, and capable of nothing. There is nothing tragic about a supposed struggle for survival already indentified by the person closest to it as not being "worth it" in the first place. Any emotion felt for the fallen hero should be productive and insightful, but under the modern vision ours can be a useless pity that consumes itself in simply being felt. (Is this why we absorb assassinations and other real horrors so relatively fast?)

But now to try to suggest the ideal. First, as to the compound of hope and myth, we would have to resume participation in fictions and fables, in accepting the contrived invitation to rewriting present truth—as "dreamed up" and not as committed. The amalgam is quite rare, deserving the familiar descriptions of the genre as mystery. I think we do better to go farther: *the tragic vision tolerates a lie.* Someday what is idealized as tragedy may be true, but for now it is, objectively speaking, a lie. When it comes true we will have to move on to higher idealizations, for the linear time continuum never allows tragic satisfaction on a plateau. Karl Jaspers comes near the "lie" position, but through a different image, when he says tragedy "gives us comfort by pandering to our self esteem."[12] He mentions this in the context that it makes a partial but deliberate rejection of reality in favor of a grand, satisfying, fiction: "For in so far as men find release in an experience of this kind, they find it only at the price of concealing from themselves the terrifying abysses of reality. Misery . . . cries out for help. But the reality of all this misery without greatness is pushed aside as unworthy of notice by minds that are blind with exaltation."[13] The connotation is slightly extreme, perhaps, but this function is far truer to tragic vision than that of "making us submit to life." The lie is the best image after all. I would just qualify Jaspers to say that the lie, or blind exaltation, can eventually refer back to enrich advancing reality if only by drilling the image of possibility into man's brain and soul.

I do not mean "lie" in the sense of simple fiction. Technically speaking, we could reinstate the term "fable," rather than myth, for the fable is a false myth. That is still too cautious, however, for tragedy involves a far

12. Karl Jaspers, "The Tragic: etc.," in *Tragedy: Modern Essays in Criticism*, ed. L. Michel and R. B. Sewall, p. 26.
13. Ibid.

deeper and more excessive fiction. It goes out of bounds to depict what might be for man if we *lie* about his present limits. Hamlet manages and gets away with far more than we could expect from a usual (true) Prince of Denmark. Hamlet tells himself the subconscious lie that "it might be done." The lie is eventually exposed, of course, but Hamlet's stretching process—which has opened vast new speculative territory otherwise off-limits—has meanwhile been transferred to the audience. The tragic vision stubbornly believes this excess (progress) is possible. To believe in the lie of heroism, as past peoples did, there was something called "the evidence of the heart." That is still too mild when we consider that one of tragedy's lies is that we can move above life.

The ideal tragic vision is the hypothetical best *Weltanschauung* for placing oneself between present and future, as in the new dimension of form-tempo. It makes possible the following benefits of thought and feeling.

Though the moment of destruction which is necessary may be extreme and vivid, the vision views pain as well as pleasure at some aesthetic distance, so as to constantly display the author's *knowledge* of emotion. Like Hindu *Rasa*, it is the "tasting" and not the emotion itself which pleases. This allows perspective on the whole gamut of impressions we receive from the tragic story, and more depth in our reaction to the event and the *sense* of the pain or other emotion. Philosophy is possible.

The tragic vision's concept of form suggests variation and contrast in the whole linear process of confronting the potential tragedy of ever-advancing time. Things we perceive in existence in the act of questioning the sense of life interact, and action itself can produce further contrasts and shifts in experience. To understand death we will have to attempt an understanding of life, and to understand evil we must also locate the good. The vision says that change is possible.

The transfiguration we see and share is not mere escapism through artistic illusion, as in the program advocated by O'Neill's tragedies. In the first place, it is not as clear and simple a suggestion as the anaesthesia, surrender, or martyrdom reactions. We "escape"—that is, answer the challenge of life even if we don't conquer it—precisely because the hero does *not* escape. We derive nothing from a vision which releases the protagonist from final confrontation in terms of everything for which he stands. In the ideal vision, the hero must fight and confront and we inherit the discovery which forces his destruction. The vision allows us to burn the candle at both ends: we have participated in the hero's lie but live on, unpunished. If we know what to do with the hero's used ideal, we move one notch up. We have a metaphor of what could be.

Therefore, the vision exploits optimism to tempt man with hope. In hope there is action.[14] Imagine a crusade by one man, among America's two hundred millions, to absolutely annihilate prejudice. Hopeless? Absurdly beyond his power? Tragedy reminds us that we don't really *know*. Thus the vision portrays exceptionality—the protagonists are the "best" men, or the "most this" or the "most that." The crusader for brotherhood would certainly have to sin or break laws to achieve the task in his lifetime. The tragic figure tries something the spectator cannot or would not try and thus, if only very briefly, we enter a dimension or a world which we ourselves could never enter. This is obviously a dramatic, attractive, and fascinating process which impels our deepest curiosity. The tragic vision knows man is not yet mature and therefore improves himself to some purpose. What's between us and "out there"? Contrivance is a consequence of this, because only exceptional fiction can go beyond what man is capable of in natural existence in the present. This tests the limits of finitude.

We see the effect of the ideal tottering. The sight is exciting in the fullest sense of empathy (including involuntary motor response) and sympathy. The suspense is real: more than being curious about a physical or factual resolution, we are about to discover the fate of an ethical idea. The tragic vision tends to transfer a chance for saving the idea to the spectator because it is aware of the audience as coparticipant and not as a distrusted prisoner absorbing remonstrance and warning. There is some hope for our power because we know more dimensions of the situation than the tragic characters. Dramatic irony allows us to share a feeling of control. Perhaps this is where the authentic tragic vision might simply be called the most artistic, in that it allows for a dynamic interplay between the literal and the latent material of the play. Then that sight of the tottering ideal becomes insight. A positive vision and the

14. What is it like to *exceed* oneself? To be immortal? To see the future? To risk all for a needed ideal? This is a lot like Colin Wilson's solution to our negativism problem, in his discussion of "positive existentialism." (See *The Stature of Man*, pp. 145 ff.)

motivation of our own participation have meant that the ideal never tumbles all the way to the ground. The insight is a reminder that humanity is not static, because *man's special identity as an animal with a spirit comes from his ability to value ideals.* The tragic vision employs art to put this in the most undeniable framework. In Dubos's phrase, it means "to grow in the midst of dangers."[15] This is close to pure optimism and completely out of the range of pessimism.

TRAGEDY AS AN INSIGHT INTO THE FUTURE

It is fascinating to speculate on how this old attitude could nourish our future. What would it be up against? Are possibilities more closed than open because of, say, recent moral and ethical setbacks which the contrasting triumphs of science cannot overcome or to which they have no relevance? Proliferating violence is just one image which may tell John Doe to give up, outdating a belief that active work and advocacy leads to a better future. Does current reality rewrite a vision of the future utterly against the fables of authentic tragedy? Or can tomorrow be *made* brighter? How must we, and playwrights, behave in terms of whichever prognosis we favor?

Tragedy is an insight on the future which can prevent our giving it up. In the spaciousness of change possible in the world of art, I suggest we have a site for contemplating both what the future can hold and what we do with ourselves on the way there, leading to an atmosphere in the real world where active struggle toward progress can again be a confident rule. A new teaching through art could change the way of the world. If we could really know tragedy again, its aesthetic could teach us a lesson of outlook, because it is a complete self-contained imaginative concept of the possibilities in effort aimed at the ideal of the future. Until actual new tragedy is written, as I expect it will be someday, we can still *think in the manner* of tragic expression. After living with several generations of tragedy based on man's inability to cope with his present, imagine the effect conceiving a positive tragedy would have on our culture and our world, to give us a contrasting image of where we might go. Enough critics have said that even the paragon classic tragedies have nothing to

15. As quoted in his article in Brinton, *The Fate of Man*, p. 481.

do with prophecy, that, like *Macbeth,* many of them end in plain and simple defeat: I must seem incautious. But is Scotland defeated? The world? Anything but; it is certain that those witnessing Malcolm's coronation at Scone can look to a Scottish future with more hope and resolve than they have dared in years. There is a new beat after every "final" defeat: if not a literal cleansing of the play's world at least an aesthetic suggestion of a new and somehow better movement for the enlightenment gained.

Why not simply say it's a matter of needing optimism which will keep us going despite the shocks of daily existence, which will at least keep man "in there trying" while pessimistic acceptance of a judgment on our present reduces striving for the changes which are so obviously needed to improve spiritual and actual life? Is true-tragedy-as-insight much more than a vote for The Power of Positive Thinking? Yes, it is; and the reason is that it is increasingly difficult to understand, and live with, the dynamics and dimensions of optimism in a sophisticated age. We now have too many educated responses to such mottoes as "there's no such word as 'can't.' " In older ages, mythic dogma in religion was the imagination's response to a satisfying program of working toward one's future. Nowadays, in a popularity poll at any rate, art clearly outranks religion as a comment on living based on the life of the imagination, for thinking the big thoughts of destiny and human purpose—even though tragic art views those rather negatively at the moment. And in art, tragic vision contains a marvelous metaphor for how progress can happen. That, when it will cease being underrated, is its potential new relevance.

The condition of our politics, spirit, and humanity urges the same change implicit in tragic make-believe: we must renew the world. That is what mythmaking is all about, and tragedy as fable is even more audacious. The thing we need to recapture is what religion can no longer say to most of us—that make-believe conduct and carefully idealized pictures of destiny can have a very practical, constructive application to living. It *is* a big jump from the lessons of history, but the metaphysics are so difficult in accepting this anyway that the size of the dilemma doesn't matter. Regardless of how much more impossible the world may seem to be in our own historic moment, we must still renew it; if you can believe you are going to work a miracle, the greatest miracle requires no greater stretch of belief than the simplest. The new credos that will go with a vision which sees man as surviving and growing are akin to those of authentic tragic vision because they will involve faithful leaps of imagination—as in grasping aesthetic ideals. I will repeat Whitehead: "All order is aesthetic order . . . and the aesthetic order is derived from the immanence of God." That is: God, or at least something inconceivable without some "irrational" faith. Is social science's insight via natural law and observation any better? Sidney Hook's *The Hero in History* is very significantly subtitled *A Study in Limitation and Possibility* and throughout the book he cautions that historians and those reacting to history must admit that "ifs" and "what might bes" are present in the range of human action. His themes are directly contrary to *The Future as History*, even though he writes at the height of World War Two. One key conclusion is this:

> There is no complete catalogue of the mistakes men commit when they make history. But in the light of the past we can list the most common among them. They are the failure to see alternatives when they are present; the limitation of alternatives to an over-simplified either-or where more than two are present; false estimates of their relative likelihoods; and, as a special case of this last, a disregard of the effects of our own activity in striving for one rather than another. What these mistakes amount to is a systematic underestimation of man's power to control his future.[16]

These mistakes are in force right now in some of our current tensions and debates and Hook's list is an apt description of the century's mistaken tragic vision. If we solve our existence-problems of insane escalation of weaponry "balances," pointless militarism, and the like, they will be solved by atmospheres of creed more voluminous than man needs or can explain at his present moment. Actually and symbolically, he will have more room for diplomatic maneuvering. Spiritually, he will find himself tempted once more by overlarge dreams. Significant progress can hardly evolve from the pessimistic marking of time, accepting the tempo of past and present. We may note an insight Plato developed in moving from the *Republic* to the *Laws*: that good statesmanship and other down-to-earth processes were insufficient to improve man's movement through

16. Sidney Hook, *The Hero in History* (New York, 1943), p. 266.

time, that myth had to be used to convey the essence and the promise of existence. There is no direct link possible, however long the wait, between realistic admission of impotence for making history and the faithful state of mind which will permit man to experiment once more—and not merely by his technics—with the advancing of his humanity.

Will a significant movement on and up be imaginary, as in Utopianism or the naïvest idealism? Imagination does precede certain kinds of practical thought and action. *Imagine* the human intellect's solution of a scientific puzzle, for instance, and the *actual* solution can be achieved. Or take the war problem mentioned earlier; the impulse for war is eternal, we say, because there will always be at least a few evil men to set upon the good. This, however, is one of the erroneous limitations corrected by Hook: there may be *other ways* to the ideal of unanimously pacific man. For example: "The frequency and intensity of wars can be diminished in a world society in which through peaceful social processes men can actually get at a lesser cost the things they believe—often mistakenly— that war can win for them."[17] First, imagine. The next goal is the reinstatement of this prerequisite imagination toward our conquest of the central moral and ethical problems of moving forward in time. Again the tragic artist can conceive of the parallel most readily: in a "going" society, he comes up with a philosophically concerned myth.

To cure ourselves of the present, as Crane Brinton writes in *The Fate of Man*, "we all need a new faith, a faith not in flux, not in the relativism of natural science—*a faith that Truth is to be found, not just invented.*"[18] But first the "Truth" must be imagined as a potential. Later it could *come* true. Only imagination can both invent and find, as in religion—and in the most destiny-oriented art, tragedy.

Will or must a new Shakespeare or Sophocles rise from the ashes of our violence, say, sometime in the 1980s? Will or must some great renaissance of such art change the world? Or will some reform of the culture and society spawn the new tragedians? Or—perhaps we can make it to the 1990s or the twenty-first century without the new nativity. These specifics are secondary: my conception of this much-needed return to optimistic and philosophical vision is, obviously, mostly metaphoric. And yet perhaps some tangible expectations could also be risked, because there is

17. Ibid., p. 257.
18. *The Fate of Man*, p. 521.

logic for saying that something will have to give, that only certain alternatives will remain in future conditions, because of the present in extremis.

The suggestion is that the future can exist only if favorable influences for future-thinking are allowed to arise. For tragedy, this means it can logically be reborn, improve, and probably even spread past its traditional boundaries in Western culture, for the first time becoming relevant to antitragic Indian and Oriental art; that is, it could become truly universal. Either we have this or the major premise of the logic doesn't apply. There would be no existence because, in Edwin Burtt's phrase, "there is no sane alternative to faith."[19] Elaborating the logic, there is no universe-preserving path we can follow much longer which does not start to embrace faith, for faith and progress *are* codependent. We will attempt the necessary progress when we begin to believe in its possibility and its fruits. Gradually, more humane methods of conducting the world and reaching decisions will have to evolve—or we will end it all. Much less gradually, violence and extortion must become unequivocally impractical. Politicians will get elected because they speak for a broader and broader constituency—the family of man, if you will. They will be unable to ignore *world* citizenry and will be sensitive to its needs. And necessarily there will have to be a synthesis of humanism and technologism—as Roderick Seidenberg calls it, "a creative harmony of faith and reason, a fruitful amalgam of instinct and intelligence."[20] In former history, when man chose the opposite path he led himself into a Dark Ages, an Inquisition, or a Puritan tyranny; now he would fall into a Nothing. Is the improvement path an unrealistic disregard of man's innate aggressiveness? Certainly—as far as we know now. Tragic myth offers equally unreal prescriptions for the future. Although Muller, for example, says it is nonsense to keep believing Fortinbras will restore health to Denmark, the Danes, or more directly speaking the Elizabethans, know more than Hamlet at the end of the play.

We go back to be thus progressive. We must again be open to "old" ideals. The kind of mystical rebirth which occurs in solid contemplation of tragic thinking means becoming receptive to the idea that one has a

19. Edwin A. Burtt, *In Search of Philosophic Understanding* (New York, 1965), p. 297.
20. Roderick Seidenberg, *Posthistoric Man* (Chapel Hill, N.C., 1950), p. 205.

mysterious and very underworked spirit. My interest is that we be open to it, that the supposed antihistorical posture of optimism be reconsidered, and that we reevaluate its mightiness in the spirit of art to permit it to open our tomorrows. We are caught, in cynical pessimism, between existence-value and universe-value, and the propaganda of tragedy seems capable of reminding us of the way out. If momentary existence fluctuates in apparent value, I should think good philosophy or theology would not leap to revise the *absolute* value of the universe.

The new thinking can happen, if something can show us the vision (which we nonetheless do not prove or totally understand) which sets stages for active progressing on the scale of being human—which is our pretense to demigodhood. It will require new people, artists, willing to take a less hysterical view of the present, trying to focus on universal man, achieving perspective on time and then surpassing it with the depth and serenity of a perspective on destinies. In the tragic theatre, and perhaps in theatre generally, I think it will call for acceptance of the fact that we lean to the magical and the childlike, not the authenticated or the parental. And I do not mean childlike to the detriment of thought, as in the studied innocence of current counterculture. The new heroes will be creative positivists, and along with the artists who will have to attempt to think once again like true tragedians, there could be others who indulge, a bit, the mystery of progress-thinking. Perhaps political leaders; there will never be a shortage of dissenting intellects to counteract any "blind" optimism—for that balance must be ensured too. In any case, only in an atmosphere of possibility will we have the means to perform significant actual acts in favor of our future.

Works performed and ideals held under a philosophy which happens to be neatly summarized by old tragic vision promise greater progress than those undertaken in defensive, pessimistic reaction to our present. Of course, below the level of fable and myth, it is absurd to attempt the impossible. Then too, what man is invited to believe about himself in the ultimate ideas of the truest tragedies is preposterous. On the other hand, considering tomorrow, and the statement of contemporary American tragedy, what is the alternative?

APPENDIXES

Appendixes suggest compilations of mechanical data, and this could make for a tainted postscript to so subjective a study as the quality of modern tragedy. I include various sets of data here for what they are worth as tabulated results from the most relevant parts of the systematic study which preceded and underlay *Tragedy and Fear*. Even in an Appendix, however, I hesitate to take the time and space to document or "prove." Here are simply "my findings"—of value insofar as a semiscientific method of study can contribute to my subject.

A. MODERN AMERICAN TRAGEDIES

Most of the plays I list here are not tragedies, as the theatregoers of the past fifty years or so have known. They would probably best be described as "high melodramas." My point in identifying them is that most of them aspired to tragedy—if in the peculiar context and attitude of our century—and those I list here provide a basis for argument because they meet a permissive working definition of tragedy. (See Introduction.) The arrangement is according to Broadway production date.

1919–20: *Beyond the Horizon,* Eugene O'Neill
1920–21: *The Emperor Jones,* Eugene O'Neill
          Diff'rent, Eugene O'Neill

Gold, Eugene O'Neill
John Hawthorne, David Liebovitz
1921–22: *Anna Christie*, Eugene O'Neill
The Hairy Ape, Eugene O'Neill
The Verge, Susan Glaspell
The Hand of the Potter, Theodore Dreiser
1922–23: *The Adding Machine*, Elmer Rice
1923–24: *The Shame Woman*, Lulu Vollmer
White Desert, Maxwell Anderson
The Right to Dream, Irving Kaye Davis
1924–25: *Desire Under the Elms*, Eugene O'Neill
Wild Birds, Dan Totheroh
1925–26: *The Great God Brown*, Eugene O'Neill
1926–27: *In Abraham's Bosom*, Paul Green
1927–28: *Strange Interlude*, Eugene O'Neill
Out of the Sea, Don Marquis
1928–29: *Street Scene*, Elmer Rice
Machinal, Sophie Treadwell
Gypsy, Maxwell Anderson
Dynamo, Eugene O'Neill
Gods of the Lightning, Maxwell Anderson and
Harold Hickerson
1929–30: None
1930–31: *Elizabeth the Queen*, Maxwell Anderson
Brass Ankle, DuBose Heyward
1931–32: *Mourning Becomes Electra*, Eugene O'Neill
Night Over Taos, Maxwell Anderson
1932–33: None
1933–34: *Mary of Scotland*, Maxwell Anderson
1934–35: *The Children's Hour*, Lillian Hellman[1]
The Petrified Forest, Robert Sherwood
Panic, Archibald MacLeish
1935–36: *Winterset*, Maxwell Anderson
Ethan Frome, Owen and Donald Davis
1936–37: *The Wingless Victory*, Maxwell Anderson
The Masque of Kings, Maxwell Anderson
Daughters of Atreus, Robert Turney

---

1. This and *The Glass Menagerie* are doubtful cases, but they are included here because they have more "tragic material" than other borderline plays.

1937–38:   *Golden Boy*, Clifford Odets
           Of Mice and Men, John Steinbeck
1938–39:   None
1939–40:   *There Shall Be No Night*, Robert Sherwood
           Key Largo, Maxwell Anderson
1940–41:   *The Cream in the Well*, Lynn Riggs
1941–42:   *Clash by Night*, Clifford Odets
1942–43:   None
1943–44:   None
1944–45:   *The Glass Menagerie*, Tennessee Williams
1945–46:   None
1946–47:   *All My Sons*, Arthur Miller
           The Iceman Cometh, Eugene O'Neill
           The Story of Mary Surratt, John Patrick
1947–48:   *A Streetcar Named Desire*, Tennessee Williams
1948–49:   *Death of a Salesman*, Arthur Miller
           Anne of the Thousand Days, Maxwell Anderson
           Big Knife, Clifford Odets
           Summer and Smoke, Tennessee Williams
1949–50:   None
1950–51:   None
1951–52:   None
1952–53:   *The Crucible*, Arthur Miller
1953–54:   None
1954–55:   None
1955–56:   *The Lovers*, Leslie Stephens
1956–57:   *Long Day's Journey into Night*, Eugene O'Neill
           (Written 1940)
           Orpheus Descending, Tennessee Williams
           A Moon for the Misbegotten, Eugene O'Neill
           (Written 1940s)
1957–58:   None
1958–59:   *Sweet Bird of Youth*, Tennessee Williams
           J. B., Archibald MacLeish

Since the end of the 1950s, only a few borderline tragic dramas might be mentioned, plus O'Neill's *More Stately Mansions*—which was a development of the rough draft done in the mid-1940s. Miller's *A View from the Bridge* meets my definition, but this longer version was based on the 1955 one-act of the same name. *After the Fall* attempts some effects of tragedy but not its ultimate function. Other partial cases are Miller's *Incident at Vichy*, and Edward Albee's *Tiny Alice* and *Who's Afraid of Virginia Woolf?* However, I think the playwrights themselves would agree that no one was really aiming for tragedy in the 1960s.

B. NEW TRAGEDIES AND NEW VISIONS

The plays identified as "tragic dramas" are listed in this table according to the primary tragic vision expressed in each play—the condition which causes the destruction. See chapter 2 for my descriptions of these "new visions."

TRAGEDIES OF ILLUSORY IDENTITY

Beyond the Horizon, Eugene O'Neill
The Emperor Jones, Eugene O'Neill
The Hairy Ape, Eugene O'Neill
Dynamo, Eugene O'Neill
Golden Boy, Clifford Odets
The Big Knife, Clifford Odets
All My Sons, Arthur Miller
Sweet Bird of Youth, Tennessee Williams

TRAGEDIES OF IRRESPONSIBILITY[1]

The Hand of the Potter, Theodore Dreiser
The Verge, Susan Glaspell
Of Mice and Men, John Steinbeck

TRAGEDIES OF MARTYRDOM

Winterset, Maxwell Anderson
Elizabeth the Queen, Maxwell Anderson
Mary of Scotland, Maxwell Anderson
Key Largo, Maxwell Anderson
The Wingless Victory, Maxwell Anderson
The Masque of Kings, Maxwell Anderson

1. There is a strong element of "irresponsibility" in virtually all of the "sex" tragedies of the 1920s and 1930s. See the Tragedies of Extremist Passions.

Anne of the Thousand Days, Maxwell Anderson
The Petrified Forest, Robert Sherwood
The Story of Mary Surratt, John Patrick
Tiny Alice, Edward Albee (?)

TRAGEDIES OF SENSITIVITY

A. *Manifest in Disorientation*

The Right to Dream, Irving Kaye Davis
The Great God Brown, Eugene O'Neill
Strange Interlude, Eugene O'Neill
The Iceman Cometh, Eugene O'Neill
The Glass Menagerie, Tennessee Williams
A Streetcar Named Desire, Tennessee Williams

B. *Manifest in Extremist Passions*

Diff'rent, Eugene O'Neill
Desire Under the Elms, Eugene O'Neill
John Hawthorne, David Leibovitz
Wild Birds, Dan Totheroh
Machinal, Sophie Treadwell
White Desert, Maxwell Anderson
Night Over Taos, Maxwell Anderson
Out of the Sea, Don Marquis
The Children's Hour, Lillian Hellman
Clash by Night, Clifford Odets
Cream in the Well, Lynn Riggs
Summer and Smoke, Tennessee Williams
The Lovers, Leslie Stephens

TRAGEDIES OF SOCIAL DISINTEGRATION

Gods of the Lightning, Maxwell Anderson and Harold Hickerson
In Abraham's Bosom, Paul Green
Panic, Archibald MacLeish
Brass Ankle, DuBose Heyward
There Shall Be No Night, Robert Sherwood
Death of a Salesman, Arthur Miller

The Crucible, Arthur Miller
Incident at Vichy, Arthur Miller (?)

TRAGEDIES OF IMPRISONMENT

A. *Manifest in Imprisonment*

The Adding Machine, Elmer Rice
Orpheus Descending, Tennessee Williams

B. *Manifest in Environment*

Street Scene, Elmer Rice
Ethan Frome, Owen and Donald Davis

TRAGEDIES OF INHERITANCE

Gold, Eugene O'Neill
Anna Christie, Eugene O'Neill
Mourning Becomes Electra, Eugene O'Neill
A Moon for the Misbegotten, Eugene O'Neill
Long Day's Journey into Night, Eugene O'Neill
The Shame Woman, Lulu Vollmer
Gypsy, Maxwell Anderson
Daughters of Atreus, Robert Turney
J. B., Archibald MacLeish
More Stately Mansions, Eugene O'Neill

C. CHARACTERISTICS OF MODERN TRAGEDIES

For my background study, I thought it would be significant to "test" the plays I identified as "modern American tragedies" by applying six key questions suggested by my basic theorem to the reading of each play. A tabular yes-no presentation of the results may not be a nice way to treat art or would-be art, and another researcher might have different ideas about my indexes and my readings. Let us just agree that the appendix is intended only to provide an illustration of some general trends and patterns on points repeatedly questioned in modern criticism but never systematically "tested."

In the table, the questions are indicated as "A" through "F" in respective columns. A seventh column contains a concise statement of what I take to be the essential philosophical dynamic, or theme, of each play.

The questions are:

A. *Is the drama pessimistic?* "Pessimism" is defined as the view which says life is hopeless because the world is basically evil and, regardless of what one does, fulfillment on earth is impossible.

B. *Is there a sudden reversal of fortune?* This question refers to the fortunes of the protagonist, and a sudden reversal is defined as relatively good or hopeful status turning suddenly to serious misfortune.

C. *Is escape possible?* Although traditional tragedy posits inevitable doom, the character has avenues of escape partly open to him which motivate his struggle. Such escape consists of a development or character having the potential to help the protagonist avoid destruction. Thus a "No" answer indicates the early hopelessness which vitiates struggle and breeds pessimism.

D. *Does the play start very late in the hero's history?* This question determines the time of the beginning of the play in relation to the crisis. A "Yes" answer indicates a drama that begins just before the crisis, or even after it, and after the suffering of the protagonist has already begun.

E. *Is there enlightenment?* This refers to the presence of enlightenment or insight either in the protagonist or the remaining characters as a result of confronting the tragic crisis. The answer determines whether or not there is understanding within the play of the meaning and value of the tragic downfall.

F. *Is there an antagonistic Character?* This question serves to identify the chief obstacle in the tragedy as another person in the play, the protagonist himself, or some intangible agency such as nature. The answer "Self" under this column indicates that the leading character is primarily self-destroyed. A "No" answer would indicate the fact that destruction and antagonism come from some agency outside the characters.

Philosophical theme. Under this heading a very brief interpretation of the play's philosophical attitude toward life, according to its given tragic vision, is stated.

(Special cases requiring amplification beyond the brief, tabular data are footnoted. The notes appear at the end of the table.)

CHARACTERISTICS OF MODERN AMERICAN TRAGEDY

Play	A	B	C	D	E	F	THEME
Beyond the Horizon	Yes	Yes	No	No	No	No	Dreams and aspirations destroy the right to survive.
The Emperor Jones	Yes	Yes	No	No	No	No	Dreams and aspirations destroy the right to survive.
Diff'rent	Yes	No	No	No	No	Self	Life is a sexual hell.
Gold	Yes	No	No	No	No	Self	Dreams and aspirations destroy the right to survive.
John Hawthorne	Yes	No	No	No	No	Yes	Life is a sexual hell.
Anna Christie	Yes	No	Yes	Yes	No	No	Life is an inescapable treadmill of sin and guilt.
The Hairy Ape	Yes	Yes	No	No	No	Self[1]	Man has neither the right nor the ability to climb out of his low station.
The Verge	Yes	No	No	Yes	No	Self	Life is a meaningless treadmill. Man is not responsible for his aberration.
The Hand of the Potter	Yes	No	No	Yes	No	Self	Life is a sexual and psychological hell. Man is not responsible for his aberration.
The Adding Machine	Yes	No	No	Yes	No	No	Man is trapped and deranged by the meaningless treadmill of his existence.
The Shame Woman	Yes	No	No	Yes	No	Yes	Life is an inescapable treadmill of sin and guilt.
White Desert	Yes	Yes[2]	Yes[3]	No	No	No	Life is a sexual hell.

Characteristics of Modern American Tragedy–*Continued*

Play	A	B	C	D	E	F	THEME
The Right to Dream	Yes	Yes	No	No	No	Self	The sensitive are always destroyed by the insensitive majority.
Desire Under the Elms	Yes	No	Yes	No	No[4]	No	Life is a sexual and psychological hell.
Wild Birds	Yes	No	No	Yes	No	Yes	Life is a sexual hell.
The Great God Brown	Yes	No	No	Yes	No	No	The sensitive are always destroyed by the insensitive majority.
In Abraham's Bosom	Yes	No	No	No	No	No	Man cannot control his hatreds and prejudices and is unable to climb out of his low station.
Strange Interlude	Yes	No	No	No	No	Self	Sensitivity tortures man in the inability to endure sexual and psychological tensions.
Out of the Sea	Yes	No	No	No	No	Self	Life is a sexual hell. The sensitive are destroyed by the insensitive majority.
Street Scene	Yes	No	No	Yes	No	No	Man is trapped by the treadmill of his existence. Life is a sexual hell.
Machinal	Yes	No	No	Yes	No	Self	Life is a sexual hell.
Gypsy	Yes	No	No	Yes	No	Self	Life is an inescapable cycle of sin and guilt. Life is a sexual hell.
Dynamo	Yes	No	No	Yes	No	Self	Dreams and aspirations destroy the right to survive in a godless universe.

Characteristics of Modern American Tragedy–*Continued*

Play	A	B	C	D	E	F	THEME
Gods of the Lightning	Yes	No	No	Yes	No	No	Man is incapable of justice and humanity.
Elizabeth the Queen	Yes	Yes	Yes	No	No	Self	The able and the ambitious must perish, leaving the world to the petty and mean.
Brass Ankle	Yes	Yes[5]	No	Yes	No	No	Man's prejudices and social fears destroy his humanity.
Mourning Becomes Electra	Yes	No	No	Yes	No	Self	Man's weakness and pride curses him, and life becomes a cycle of sin and guilt.
Night Over Taos	Yes	No	No	Yes	No	Self	Life is a sexual hell. Man is trapped by his pride.
Mary of Scotland	Yes	No	No	Yes	No	Self	Principles of justice are meaningless. Man is trapped by his pride.
The Children's Hour	Yes	Yes[6]	No	Yes	No	Yes[7] Self	Life is a psychological and sexual hell.
The Petrified Forest	Yes	No	No	Yes	No	Self	The sensitive must perish. Man has made his life meaningless.
Panic	Yes	No	No	Yes	No	No	Social complexity destroys humanity and selflessness.
Winterset	Yes	No	No	Yes	No	Self	Life is meaningless because man is incapable of justice and humanity.

Characteristics of Modern American Tragedy–*Continued*

Play	A	B	C	D	E	F	THEME
Ethan Frome	Yes	No	No	Yes	No	Self	Man is trapped by the tread-mill of his existence.
The Wingless Victory	Yes	No	No	No	No	Self	Man's prejudices and social fears destroy his humanity.
The Masque of Kings	Yes	No	No	Yes	No	Self	Nobility and justice are crushed by the majority.
Daughters of Atreus	Yes	Yes	No	Yes	No	Yes	Life is a cycle of sin and guilt. Life is a psychological hell.
Golden Boy	Yes	No	No	Yes	No	Self	Dreams and aspirations destroy the right to survive.
Of Mice and Men	Yes	No	No	Yes	No	Self[8]	Man is not responsible for his aberration. Dreams of peace cannot be realized.
There Shall Be No Night	No	No	Yes	Yes	Yes	No	Man will learn humanity from witnessing the ultimate act of his present inhumanity.
Key Largo	Yes	No	No	Yes	No	Self	Man's weakness and sin make his life meaningless.
Cream in the Well	Yes	No	No	Yes	No	Self	Life is a sexual and psychological hell. Man is not responsible for his aberration.
Clash by Night	Yes	No	No	Yes	No	No	Life is a sexual hell.
The Glass Menagerie	Yes	No	No	Yes	No	No	The sensitive do not succeed and survive.
All My Sons	Yes[9]	Yes[10]	No	Yes	No	Self	Dishonest dreams destroy the right to survive.

Characteristics of Modern American Tragedy–*Continued*

Play	A	B	C	D	E	F	THEME
The Iceman Cometh	Yes	No	No	Yes	No	Self	Sensitivity assures man's pain. Life and love are totally meaningless.
The Story of Mary Surratt	Yes	Yes	No	No	No	No	Man is incapable of justice and humanity.
A Streetcar Named Desire	Yes	No	Yes	Yes	No	Yes[11] Self	The sensitive are always destroyed by the insensitive. Life is a sexual and psychological hell.
Death of a Salesman	Yes	No	No	Yes	No	Self	Social complexity destroys humanity. Man is unable to rise above his meaningless existence.
Anne of the Thousand Days	Yes	Yes	No	No	No	Yes[12] Self	Weakness and pride doom man. Sexual sensitivity assures pain.
The Big Knife	Yes	No	No	Yes	No	Self	Contemporary social values are destructive.
Summer and Smoke	Yes	No	No	Yes	No	Self	Life is a sexual hell.
The Crucible	No	Yes	No	No	Yes	Yes	Man destroys man through injustice and social fears.
The Lovers	Yes	Yes	No	No	No	Yes	Life is a sexual hell.
Long Day's Journey into Night	Yes	No	No	Yes	No	Self	Life is an inescapable treadmill of sin, guilt, and bad fortune. Sensitivity assures pain.

Characteristics of Modern American Tragedy–*Continued*

Play	A	B	C	D	E	F	THEME
Orpheus Descending	Yes	No	No	Yes	No	No	The world is corrupt.
A Moon for the Misbegotten	Yes	No	No	Yes	No	Self	Man's heritage is weakness and guilt.
Sweet Bird of Youth	Yes	No	No	Yes	No	No	Dreams and aspirations destroy the right to survive.
J. B.	No	Yes	Yes	No	Yes	Yes	Life is a constant challenge to faith.
A Touch of the Poet	Yes	No	No	Yes	No	Self	Dreams and aspirations destroy the right to survive.

1. Although Yank is killed by the ape, Yank's action in going to the cage and opening it can be interpreted as a symbolic self-destruction.

2. There is a sudden reversal only in the sense that the Kanes are unaware of their jealousies and hidden passions until they move to their new home and the wife becomes involved with another man.

3. There is a slight possibility of escape during the last act of the play where the husband wavers on the point of forgiving his wife her infidelity.

4. The young lovers profess to know something as a result of their cirmes of passion, but they are led to their doom in a conclusion that directly contradicts their feelings.

5. There is a sudden reversal only in the sense that the heroine's discovery of her Negro blood is a sudden change in the situation. Her fortunes were not high prior to the discovery, but were different.

6. The heroines' fortunes are not high at the beginning of *The Children's Hour* because their emotional fears are old. But the little girl's accusation does constitute a sudden change in the situation, although it cannot be considered a reversal of fortune in the traditional sense.

7. The malicious child may be considered an antagonist, but there is an element of self-destruction in the play's conclusion that stems from the innate psychological fears and weaknesses of the heroines.

8. Lennie is actually killed by George as an act of mercy, but the essential developments of Lennie's destruction are in his own psychological helplessness.

9. Miller's play is not pessimistic to the point that it generalizes a worldwide pessimistic view from its story. However, there is no optimistic note to the conclusion or meaning.

10. There is a sudden reversal only in the sense that there is a sudden discovery of Keller's dishonesty. Keller's fortunes are thus changed on the surface, although the play begins with his moral degradation already begun.

11. Stanley may be considered an antagonist, but at least equal share in the destruction is found in Blanche's delusions and psychological vulnerability.

12. King Henry is a source of antagonism, although the play's ending also includes martyrdom.

D. DESCRIPTIVE LIST OF PLAYS

This list includes very brief sketches of the plays I have referred to in this book as American "tragic dramas." Listing is alphabetical.

In Abraham's Bosom, Paul Green

Abraham, an illegitimate mulatto, reflects the Negro problems in a world full of prejudice and suppression. He is antagonized by his white father, and he determines to establish a school with which to educate his people to help them out of their despair. When Abe whips a Negro pupil, he loses his school. Years later he is still trying to help the Negroes but his own egotism and pride, and his errant son, betray him to the white people.

The Adding Machine, Elmer Rice

Mr. Zero has spent most of his life as a servile accountant. Only the harangues of his wife break the monotony of his life. He falls in love with an equally beaten woman clerk at the office. Automation comes to take away Zero's job. Zero goes mad, and kills his boss. He is caught and tried. After his execution, he is seen in heaven with the clerk, who killed herself to be with him. But even in the afterlife, his hopeless conformity is seen as his destruction.

All My Sons, Arthur Miller

During the second World War, factory-owner Joe Keller allows defective airplane parts to be shipped, resulting in the death of several fighter pilots. He further allows his partner to take the blame while he goes on to prosper. One son, overseas, kills himself when he finds out about his father's act. The other son discovers the truth later and, when his guilty secret and whole false life are revealed before all, Keller shoots himself.

Anna Christie, Eugene O'Neill

A retired sailor, Chris Christopherson, is now a barge captain. He has not been a good father, and his daughter Anna has become a prostitute. Chris does not know this, and she comes to visit him as a last resort at escaping her past. He lives with her on the barge, and she becomes almost happy again. But when she falls in love with a sailor, Chris's fear of the seaman's lot threatens the love. Anna fatalistically tells the sailor of her past, and he is shattered. But eventually the trio makes a compromise and they accept each other. But the play ends with the idea that they cannot escape doom symbolized by the sea.

Anne of the Thousand Days, Maxwell Anderson

This is the story of the fateful love of Anne Boleyn and King Henry VIII, told from the moment Henry first declares his intention to have Anne to the moment he realizes she is dead by his own decree.

Beyond the Horizon, Eugene O'Neill

On a New England farm, two brothers love the same girl, Ruth Atkins. Robert Mayo is a frail dreamer who wants to go on a voyage to satisfy a longing to go "beyond the horizon." Andrew Mayo is satisfied with being a very good farmer. Robert assumes Ruth loves his more vigorous brother but, as he is about to leave, he discovers that Ruth loves him. So Robert stays on the farm and Andrew goes on the voyage. The reversal of roles makes everyone almost immediately wretched. Robert's incompetence on the farm incites his father's hatred. Ruth quickly realizes she loved Andrew after all. The farm goes to ruin. The crisis comes as Andrew returns to the farm after years of wandering—the symbol of what might have been. Overwork and the hopelessness of his situation aggravate Robert's frail health into tuberculosis and he dies speaking of the places he never got to see.

Big Knife, Clifford Odets

Charlie Castle, a movie star, wants to get away from Hollywood because of his wife's wishes and his own recognition of the falseness of stardom and the values employed by his industry in creating popular appeal. But he is bound by a long-term contract, and his studio warns him that attempts to break away will be met with his exposure as a drunken-driving killer. Choosing the only way out, Castle kills himself.

Brass Ankle, DuBose Heyward

Ruth Leamer discovers with the birth of her second child that she has

Negro blood. Her husband, a champion of the whites, is crushed. Sensing the criticism of his friends and the resulting social ostracism, he hysterically proclaims his parentage of the baby. Ruth, to save them, calls the neighbors together and announces that she has had a Negro lover who fathered the black child. Her husband, in rage, kills both Ruth and the infant.

The Children's Hour, Lillian Hellman

Two sensitive women schoolteachers are destroyed by the evil story circulated by a satanic little girl student, reacting against a minor punishment. The women are suspected of homosexuality, and their school is ruined. One of them commits suicide, partly because of latent fears about her relationship with the other young woman.

Clash by Night, Clifford Odets

Mae Wilenski is disappointed with life and her stupid but honest husband Jerry. When a more attractive man comes to board with the Wilenskis, Mae, after a short struggle, decides to submit to his advances. Jerry slowly comprehends the situation, then stalks down his wife's lover and kills him.

The Cream in the Well, Lynn Riggs

In the Sawter family, living on an Oklahoma farm, incest and perversion try the understanding of simple people. One daughter sadistically goads her brother's fiance into suicide. She marries and drives him to drink by her frigidity and sadism. The disgusted brother comes home after debasing himself sexually. The two perverts are drawn together, but this ends in the girl's suicide.

The Crucible, Arthur Miller

John and Elizabeth Proctor are caught as helpless victims of the Salem witch trials, begun by a pure fiction told by a malicious young girl to cover up her own lascivious activities. The community goes mad with fear and suspicion until several innocent people are destroyed. Finally, Proctor goes to his death rather than make a false confession which could only allow the madness to spread further.

Daughters of Atreus, Robert Turney

Turney's play retells the classic story of the tragedy and family curse of the house of Atreus. The drama runs from the sacrifice of Iphigeneia to the murder of Klytaimnestra.

Death of a Salesman, Arthur Miller

Willy Loman is living out his last days, having been a failure as a father and a salesman. His sons, fed with Willy's false pride and dishonest values, are reflections of his own failure. Last desperate attempts to start his boys in a successful business fail, and the hopelessness of the Lomans' existence seems unbearable. To provide his family with the money from his insurance policy, Willy kills himself.

Desire Under the Elms, Eugene O'Neill
Ephraim Cabot, the sour patriarch of a New England farm and a widower, is hated by his sons. When Cabot, at seventy-six, marries a pretty young woman, two sons leave. The third, Eben, feels Cabot cheated and overworked Eben's mother. The young wife falls in love with Eben and when she bears a son, it is found to be Eben's rather than Cabot's. The child is killed by its mother and finally she and Eben are led away, leaving Ephraim bitter and lonely.

Diff'rent, Eugene O'Neill
Emma Crosby is a victim of her Puritanism. As a young girl she rejects her faithful suitor, Caleb, because he falls short of the ideal lover she has found in books. A sea captain, Caleb admits that once, on a voyage to the south seas, he was seduced by a native girl. Emma cannot forgive him. Years later, Emma falls in love with a worthless young man. Caleb, who has waited all these years hoping Emma will marry him if he proves his love by remaining true to her, discovers her passion for the young man. His picture of Emma as the pure virgin is shattered and he hangs himself. When Emma discovers that her young lover only wants her money and that Caleb is dead she too commits suicide.

Dynamo, Eugene O'Neill
Reuben Light seeks a new god in a frustrating world, and thinks he finds it in machine-worship. His religious fanaticism and insanity is a combination of family traumas and oversensitivity to the world. He ends his life a suicide, electrocuted by the machine he worships.

Elizabeth the Queen, Maxwell Anderson
This play dramatizes the fateful love of the Earl of Essex and Queen Elizabeth I. Essex battles the conniving "rats" who run Elizabeth's government and the fierce pride of Elizabeth. Finally, the political differences of the lovers lead Essex to his death on Elizabeth's execution order.

The Emperor Jones, Eugene O'Neill
Jones, an ex-convict and ex-Pullman porter, goes to the West Indies where he establishes himself as the emperor of the natives. He enslaves them for his profit. The natives grow suspicious of his authenticity and put him on trial. Jones escapes again, but is eventually caught in the jungle and shot.

Ethan Frome, Owen and Donald Davis

On a bleak New England farm Ethan Frome is trapped by his work and his responsibilities to the women of his family. After a hopeless love affair undertaken to salve the pain of his empty marriage, Ethan and his lover attempt suicide. The attempt fails, and they live out their dreary lives physically and psychologically maimed.

The Glass Menagerie, Tennessee Williams

A pathetic southern woman clings to recollections of better days in the world. Her main problem is her extremely shy and crippled daughter, for whom she is trying to find a suitor. Her restless, poetic son attempts to bring home a gentleman for his sister, but the affair ends in failure. Tiring of arguing with his mother, the son leaves.

Gods of the Lightning, Maxwell Anderson and Harold Hickerson

Macready and Capraro, the former a fiery leader of the strikers in a mill town walkout, the latter a passive but fervent anarchist, are arrested for the murder of a payroll messenger. Their trial is unjust, and they are "framed" and sent finally to their electrocution while their comrades mourn their passing and all that is related to it.

Gold, Eugene O'Neill

Captain Bartlett, wrecked on an island with the crew of his whaling ship, believes he has discovered treasure. In hiding his find, two murders are necessary to ensure the secret. After being rescued, Bartlett plans to return for his gold. But before he can get away, his guilt affects his mind. His deranged mutterings allow his wife and son to learn his secret. His refusal to confess causes the death of his sick wife, but his son grows greedy for the gold and also goes mad. The treasure is discovered to be worthless, and Bartlett dies of remorse.

Golden Boy, Clifford Odets

Joe Bonaparte is undecided between careers as a violinist and a prizefighter. In the boxing world, his character gradually decays and he realizes that false ideals and his broken hands have ruined his chances for happiness and disappointed his father's dreams for him. Joe kills his opponent in a fight, drives away from the scene in a car, and, speeding, kills himself.

The Great God Brown, Eugene O'Neill

Two men—one gifted and poetic, the other practical and hard-working —love the same girl, Margaret. Margaret marries the artist Dion, and Dion sells his share of a family business to Brown. Dion dissipates himself, and ends up working in Brown's office. Brown tries to keep Dion faithful to Margaret. Dion dies, and his mask is put on by Brown who takes Dion's place with Margaret, making her happy again. When the deception is discovered, Brown is accused of murder and, in a chase, is shot. Margaret lives on.

Gypsy, Maxwell Anderson

This is the Freudian story of a woman who carries out the promiscuousness learned from her mother as a nymphomaniac. Married and yet carrying on extramarital affairs, she fears sexual restriction. She leaves her husband, but is eventually abandoned by all her lovers, and she kills herself.

The Hairy Ape, Eugene O'Neill

Yank is a ship's stoker. A sudden, humiliating contact with the aristocracy leads the uneducated, self-pitying Yank to revolt. Trying to pick fights with the upper classes and dabbling in socialism, he only makes a fool of himself. In every defiant gesture he makes, Yank finds he is out of his class and over his depth except in the hold of the ship, where he can tyrannize the other stokers. A dream leads him to the zoo, where he attempts to talk to an ape. Yank lets the beast out of the cage, and is crushed to death.

The Hand of the Potter, Theodore Dreiser

Isadore Berchansky is a victim of his perverted sexual drives. Convicted of sexual assault on a little girl, he tries to adapt to his family and society once again. But his madness persists, and he assaults another little girl, this time killing her. His family is forced to abandon him, and the strain of police pursuit and the awareness of his own insanity leads him to suicide.

The Iceman Cometh, Eugene O'Neill

In naturalistic detail, several human derelicts are seen trying to sustain themselves with last-chance delusions. They are disillusioned by life and love, and live out their meaningless existence in a skid-row atmosphere of total nihilistic despair.

J. B., Archibald MacLeish

A modern Job suffers trials set upon him by a contemporary version of God until he nearly breaks down under the strain. But, finally overcoming the destructive effects of psychological and other tortures, he begins to see the key to existence in the modern world.

John Hawthorne, David Liebovitz

A lonely mountain girl, Laura, marries a rich but stern old farmer. She falls in love with a farmhand, John Hawthorne. John tries to free himself, but Laura pretends concern for his salvation. The husband discovers the lovers, and a quarrel ends in John's killing the older man.

John and Laura try to run away, but Laura becomes fanatic over John's sin. Since she cannot convert him, she betrays him to the sheriff with the idea she is saving his soul.

Key Largo, Maxwell Anderson

King McCloud, feeling guilty over deserting his comrades during the Spanish Civil War, goes on a self-abasing tour of the survivors left by the dead soldiers. Visiting the last bereaved family, he finds the father and sister prisoners of a gangster. He sacrifices himself, taking the gangster with him, to make some retribution for his guilt.

Long Day's Journey into Night, Eugene O'Neill

The members of the Tyrone family live out their pitiful and useless lives in the Tyrone summer home in New England. The mother is a dope addict, the father an artistically destroyed actor, one son a drunken lout, and the other son tubercular and hopelessly morbid. They realize for the final time that each one's weakness will combine with the vices of the others, and they must live on in their slow death.

The Lovers, Leslie Stephens

Following the marriage of two peasants in twelfth-century France, the lord of the neighborhood invokes the custom of the *droit du seigneur*. Battling their passions and the lust of the lord, the couple is destroyed. In the end the bride kills herself, and the husband and the lord kill each other.

Machinal, Sophie Treadwell

A young woman is confined in a sexual hell by the conditioning of her upbringing. Her frigidity makes her marriage a torture, and childbirth still worse. Rejecting her revolting husband, she eventually becomes involved with a murderous young man who gives her the idea of killing her husband. She does so, but is betrayed by her lover and goes to her death.

Mary of Scotland, Maxwell Anderson

Queen Mary is destroyed, in a contest for power, by the old and hardened Queen Elizabeth. Elizabeth's ruthlessness symbolizes the nature of politics in contrast to the sympathetic portrait of Mary as a martyr.

The Masque of Kings, Maxwell Anderson

The idealistic Prince Rudolph of Austria sees his court stifled by the old political traditions represented by his father, the Emperor Franz Joseph. Against a background of romance and intrigue, he resolves to revolt, even if it means sacrificing the Emperor. The old Hapsburg actually takes heart at Rudolph's idealism, but practical politics do not work the same as ideals. Rudolph, frustrated in love and revolution, abdicates before he is crowned. He is found dead in his hunting lodge.

A Moon for the Misbegotten, Eugene O'Neill

This is the story of the fading life of Jim Tyrone, who found a strange love and a false peace before he died. Tyrone inherits a crumbling New England farm, tenanted by the drunken Mike Hogan and his matronly daughter Josie. Tyrone joins Hogan in drunken escapism, and soon comes under the influence of Josie's mother-love. When Tyrone threatens to sell the farm, Hogan and Josie thwart him, primarily by distracting him with Josie's attentions. Tyrone is symbolically absorbed by the mother-figure as the play ends.

Mourning Becomes Electra, Eugene O'Neill

O'Neill's play recasts the classical tragedy of Electra in a Civil War period setting. Lavinia (Electra) hates her mother for her affair with a sea-captain with whom Lavinia is also in love. When the father returns, the wife kills him. Lavinia's brother joins her in revenge, beginning with the murder of the mother's lover. Lavinia's mother then commits suicide. The brother and sister live out the family curse, plagued by guilt, remorse, and their incestuous feelings.

Night Over Taos, Maxwell Anderson

Don Pablo Montoya, the last leader of the Spanish grandees in Taos, New Mexico, in 1874, seeks to rally his people to a defiant defense of their ranches and their ancient feudalism against the encroaching American government. Don Pablo's eldest son, Federico, would betray his father, and is killed. The younger son, Felipe, tries to marry a woman Montoya intended for his own. Montoya offers the young lovers a cup of poison but, sick of love frustrations and defeat, he drinks the poison himself.

Of Mice and Men, John Steinbeck

The play depicts the strange comradeship of Lennie, a giant with a child's mind, and George, the itinerant worker who looks after him. They dream of having a small homestead somewhere, where Lennie can raise the soft and furry animals he loves to pet. They are near to buying such a place, when Lennie, without meaning to, kills the flirtatious wife of a ranch foreman and George mercifully kills him before the lynch mob arrives.

Orpheus Descending, Tennessee Williams

Val Xavier, a young wanderer, finds himself the center of passions and prejudices in a small southern town. He becomes involved with a deranged woman painter and a married proprietress of the local store. Against a background of racial tensions and helpless hatreds, Val and his lover are destroyed by the woman's racist husband and the rabid community appointed to punish the lovers' sins.

Out of the Sea, Don Marquis

John Marstin, an American poet visiting Cornwall, meets and falls in love with Isobel, the desperate wife of the brutal Mark Tregesal. Carrying out the Tristan and Isolde parallel, Tregesal swears to master Isobel and make her love him. Marstin and the girl try to elope but do not succeed. Isobel stabs Tregesal and, realizing there is now no chance for happiness, drowns herself.

Panic, Archibald MacLeish

The play depicts the last stand of Banker McGafferty against the forces of fear that engulfed him the time that the banks were closing and there was little hope in man. McGafferty, the leading industrialist and financier of his time, goes into conference with his fellow bankers to induce them to pool their credits and halt the threatened financial collapse. The bankers are interested only in saving themselves. Panic finally takes hold of McGafferty and he is crushed.

The Petrified Forest, Robert Sherwood

In a gas station in the desert Southwest, a dramatic variety of people is terrorized by a band of escaping gangsters, led by Duke Mantee. This crisis is a catalyst for studying the people's reactions. Among them are a penniless and disillusioned young writer, Squier, and the proprietor's daughter, whom he befriends. When the posse arrives, and bullets begin to fly, the young couple takes final stock of life. Squier asks for death at the hands of Mantee as his negation of man's inhumanity and his existence.

The Right to Dream, Irving Kaye Davis

Against her family's wishes, a rich girl marries a young writer and starves with him in a tenement while he tries to fulfill himself. When their life becomes too wretched, the girl's mother interferes, and the writer takes a degrading job as editor of a mystery magazine. Soon he is rich but artistically destroyed. He kills himself.

The Shame Woman, Lulu Vollmer

Lize Burns has lived twenty years in an isolated mountain cabin, escaping from the shame of being seduced by the son of the local mayor. She loses herself in her adopted daughter, but when she discovers the daughter has been meeting a man, Lize confesses her past in the hope of saving the girl from a similar fate. It comes out that the girl has already been seduced, and the daughter kills herself. Lize discovers the guilty man is the same one who seduced her years ago. She kills him when he threatens to brag about it. Rather than bring her daughter's name into the case, she goes to the gallows in silence.

The Story of Mary Surratt, John Patrick

An innocent woman, whose foolish son got himself involved in Booth's plot to kill Lincoln, is herself implicated by a blood-hungry justice. Her trial is a mockery wherein her fate is decided in advance. She is executed.

Strange Interlude, Eugene O'Neill

Nina Leeds is trying to live a life of complex romantic ideals confused by sexual frustration. Only her dead lover satisfied her, and she tries to find completion in a combination of men, including her husband and son. By the time she discovers an ideal relationship, she is in middle-age and past her sexual capacity for love.

A *Streetcar Named Desire*, Tennessee Williams

Blanche DuBois, debauched but still more human and sensitive than most of the people in her world, is forced to seek protection with her sister in New Orleans. She finds her married to a brute named Kowalski. The sensitivity of Blanche immediately clashes with the symbolic insensitivity of Kowalski. Kowalski finds Blanche a threat to the simple gratification of his animal world. Ultimately, he destroys her reputation and his rape of her is Blanche's ultimate psychological shock. Rather than believe Blanche's story about the attack, her sister commits her to a mental hospital.

Street Scene, Elmer Rice

Anna Maurrant is persecuted by her brutal and unloving husband. Trying to find some kindness and tenderness in their miserable tenement existence, Anna allows herself to become involved with another man. Maurrant sets a trap for her and, confirming his suspicions about her infidelity, he kills her lover and mortally wounds her. He himself is pursued and killed after the murder.

Summer and Smoke, Tennessee Williams

Alma Winemuller cannot realize love because of her pristine and pure values and latent frigidity. Yet she is attracted to John Buchanan, a lusty, sensual, and aggressive young doctor. Keeping him at a distance too long, she loses him by the time she feels able to let down the barriers of her fear. Then she begins a desperate affair with a young stranger, starting down the road to her full psychological ruin.

Sweet Bird of Youth, Tennessee Williams

Chance Wayne has an affair with a fifteen-year-old girl, whose father is the political boss of Chance's southern home town. Because Chance is poor and unimportant, the father thwarts the romance. Chance goes to New York in the hope of becoming an actor to impress the people back home. But he only becomes a gigolo, and he follows this career to Florida, where he squires a fading movie star with the thought she can get him his start in Hollywood. Bringing the movie queen to his home town to make an impression, he becomes involved again with his former sweetheart. He has infected her with venereal disease, and her father has her sterilized. The actress returns to Hollywood, but the youth she and Chance sought in each other is destroyed, and Chance is castrated for his sin by the girl's father.

There Shall Be No Night, Robert Sherwood

Sherwood's play is a story of the Russo-Finnish war, and the results of political and military inhumanity. A pacifist scientist is turned into a heroic opponent of fascism, and his perception of war is seen as a hope that the act of war will exhaust man's bestiality and become his great human awakening.

A Touch of the Poet, Eugene O'Neill

A onetime major in the Duke of Wellington's army still affects the dashing part of the gallant soldier. In his tavern, drink and the memories of his colorful career are his escape from a dismal reality that includes a subservient wife and a defiant daughter. When his daughter becomes involved with the son of a Yankee family, the hero carries his haughty illusion to extremes. His pose is eventually unmasked and he is defeated. Ironically, the daughter mourns the death of his destructive illusion.

The Verge, Susan Glaspell

Claire Archer, experimenting with plant science, tries to force life into new forms even at the expense of forms that exist. As she is interested in creating new plant life, she also tries to find her soul. She is thwarted in her experiments by a practical, ordinary husband and the conformity of her family. She wants to "go mad" to effect her breakthrough. Eventually, her perversion causes her to destroy her husband, and the play ends with her complete psychological derangement.

White Desert, Maxwell Anderson

The Kanes have moved to a North Dakota homestead. The midwinter atmosphere is barren. Their only neighbors are the Petersons. Peterson is attracted to Kane's wife, and jealousy and suspicion grow. Kane's recollection of his wife's premarital looseness with him makes him fear her conduct with Peterson, and he finally accuses her. Resentful, his wife avenges herself by being promiscuous with Peterson when

Kane is away. Later, she confesses, and Kane tries to start over with her. But the memory eventually taunts him to kill his wife.

Wild Birds, Dan Totheroh

Mazie, a young orphan, lives with the grim Slag family on a farm. She is enslaved by the brutal Slag. A boy, escaped from reform school, comes to the farm, and Slag bonds him to labor in return for secrecy. The boy and Mazie fall in love and they run away when Slag refuses to let them get married. Slag catches them but, later, when he finds Mazie is pregnant he whips the boy to death in a sadistic frenzy. Mazie kills herself.

The Wingless Victory, Maxwell Anderson

An adventurous sea-captain returns home from the south seas, bringing with him a dark-skinned exotic wife. In the provincial atmosphere of Salem, the interracial marriage stirs tensions, prejudices, and social fears. Against the background of Puritan pride fighting Christian humanity, the wife commits suicide.

Winterset, Maxwell Anderson

Mio Romagna seeks to avenge his father's unjust execution by tracing evidence that might clear his father's name. He seems to get the truth from the deranged Judge Gaunt and also meets the gangster, Trock, who was the real guilty party. However, his love affair with Miriamne turns him from his quest, and he is killed by Trock's men.

SELECTED BIBLIOGRAPHY

Bentley, Eric. *The Dramatic Event*. Boston, 1954.
———. *The Life of the Drama*. New York, 1967.
Bradley, A. C. *Shakespearean Tragedy*. New York, 1955.
Brinton, Crane, ed. *The Fate of Man*. New York, 1961.
Burtt, Edwin A. *In Search of Philosophic Understanding*. New York, 1965.
Cargill, Oscar, et al. *O'Neill and His Plays*. New York, 1961.
de Chardin, Pierre Teilhard. *The Future of Man*. New York, 1964.
Dreiser, Theodore. *Hey Rub-a-Dub-Dub: A Book of the Mystery and Wonder and Terror of Life*. New York, 1920.
Dudley, Donald R. *A History of Cynicism*. London, 1937.
Edelstein, Ludwig. *The Idea of Progress in Classical Antiquity*. Baltimore, 1967.
Eliade, Mircea. *Myth and Reality*. New York, 1963.
Engel, Edwin. *The Haunted Heroes of Eugene O'Neill*. Cambridge, Mass., 1953.
Erikson, Erik. *Insight and Responsibility*. London, 1964.
Falk, Doris V. *Eugene O'Neill and the Tragic Tension*. New Brunswick, N.J., 1958.
Flexner, Eleanor. *American Playwrights, 1918–1938*. New York, 1938.
Freud, Sigmund. *Civilization and Its Discontents*. London, 1963.
Frye, Northrop. *Anatomy of Criticism*. New York, 1966.

Gassner, John. *Theatre at the Crossroads.* New York, 1960.
———. *The Theatre in Our Times.* New York, 1954.
Gaster, Theodor H. *Thespis: Ritual, Myth, and Drama in the Ancient Near East.* New York, 1950.
Goodman, Randolph. *Drama on Stage.* New York, 1961.
Harris, Mark. *The Case for Tragedy.* New York, 1932.
Heilbroner, Robert. *The Future as History.* New York, 1960.
Henn, T. R. *The Harvest of Tragedy.* London, 1956.
Hewitt, Barnard. *Theatre U.S.A., 1668 to 1957.* New York, 1959.
Hook, Sidney. *The Hero in History.* New York, 1943.
Kaufmann, Walter. *From Shakespeare to Existentialism.* Garden City, N.Y., 1960.
———. *Tragedy and Philosophy.* New York, 1969.
Kierkegaard, Søren. *Fear and Trembling: The Sickness Unto Death.* Translated by Walter Lowrie. Garden City, N.Y., 1954.
Krutch, Joseph Wood. *The American Drama Since 1918.* New York, 1957.
———. *The Modern Temper.* New York, 1929.
Kubler, George. *The Shape of Time.* New Haven, 1962.
Langer, Susanne K. *Philosophy in a New Key.* Cambridge, Mass., 1942.
Lucas, F. L. *Tragedy in Relation to Aristotle's Poetics.* rev. ed. New York, 1957.
Mandel, Oscar. *A Definition of Tragedy.* New York, 1961.
Michel, L., and Sewall, R. B., eds. *Tragedy: Modern Essays in Criticism.* Englewood Cliffs, N.J., 1963.
Moses, Montrose J., ed., *American Theatre.* New York, 1934.
Muller, Herbert. *The Spirit of Tragedy.* New York, 1956.
Myers, Henry A. *Tragedy: A View of Life.* Ithaca, 1956.
Nietzsche, Friedrich. *The Birth of Tragedy: Hellenism or Pessimism.* Translated by William A. Haussman. London, 1911.
O'Connor, William Van. *Climates of Tragedy.* Baton Rouge, La., 1943.
O'Hara, Frank. *Today in American Drama.* Chicago, 1939.
Owen, John. *The Five Great Skeptical Dramas of History.* London, 1896.
Peacock, Ronald. *The Poet in the Theatre.* New York, 1960.
Peckham, Morse. *Beyond the Tragic Vision.* New York, 1962.
Pei, Mario. *The Story of Language.* New York, 1960.
Read, Herbert. *Art and Alienation.* London, 1967.
Rodman, Selden. *The Insiders: Rejection and Rediscovery of Man in the Arts of Our Time.* Baton Rouge, La., 1960.
Rosenheim, Richard. *The Eternal Drama.* New York, 1952.

Schopenhauer, Arthur. *The World as Will and Idea.* Translated by R. B. Haldane and J. Kemp. Garden City, N.Y., 1961.

Schweitzer, Albert. *The Philosophy of Civilization.* Translated by C. T. Campion. New York, 1960.

Selden, Samuel. *Man in His Theatre.* Chapel Hill, N.C., 1957.

Sievers, W. David. *Freud on Broadway.* New York, 1955.

Steiner, George. *The Death of Tragedy.* New York, 1961.

Stevens, Wallace. *The Necessary Angel.* New York, 1951.

Stoll, E. E. *Shakespeare and Other Masters.* Cambridge, Mass., 1940.

Styan, J. L. *The Elements of Drama.* Cambridge, England, 1963.

Unamuno, Miguel de. *The Tragic Sense of Life in Men and Peoples.* London, 1921.

Whitehead, Alfred North. *Alfred North Whitehead: An Anthology.* Selected by F. S. C. Northrop and Mason W. Gross. Cambridge, England, 1953.

Wilson, Colin, *The Outsider.* New York, 1956.

———. *The Stature of Man.* New York, 1959.

INDEX